Barron's Review Course Series

Let's Review:

English

2nd Edition

Carol Chaitkin
English Department Head
Great Neck North High School
Great Neck, New York

BARRON'S

Acknowledgments

Page 79: "Pitcher" from *The Orb Weaver* by Robert Francis © 1960, Wesleyan University Press. By permission of University Press of New England.

Page 82: "Old Photograph of the Future" from *New and Selected Poems* 1923–1985 by Robert Penn Warren © 1985. Reprinted by permission of Random House, Inc.

Page 84: "Child on Top of a Greenhouse" from *The Collected Poems of Theodore Roethke* by Theodore Roethke © 1946 by Editorial Publications, Inc. Used by permission of Doubleday, a division of Bantam Doubleday Dell Publishing Group, Inc.

Page 84: "The Sleeping Giant" from *Old and New Poems* © 1990 by Donald Hall. Reprinted by permission of Ticknor & Fields/Houghton Mifflin Company. All rights reserved.

Page 87: "Juke Box Love Song" from *Montage of a Dream Deferred* by Langston Hughes. Reprinted by permission of Harold Ober Associates Incorporated © 1951 by Langston Hughes. Renewed 1979 by George Houston Bass.

Page 89: "As You Say (Not Without Sadness), Poets Don't See, They Feel" from *Selected Poems* © 1964, 1985 Karl Shapiro by arrangement with Wieser & Wieser, Inc. New York.

Page 93: "The Bean Eaters" from *Blacks* by Gwendolyn Brooks © 1991, Third World Press, Chicago.

All inquiries should be addressed to:
Barron's Educational Series, Inc.
250 Wireless Boulevard
Hauppauge, NY 11788
http://www.barronseduc.com

International Standard Book Number 0-7641-0100-5

Library of Congress Catalog Card Number 98-42411

Library of Congress Cataloging-in-Publication Data
Chaitkin, Carol.
   Let's review. English / Carol Chaitkin. — 2nd ed.
     p. cm. — (Barron's review course series)
   Includes bibliographical references and index.
   ISBN 0-7641-0100-5 (alk. paper)
   1. English language—Examinations—Study guides. I. Title.
  II. Title: English. III. Series.
  LB1631.5.C52   1999
  808'.042'076—dc21   98-42411
                              CIP

PRINTED IN THE UNITED STATES OF AMERICA
987654321

TABLE OF CONTENTS

PREFACE TO THE SECOND EDITION

Let's Review: English is designed as a handbook for high school English courses and as a review book to prepare students for the new New York State Examination in Comprehensive English. *Let's Review* also offers students and teachers a detailed outline of the new Regents Learning Standards for English Language Arts.

Because the Regents exam in English is not a test of a specific curriculum but an assessment of skills in reading, listening, literary analysis, and composition, *Let's Review* offers a comprehensive guide to essential language, literature, critical reading, and writing skills all high school students should seek to demonstrate by the end of junior year.

HOW CAN THIS BOOK HELP ME?

First, *Let's Review* gives you a comprehensive review of the concepts, language, and skills you need to do well—and enjoy!—your high school or college courses in literature and composition. You will find everything from tips on how to study vocabulary to suggestions for writing about poetry, from tips on how to listen well to a helpful review of literary elements and techniques. There is a detailed index to help you find whatever you need. Second, *Let's Review* is specifically designed to help you prepare for the new Regents exam. You will find a chapter for each part of the new exam, with sample questions and answers and sample essays with commentary and scoring.

QUESTIONS AND ANSWERS ABOUT THE NEW REGENTS COMPREHENSIVE EXAMINATION IN ENGLISH

Why all the changes in the English Regents?

The test is being revised to assess New York State students' ability to perform a broad range of language functions, critical thinking, and writing skills. It represents the more rigorous level of expectation reflected in the new Learning Standards for English Language Arts.

What does the new exam look like?

The exam will be in **four parts** or "tasks," and **each will include an essay response**. The first three parts require you to listen to or read extended passages of informational text or literature, answer multiple-choice questions on those passages, and write an essay for a particular purpose and audience. For the fourth part you must write an essay of critical analysis and evaluation of two works of literature you have read. All written responses require effective use of language and standard written English.

How and when will the new exam be given?

The new English Regents exam will be completed over two days of three-hour sessions each, with two tasks per session. It is scheduled to be given for the first time in June 1999 and will continue to be offered in January, June, and August of each year.

Why is the new exam six hours long?

Each of the four tasks on the new English Regents exam is designed to take most students about one hour to complete. The additional time gives you the opportunity to do your best work.

Why is doing well on this exam important to me?

Beginning with the high school class of 2000, passing the English Regents exam is a requirement for a high school diploma in New York State. (Students who pass the "old" exam in January 1999 will meet this requirement.)

WAYS TO USE *LET'S REVIEW: ENGLISH*

As a handbook for literature study in high school and college courses, see especially:

> Chapter 3—Reading Prose
> Chapter 4—Reading Poetry
> Chapter 5—Writing About Literature: A General Review

As a handbook for writing, see especially:

> Chapter 2—Reading and Writing for Information and Understanding
> Chapter 5—Writing About Literature: A General Review
> Chapter 7—Grammar and Usage for the Careful Writer
> Chapter 8—Punctuation: Guidelines and Reminders

As a guide to listening, reading, and language skills, see especially:

> Chapter 1—Listening and Writing for Information and Understanding
> Chapter 2—Reading and Writing for Information and Understanding
> Chapter 3—Reading Prose
> Chapter 9—Vocabulary
> Chapter 10—Spelling

As a review text for the new English Regents exam, see especially:

> Chapter 1—Listening and Writing for Information and Understanding: Part I of the New Exam
> Chapter 2—Reading and Writing for Information and Understanding: Part II of the New Exam
> Chapter 6—Writing About Literature on the Regents Examination: Parts III and IV of the New Exam
> Appendix A—The New York State English Language Arts Learning Standards
> Appendix F—Scoring Rubrics
> Model Regents Examinations

Chapter 1

LISTENING AND WRITING FOR INFORMATION AND UNDERSTANDING

People told stories long before they wrote them down. Although much of the oral tradition has been replaced by print and electronic media, students still learn a great deal simply by listening: to lectures, discussions, instructions—and to one another. Much of what we know has been acquired by listening.

HOW TO LISTEN WELL

As author and teacher William H. Armstrong points out, "While listening is the easiest and quickest . . . way to learn . . . it is the hardest of all the learning processes to master." Listening well requires a concentration and a discipline that allow you to "hold your mind on the track of the speaker." Here are some tips on how to do that:

How to Listen Well

If you are listening to a speech or a reading from a memoir, keep the following questions in mind:

What is this piece about? What is the main idea or purpose?

What does the author say? believe? recall? value? assert?

What does the author mean? imply? suggest? agree with? disagree with?

How are language and imagery used?

To what conclusions or inferences is the reader led?

What experience is meant to be shared and understood?

If you are listening to a lecture or a passage from a text, ask yourself:

What is the subject? What do I already know about this subject?

What main idea or theme is being developed? What phrases or terms signal the main thought?

What is the purpose? inform? persuade? celebrate? guide? show a process? introduce a new or unfamiliar subject?

1

These questions summarize much of what is meant by comprehension. They summarize what we are meant to understand and appreciate. Keep them in mind as you listen to any kind of presentation, and use them as reminders of what to include when you take notes. You should also review them as you prepare for the listening and reading comprehension parts of the new Regents exam.

The first part of the new New York State Regents Comprehensive Examination in English is designed to assess skills in listening and writing for information and understanding. You are expected to analyze and interpret a passage by noting salient information and by drawing inferences. *Noting salient information* means noting the key ideas, the most significant points; *drawing inferences* means forming conclusions and general understandings to which the text leads.

In addition to answering five or six multiple-choice questions on key ideas, you must also be able to compose an extended written response that conveys, to a given audience for a given purpose, the information and understanding you have gained. The selected passages may come from speeches and memoirs, lectures, or texts on the arts, history, or social sciences. They are often passages with distinctive voices, which are meant to be heard.

LISTENING PASSAGES AND QUESTIONS FOR REVIEW

Below are three examples of listening passages from past Regents exams. Each is followed by multiple-choice questions and analysis. Use these questions to help you understand what is meant by the terms *salient information* and *drawing inferences;* note also the questions about vocabulary and literary elements or techniques. Sample listening and writing tasks from the new Regents exam follow these examples.

If possible, have someone read the passages to you while you take notes; then, compare your notes with the ideas and information featured in the questions.

Listening Passage A

The following is adapted from "Writing for Monkeys, Martians, and Children," by Sandy Asher.

As a child, I sensed there was something I desperately needed from books. As a writer for young readers, I've tried to figure out what that something was. It turned out to be a combination of three things: companionship, a sense of control, and magic.

2

First, companionship. Life can be a lonely journey, and adolescence the loneliest stretch of all. Books, novels, and stories are one way to reach out to one another without losing face, a way of saying, "We are all in this alone together." A story that reminds us of this can be the best friend a teenager has. The characters in that story understand—and they won't let you down.

A sense of control is the second thing we crave from books. Life is chaotic. Adults pretend to be in control, yet we're not. The minute we think we've got it all together, someone shoots down a plane full of innocent people, a child disappears without a trace, or we find out the last three things we ate, drank, or breathed cause cancer. Children and adults would go stark raving mad if they had to deal with life exactly as it comes. It's too hard, too fast, too overwhelming, and far too complex. Since the days of the cave dwellers, we've listened to and told stories as a way of making life hold still long enough for us to make sense of it, to decide where we fit in and what to do. Fiction is not a luxury. It is an absolute, sanity-preserving necessity.

Companionship, a sense of control, and finally, there's magic, the third ingredient in stories. Magic, the illusion of traveling outside oneself and into another life in another world, beyond the limits of probability and into the excitement of possibility. As a child, when I read a good book, I climbed inside and lived there and hated it when the time came to climb back out.

The magic doesn't really take place between the covers of a book; it actually takes place in the mind of the reader. It's our ability to imagine the impossible that makes the trick work. That's why we love great magicians and writers, not because they fool us, but because they remind us that the most wonderful, most unlimited, most miraculous thing of all is our own mind.

Magic, companionship, a sense of control. The wonder of ourselves, of each other, and of life—this is the true subject matter of all novels. The best children's literature speaks not only to children but to the human condition. Writing for children simply means writing for human beings in the beginning, when you can still take part in creation, before habit, cynicism, and despair have set in, and while there is still hope and energy, a willingness to learn, and a healthy sense of humor. These qualities I find irresistible in the young people I write about and for, qualities I want to hang onto and to cultivate in myself. So I write for children, not just for their sakes—but for my own.

QUESTIONS

1 With which statement about adolescents would the speaker most likely agree?
   1 They should write books in order to understand themselves.
   2 They need to understand that life is often lonely.
   3 They see fiction as useless in their lives.
   4 They believe they are in control.

2 According to the speaker, some teenagers enjoy reading because
   1 books provide a sense of friendship
   2 books show that adults are not in control
   3 teenagers like to read about themselves
   4 teenagers can learn about the past

3 Air disasters and the disappearance of children are cited as evidence of
   1 loneliness in America
   2 the insanity of terrorists
   3 information we can obtain from reading
   4 our lack of control over events

4 The speaker implies that insanity is a threat because our lives are
   1 complex
   2 dreamlike
   3 lonely
   4 meaningless

5 According to the speaker, why do we love magic?
   1 We love to be entertained.
   2 We are mystified by it.
   3 It reminds us of our possibilities.
   4 It makes us feel less alone.

6   The speaker says we love great writers because they
    1   answer our questions about life
    2   make the impossible probable
    3   show us the magic inside us
    4   are able to fool us

7   According to the speaker, what is the true subject matter of novels?
    1   an adult sense of control
    2   the wonder of ourselves and of life
    3   miraculous occurrences
    4   ideas that appeal to children

8   According to the speaker, what does the best children's literature do?
    1   It encourages children to write.
    2   It creates the illusion of magic.
    3   It projects hope for the future.
    4   It represents the human condition.

9   The speaker implies that she benefits from writing children's books because she
    1   retains and cultivates her youthful outlook
    2   enjoys performing magic
    3   feels rewarded in getting to know young people
    4   likes sharing her knowledge and experiences

10 The speaker's purpose in writing this speech most likely is to
    1   persuade us to read more books
    2   explain her childhood addiction to reading
    3   explain why she writes children's books
    4   show how books can be our friends

LOOKING AT THE QUESTIONS: PASSAGE A

Note the key terms.

1   With which statement . . . would the *speaker most likely agree*?
    (The answer should restate a point made by the speaker.)
    2 "They need to understand that life is often lonely." The second para-
    graph is about the power of books to enable us to "reach out to one
    another . . . [to say] '[w]e are all in this alone together.' " It is easy to elimi-
    nate the other answers because none reflects a point made by the speaker.

2   *According to the speaker,* some teenagers enjoy reading because
    (The answer requires recall of what the speaker actually said.)
    1 "books provide a sense of friendship" The speaker states, "A story . . .
    can be the best friend a teenager has . . . . The characters . . . won't let you

5

down." Students should be cautioned that, while each of the other statements may in fact be true, none is specifically made in this passage.

3 Air disasters . . . are *cited as evidence of*
(The answer requires understanding *how specific details support* the speaker's point.)
4 "our lack of control over events" The second point the speaker develops is the theme, "Life is chaotic. Adults pretend to be in control." Again, students must be cautioned not to select answers that are generally true statements—or that express ideas they agree with—but rather to select answers that are supported by the passage itself.

4 The speaker *implies* that insanity is a threat because our lives are
(The answer requires stating explicitly what is suggested by the passage.)
1 "complex" This is a relatively easy connection to make because, as the speaker asserts, "[Life is] too hard, too fast . . . too complex," and because stories are a way of helping us "make sense of it . . . . Fiction is . . . an absolute, sanity-preserving necessity."

5 *According to the speaker,* why do we love magic?
3 "It reminds us of our possibilities." She says, "We love . . . magicians and writers . . . because they remind us that the . . . most miraculous thing of all is our own mind."

6 *The speaker says* we love great writers because they
3 "show us the magic inside us" This is a reiteration and emphasis of question 5 and its supporting passage. Choice 1, while true, is not the point the speaker is making; choice 2 must be rejected because writers do not make the impossible *probable*. Students must read the choices carefully and avoid selecting an answer simply because it includes a key term from the passage.

7 *According to the speaker,* what is the true subject matter of novels?
2 "the wonder of ourselves and of life" This is nearly a direct quote from the passage.

8 *According to the speaker,* what does the best children's literature do?
4 "It represents the human condition." This too is taken from the passage itself: "The best children's literature speaks . . . to the human condition."

9 *The speaker implies* that she benefits from writing children's books because she
1 "retains and cultivates her youthful outlook" As the passage comes to an end, the speaker *says*, "These qualities I find irresistible in the young people I write . . . for, qualities I want to hang onto and to cultivate in myself."

10 *The speaker's purpose* in writing this speech most likely is to
3 "explain why she writes children's books" Although she does indeed explain her "childhood addiction to reading," and she does show how

books can be friends (and she might hope she has persuaded us to read more books), the title of the passage, the introduction, and the main clause in the concluding sentence, "So I write for children," make it clear that this is the overall purpose of the piece.

Comment

This is a good passage to begin a review with because it offers direct and clear organization. The opening paragraph reveals that the speaker "sensed there was something I desperately needed from books" and that "it turned out to be a combination of three things." The listener expects to hear what those three things are, and each of the next three paragraphs begins with one of the key ideas and an indication of where we are in the discussion—"first, . . . second, . . . and finally."

Students should expect the listening passages on *the new* Regents exam to be more complex, both in language and in structure, but should keep in mind that they *may take notes during the reading.* The second example is from a work of fiction; the questions require both recall and interpretation.

Listening Passage B

The following is adapted from the novel *Braided Lives,* by Marge Piercy.

She works hard, my mother in her little house. She sits nearsightedly squinting at the old sewing machine, shortening a coat she bought too large at a rummage sale. She is always making over, trying to create something nice and pretty or at least serviceable out of what somebody with more money has discarded or sold off cheap. Things break and she fixes them, mends the old chair, glues the cracked plate, darns the worn sock. All day she scrubs and cleans and mutters. The bills come in and she mutters. She wants it nice, the house, her life. She irons even the sheets and towels. She is still showing her mother she can do it better. She was angry at her mother, she stayed angry. Not enough in a family of twelve for any particular girl child.

He works hard, my father, long hours. His hands are relief maps of burns and scars. His back is stooped from peering forward into engines. He has a permanent hacking cough from smoking and from breathing exhaust

7

fumes. His light gray eyes are squinted as if against a glare; they have the air of having wanted to look into distances rarely offered them. At fourteen he worked evenings and weekends and he has worked ever since.

With my books and my papers and my ever more peculiar interests and passions and ambitions, my friends they mistrust, I come into this house like a hot wind, casting dust in their eyes and spoiling their food. I want to make them happy. I pursue them around the house trying to share my ideas, to please, and I terrify. I am nothing they know what to do with.

I want to say, *Look, I love you,* but it comes to me that is the last thing I can say directly. It is not said in this house. The flimsy walls would crack with shame if I spoke it. We have channels between us for insult, channels for negotiation and innuendo, for push and pull, even for comfort after injury, but none for affection. I am a daughter who does not fit into the narrow slot marked Daughter and they cannot rejoice in me.

QUESTIONS

1 According to the narrator, why does her mother sew?
  1 It is a way to escape reality.
  2 It brings in extra money.
  3 She saves money by doing it.
  4 She cannot find employment outside the house.

2 The narrator implies that her mother's attitude toward her own childhood was a result of her being
  1 married at a young age
  2 the only child kept out of school
  3 forced to work long hours
  4 a girl among many children

3 What literary device is used to describe the father's hands?
  1 metaphor
  2 understatement
  3 contrast
  4 irony

4   The narrator's description of her father suggests that he
1   resents his life of constant work
2   sometimes dreams of a different life
3   dislikes his wife
4   complains about his poor health

5   The narrator implies that the lives of both her mother and father are dominated by their
1   family
2   ambitions
3   labors
4   home

6   The narrator's purpose in saying that she comes into her parents' house "like a hot wind, casting dust in their eyes and spoiling their food" most likely is to
1   emphasize the differences between the narrator and her parents
2   demonstrate the hostility the narrator feels toward her parents
3   show that the narrator has a violent temper
4   emphasize the narrator's abundant energy

7   The narrator states that she follows her parents around the house in order to
1   attract their attention
2   share her ideas with them
3   help in their daily tasks
4   tell them she loves them

8   The narrator states that she is reluctant to tell her parents that she loves them because they
1   do not openly express affection
2   know she really does not love them
3   would not believe her
4   have never heard her say it before

9   What does the narrator imply about her parents?
1   They demand hard work of her.
2   They favor her brothers.
3   They admire ambition in all young people.
4   They have conventional attitudes toward her.

10 The narrator's attitude toward her father and mother can best be described as
1 optimistic
2 scornful
3 loving
4 fearful

LOOKING AT THE QUESTIONS: PASSAGE B

Note the key terms.

1 *According to the narrator,* why does her mother sew?
3 "She saves money by doing it." This question requires both recall and some interpretation. The key is in the reference to "somebody with more money." The opening section also makes it clear that what the mother makes over is for the family's own use.

2 *The narrator implies* that her mother's attitude toward her own childhood was a result of being
4 "a girl among many children" This restates the close of the first section. None of the other points is made in the passage.

3 *What literary device* is used to describe the father's hands?
1 "metaphor" The narrator says, "His hands are relief maps." This is a clear example of direct comparison. (See A Glossary of Poetic Terms and Techniques, Chapter 4.)

4 The narrator's description of her father *suggests* that he
2 "sometimes dreams of a different life" This question requires interpreting the description of the father's eyes as "[having] the air of having wanted to look into distances rarely offered them." Note that the rest of the passage is description, without comment. There is no reference to resentment, dislike, or complaint in the father. Again, students must be careful not to interpret a passage in terms of what they think a character *might* feel.

5 The narrator *implies* that the lives of both her mother and father are dominated by their
3 "labors" This is the precise term here, as both parents are introduced by the phrase "works hard." The father has worked since he was fourteen.

6 The narrator's purpose in saying that she comes into her parents' house "like a hot wind, casting dust in their eyes and spoiling their food" most likely is to
1 "emphasize the differences between the narrator and her parents" Students must interpret the simile of "a hot wind" in the larger context of the passage, which is about all the ways the narrator is different

10

from her parents. (Her statement that she "want[s] to make them happy" eliminates choices 2 and 3.)

7   The narrator states that she follows her parents around the house in order to
2 "share her ideas with them" This is a reiteration of what she actually says. While choices 1 and 4 are appropriate interpretations of the passage, they are not answers to the specific question.

8   The narrator states that she is reluctant to tell her parents that she loves them because they
1 "do not openly express affection" She says, "We have channels . . . but none for affection."

9   What does the narrator *imply* about her parents?
4 "They have conventional attitudes toward her." Here the answer is in understanding the final statement: "I am a daughter who does not fit into the narrow slot marked Daughter . . . ."

10 The narrator's *attitude* toward her father and mother can best be described as
3 "loving" Students must recall the narrator's efforts to please them and her wish to say, "I love you." Indeed, the entire passage is the narrator's effort to tell her parents she loves them.

Listening Passage C

The following is from *Pilgrim at Tinker Creek,* by Annie Dillard, a field naturalist and author.

When I was six or seven years old, I used to take a precious penny of my own and hide it for someone else to find. It was a curious compulsion. For some reason I always "hid" the penny along the same stretch of sidewalk up the street. I'd take a piece of chalk and, starting at either end of the block, draw huge arrows leading up to the penny from both directions. I was greatly excited, during all this arrow drawing, at the thought of the first lucky passerby who would receive in this way, regardless of merit, a free gift from the universe. I'd go straight home and not give the matter another thought, until, some months later, I would be gripped by the impulse to hide another penny.

There are a lot of things to see, unwrapped gifts and free surprises. The world is fairly studded and strewn with pennies cast broadside from a generous hand. But—and this is the point—who gets excited by a mere penny? If you follow one arrow, if you crouch motionless on a riverbank to watch a tremulous ripple thrill on the water, and are rewarded by the sight of a muskrat kit paddling from its den, will you count that sight a chip of copper only, and go your rueful way? It is very dire poverty indeed for a man to be so malnourished and fatigued that he won't stoop to pick up a penny. But if you cultivate a healthy poverty and simplicity, so that finding a penny will make your day, then, since the world is in fact planted in pennies, you have with your poverty bought a lifetime of days. What you see is what you get.

Unfortunately, nature is very much a now-you-see-it, now-you-don't affair. A fish flashes, then dissolves in the water before my eyes like so much salt. Deer apparently ascend bodily into heaven; the brightest oriole fades into leaves. These disappearances stun me into stillness and concentration; they say of nature that it conceals with a grand nonchalance.

Nature, however, does reveal as well as conceal: now-you-don't-see-it, now-you-do. For a week this September, migrating red-winged blackbirds were feeding heavily down by Tinker Creek at the back of the house. One day I went to investigate the racket; I walked up to a tree, an Osage orange, and a hundred birds flew away. They simply materialized out of the tree. I saw a tree, then a whisk of color, then a tree again. I walked closer and another hundred blackbirds took flight. Not a branch, not a twig budged: the birds were apparently weightless as well as invisible. Or, it was as if the leaves of the Osage orange had been freed from a spell in the form of red-winged blackbirds; they flew from the tree, caught my eye in the sky, and vanished. When I looked again at the tree, the leaves had reassembled as if nothing had happened. Finally I walked directly to the trunk of the tree and a final hundred, the real diehards, appeared, spread, and vanished. How could so many hide in the tree without my seeing them? The Osage orange, unruffled, looked just as it had looked from the house, when three hundred red-winged blackbirds cried from its crown. I looked upstream where they flew, and they were gone. Searching, I couldn't spot one. I wandered upstream to force them to play their hand, but they'd crossed the creek and scattered. One show to a customer. These appearances catch at my throat; they are the free gifts, the bright coppers at the roots of trees.

QUESTIONS

1 The child's behavior in hiding the penny was a
  1 saddening experience
  2 spontaneous impulse
  3 practical joke
  4 constant mystery

2 The "generous hand" refers to
  1 fate
  2 the child
  3 the poor
  4 nature

3 The narrator seems to think that today most people's reaction to finding a penny is
  1 indifference
  2 amusement
  3 surprise
  4 exasperation

4 According to the narrator, what is the effect of "cultivating" poverty?
  1 Others provide what you need.
  2 You become receptive to small wonders.
  3 Every cent becomes a source of anxiety.
  4 You live longer.

5   The narrator suggests that opportunities to encounter the world's surprise
    wonders are
    1   infrequent
    2   controlled
    3   endless
    4   declining

6   The expression "dissolves . . . like so much salt" describes the
    1   losing of money
    2   passing of a glimpse of nature
    3   fading of a childhood memory
    4   living of a life of poverty

7   What is the effect on the narrator when the fish, deer, and oriole vanish
    from her sight?
    1   She is frightened.
    2   She feels sad and lonely.
    3   She is irritated.
    4   She becomes quietly attentive.

8   The narrator believed that the sudden appearance of the birds from the
    orange tree could be described as
    1   magical
    2   commonplace
    3   startling
    4   predictable

9   The narrator implies that the reason she could not find even one of the
    birds she had disturbed was that
    1   she did not search
    2   nature hides things well
    3   birds are too swift
    4   the birds continued to migrate

10 The phrase "force them to play their hand" most likely means to
    1   give the birds a chance to hide again
    2   watch the birds enjoy themselves
    3   cause the birds to reveal themselves
    4   continue the hide-and-seek game

LOOKING AT THE QUESTIONS: PASSAGE C

Note the key terms.

1   The child's behavior in hiding the penny was a
    2 "spontaneous impulse" While there is some element of "mystery" in
    her motives, the child accounts for the action of hiding the penny as a
    "curious compulsion," and she says later that she would be "gripped by
    the impulse" to hide another penny.

2   The "generous hand" refers to
    4 "nature" Here students should hear the metaphor that moves the
    passage from childhood anecdote to a lyrical reflection on the gifts
    nature offers the ready observer. The answer is implied in the images
    of the stream, and it is made more explicit as "nature" becomes the
    subject of the passage.

3   The narrator *seems to think* that today most people's reaction to finding
    a penny is
    1 "indifference" The author asks, "Who gets excited by a mere penny?"

4   *According to the narrator,* what is the effect of "cultivating" poverty?
    2 "You become receptive to small wonders." At this point students
    should understand the extended metaphor of found pennies as one of
    nature's "small wonders," and should realize, therefore, that cultivated
    poverty is a cultivated receptivity to those wonders.

5   The narrator *suggests* that opportunities to encounter the world's sur-
    prise wonders are
    3 "endless" This is a continuation of the thought expressed above; the
    speaker says that, "the world is in fact planted in pennies . . . ."

*NOTE: None of these questions involves simple recall only; each requires
interpretation and the ability to follow the author's metaphoric logic.*

6   *The expression* "dissolves . . . like so much salt" *describes* the
    2 "passing of a glimpse of nature" This image introduces a series of
    "disappearances" in nature and leads to the next question.

7   What is the *effect on the narrator* when the fish, deer, and oriole vanish
    from her sight?
    4 "She becomes quietly attentive." She says, "These disappearances
    stun me into stillness and concentration." The listener must not only
    appreciate what the author says but also recognize the key ideas
    expressed in different terms.

*NOTE: Questions are often posed using key words that are synonyms or
paraphrases of the original; rarely is the passage quoted directly. Thus, the
listening task also encompasses vocabulary skills.*

8   The narrator *believed* the sudden appearance of the birds from the orange tree *could be described as*
1 "magical" While the experience might be "startling," the overall description here is in terms of sudden appearance and disappearance, of leaves "being freed from a spell." (There is nothing "commonplace" or "predictable" here!)

9   The narrator *implies* that the reason she could not find even one of the birds she had disturbed was that
2 "nature hides things well" The final section is introduced with the observation that, "Nature . . . does reveal as well as conceal." And, the narrator asks, "How could so many hide?"

10 The phrase "force them to play their hand" *most likely means* to
3 "cause the birds to reveal themselves" Again, the listener must recognize the narrator's meaning in a metaphor.

PART I OF THE NEW EXAM

In this first part of the Regents exam you are applying skills that you use daily, in nearly every subject you study. The listening passages on the new exam are longer than the examples above; they range in length from 750 to 1000 words or more and require ten to fifteen minutes of careful listening. *You may take notes at any time during the reading.* The author and the source of the passage are identified before it is read, and this information helps you anticipate the sense and tone of what you are about to hear. The purpose and the audience for the written response will also be indicated and should guide you in taking notes.

Sample Passages, Tasks, Questions, and Essays

SAMPLE TASK I
[FROM REGENTS PILOT EXAM, SPRING 1996]

Overview: For this part of the test, you will listen to a speech about how an author became a writer of children's books and then will write a response based on the situation described below. You will hear the speech twice. You may take notes at any time you wish during the readings. Before you compose the report, you will answer several multiple-choice questions on the passage. These questions may help you organize your essay.

The Situation: You have been chosen by your class to attend the annual meeting of the American Library Association, where you will hear author Cynthia Rylant accept the Newbery Medal for her book *Missing May.* The Newbery Medal is an award given annually for the most distinguished children's book of the year.

Your Task: Compose a report for your class about the people and experiences that influenced Rylant's development as a writer.

Guidelines:

- *Identify* the people and experiences that influenced Rylant's development as a writer
- *Describe* the ways in which those people and experiences influenced her development as a writer
- *Support* your discussion with specific evidence from the speech
- *Provide* information from the speech that is accurate, relevant, and complete
- *Organize* your report in a logical and coherent manner
- *Use* correct grammar, spelling, and punctuation

Listening Passage

This is the biggest thank-you note I've ever had to write in my life. Believe it or not, I've never been much good with words when I've tried to express gratitude and, especially, love. Thus it is hard for me now to find words. On this momentous occasion when I am required to give a grand speech, I have been rendered nearly speechless.

I need to issue thanks to people who have made my life so beautiful that I have been inspired to write beautiful stories.

The first will be my mother, who managed, I don't know how, never to belittle or condemn any opinion I ever held. And, believe me, I held some wild opinions growing up. She loved me without judgment and patiently readjusted as I came home on holidays sometimes a vegetarian, sometimes not, sometimes a Christian, sometimes not, sometimes married, sometimes not. I had a baby when I was young and broke, and she rescued me from those times I was only steps away from the welfare office. And not once, though she had countless opportunities, has she ever said to me, "I told you so."

I was raised in an atmosphere of forgiveness, and this may be the finest gift God has given me on this earth. Knowing that I would be forgiven by my mother, my family, if I ever failed at anything I tried, gave me the courage to be a writer, the courage to place my work in the world for judgment, and the courage to keep on trying to say something important in my books.

I must thank my grandparents, who raised me for several years in Cool Ridge, West Virginia, until I was eight. There is no question in my mind that it was during those years that the writer in me was born. My grandparents gave me a small, warm, quiet house. They gave me faith in breakfast every morning and supper every night. They gave me a garden rich with the smell of carrots and potatoes and beans. They gave me the sacrifice of all their work on my behalf, and from them I learned steadfastness.

I grew up reading comic books because there was no library in my town or in my school, and I did not enter a public library until I was in my twenties. When I was twenty-three, just out of college and desperate for a job, I went to the Cabell County Public Library in Huntington, West Virginia, and asked for a job as a clerk. I was hired and assigned to the children's department.

Having grown up reading comic books and the Nancy Drew books my mother bought for me at the dime store, I did not know there was any such thing as children's literature. I had majored in English in college, and still I did not know this.

I spent only five months working in that children's room—I was, myself, growing my own baby, who would be delivered in the oranges and reds of the fall.

In those few months in that treasure chest of children's books, I discovered what I was. I was a children's book writer.

I also learned many things about libraries those months that I have never forgotten. The most important thing I learned is that they are free. That any child from any kind of house in any kind of neighborhood in this whole vast country may walk into a building which has a room full of books meant just for him and may choose whichever ones he wants to read and may take them home because they are free. And they are not free in a way which might diminish the child, not in the way of second-hand clothes or Salvation Army Christmas toys.

They are free in the most democratic and humane way. Both the poor child and the wealthy child are privileged with free libraries, and whenever they enter one, *Make Way for Ducklings* will be sitting there waiting for them both.

When I discovered I was a children's book writer, I began writing stories at home and mailing them to publishing houses in New York City. I was still living in West Virginia, had never met an author or illustrator, had only just found children's literature myself, and had not the foggiest idea how people became published. But I bought a copy of a book which listed publishers' addresses, and I mailed my stories to New York anyway. Because that's what I was put here on earth to do in 1978.

And that year I received two more gifts from God.

One, the more important, was my son, whom I named Nathaniel after one of my favorite writers. And that spirit in me which had been a little too quiet was stirred by this young child, and I found this stirring my strong writer's voice. It sounded like this:

When I was young in the mountains, Grandfather came home in the evening covered with the black dust of a coal mine. Only his lips were clean and he used them to kiss the top of my head.

And it was this voice, this writing, which led to the second gift of that year. The acceptance of my first book for children and new meaning for my life.

I have many friends here tonight: fellow writers, illustrators, editors, librarians. I have my most dear ones here—my best friend, my sweetheart, my son, and my mother—who make my life safe and who make it worth living.

I want to thank the Newbery Committee of 1993, the American Library Association, all children's book publishers, all children's librarians. I am honored to have been a part of you this past decade, and I cannot wait to see all of the beautiful books which are waiting for us in the future—which wait for the poor child and the wealthy child. And which will be given to them with love. Thank you and God bless you all.

MULTIPLE-CHOICE QUESTIONS

Directions: Answer the following questions. The questions may help you think about ideas and information you might use in your writing. You may return to these questions anytime you wish.

1   According to the speaker, the finest gift she was given by her mother was
   1   the opportunity to read many books as a child
   2   the education she received in college
   3   the atmosphere of forgiveness in which she was raised
   4   the encouragement to become a writer

2   The speaker expresses gratitude to her grandparents, saying "from them I learned steadfastness," which means
   1   patience
   2   perseverance
   3   humility
   4   faith

3   The speaker indicates that she first discovered she was to become a children's book writer when she
1   worked in a library for several months
2   began reading to her son
3   met other writers of children's books
4   began sending stories to publishers

4   When the speaker says that libraries are "free in the most democratic and humane way," she means that they
1   are like other charities in giving to the poor
2   make books available to privileged and poor alike
3   do not require membership fees
4   have books for all kinds of readers

5   At the end of her speech, Cynthia Rylant thanks children's book publishers and children's librarians for
1   supporting and encouraging her work
2   encouraging other writers
3   providing wonderful books to rich and poor children in the future
4   teaching young children to read

ANSWERS

1. 3   **2.** 2   **3.** 1   **4.** 2   **5.** 3

> Review **The Situation** and reread **Your Task** and **Guidelines.** Then write your response.

Cynthia Rylant's speech could be described as a celebration of the people and events that influenced her development as a writer of books for young people. Write a report for your class in which you discuss the people and experiences Rylant celebrates in her speech. In what ways have those people and experiences influenced her as a writer?

Sample Essay Response

Here is an example of a student essay that would receive a high score for this task:

Cynthia Rylant is certainly one of today's most prominent and talented children's authors. Her book Missing May *was recently honored at a gathering of the American Library Association where she was presented with the prestigious Newbery Medal. Her innate talent for writing children's novels was not formed in a vacuum, however. Raised until the age of 8 by her grandparents in Cool Ridge, West Virginia, the seed of her talent was planted; it was further nourished and continued to grow throughout her formative years with her mother. These caring and supportive people greatly impacted Cynthia's desire and ability to write.*

While growing up with her grandparents, Cynthia did not have great access to literature. Subsisting instead on comic books and Nancy Drew novels, she tended to her garden, never being exposed to the great and complex works of the literary giants. Her grandparents instilled in her a sense of steadfastness and almost stoic perseverance through their sacrificial work ethic, with which they hoped to provide their young grandchild a good and decent life. This perseverance helped her later in life as she sought a publisher.

Her mother may also be cited for influencing the young Cynthia to become a writer. Allowing her to grow up in an atmosphere where opinions were not questioned or rebuked dissipated the fear of failure that resides in all of us. Knowing that whatever she did would be accepted unconditionally removed the fear of failing at any endeavor she attempted.

Her job after college in the children's section of the local library introduced her to the genre that would become her profession. Not even aware that there actually was children's literature, she was intrigued with this new direction and decided to follow it. Writing several stories at her home in West Virginia, she would send them to publishers in New York. Persevering through rejections, she eventually had one of her works accepted and published in 1978, just after her son, Nathaniel, was born.

Cynthia Rylant is certainly a talented author, but that talent had to be awakened and combined with her life experiences in order for her true virtuosity to become evident. Through the influence of her mother and grandparents, as well as her life experiences, she was able to gain the tools that she would need in order to become a successful writer.

QUALITIES TO BE ASSESSED*

Meaning: the extent to which the response exhibits sound understanding, interpretation, and analysis of the task and texts

Development: the extent to which ideas are elaborated through the use of specific, accurate, and relevant evidence from the text

Organization: the extent to which the response exhibits direction, shape, and coherence

Language Use: the extent to which the response exhibits effective use of words, sentence structure, and sentence variety to convey ideas and information to a given audience

Conventions: the extent to which the response exhibits conventional spelling, punctuation, paragraphing, grammar, and usage

---

Comment

Using the Regents criteria noted above, it is easy to see why this essay would rate a high score. The task requires a report on the people and experiences that influenced Rylant's development as a writer. This essay conveys a clear and accurate description of those *people and experiences,* and it interprets and analyzes the impact of those people and experiences. The writer clearly understands the task and the speech. Note, for example, that the writer did not include Rylant's comments on the value of public libraries; those observations are not directly *relevant* to the task.

This is also a good model of the familiar five-paragraph essay: the introduction establishes the subject and context, has a clear thesis (the last sentence), and outlines in metaphor the points to be developed in the three paragraphs of example. The conclusion is also especially good because it restates, in new language, the main points of the speech, and it genuinely *concludes* by referring to Rylant as she is today. The criteria for **Meaning, Development, and Organization** are well met. Also, this student's **Language Use** is exceptionally good, and the writing is free of any significant error.

---

*These are the criteria for rating essays on all four parts of the new Regents exam. More detailed descriptions of each category are printed in the rubrics in Appendix F.

Here is a second example of a student essay for this task:

Cynthia Rylant seemed to have always been brought up in a lov-ing atmosphere. As a child, she was loved and encouraged by her mother and her grandparents. Her mother and her grandparents, she claims, inspired her the most. Cynthia's mother never belittled Cynthia's opinions, and Cynthia says that she had some pretty "wild opinions" growing up! Sometimes, later in life, Cynthia would come home a new person, a vegetarian, sometimes Christian, sometimes not, even married. Yet Cynthia's mother stood by and never said "I told you so" when something didn't work out.

Up until age 8, Cynthia was brought up by her grandparents. They lived in Cool Ridge, West Virginia. Cynthia felt that these were the years her love for writing was born. Cynthia's grand-parents sacrificed so much hard work to make her happy.

These two groups of people gave Cynthia what is so vitally important for a writer. They allowed Cynthia to feed on her own opinions, thus encouraging Cynthia's mind to grow.

As a young girl, the town Cynthia lived in had no public library. Instead of books, Cynthia read comic books. She didn't enter a public library until she was in her 20's. At age 23 she took a job as a clerk in the children's section of the public library. She was only there for 5 months because she was pregnant. Yet in that short time, she discovered what she was going to do with the rest of her life. Cynthia had discovered children's literature. She had majored in English literature, but she still didn't know about children's lit-erature. Once she had discovered it, it became her passion.

Cynthia feels that 1978 was a big year for her. It was the year her son, Nathaniel (named after her favorite author) was born, and it was also the year that her first book for children was accepted. Before her son was born she had been writing with the help of the "strong voice" inside her head. All the inspiring peo-ple in her life had combined to help her hear "the voice" in her head, thus allowing a very talented author to step forward.

Comment

While this writer has a good understanding of the speech and of the task, the essay as a whole does not have the coherence of the first one. This writer did not compose a distinct introduction or conclusion, but there is a clear structure to the essay: the writer begins with examples of the people who influenced Rylant and then moves to examples of the experiences that shaped her. The writer also shows a sense of structure in the effort to "summarize," in the third paragraph, the importance of Rylant's family. With respect to development, the writer does not

adequately discuss the period of Cynthia's growing up with her grandparents, but does make Rylant's experience of discovering children's
literature in a library vivid and relevant.

The writer makes a good effort to conclude by offering the elements of
Rylant's own conclusion: the inspiration that came from the birth of her
son and the encouragement of having a book published. This essay would
be even better if the writer had explained more clearly what Rylant meant
by "the [writer's] voice." This passage, which also recalls Rylant's growing up with her grandparents, is probably the most difficult to appreciate
on hearing only, and the writer is to be commended for trying to include it.

Some weakness in organization and development, along with several
spelling errors (corrected here), would put this essay in the 4–5 range
(see rubric in Appendix F).

SAMPLE TASK II

The task in the following example is similar to the one above; here the
speech concerns a woman's decision to enter politics.

The Situation: You have been chosen by your class to attend a meeting of
the National Women's Political Caucus, where you will hear Madeleine
Kunin, former governor of Vermont, give a talk on her life in politics.

Your Task: Listen to the speech in order to obtain information for a report
to your class about the experiences that led Ms. Kunin to pursue her political
career. You will hear the speech twice. You may take notes at any time you
wish during the readings.

Guidelines:
- *Identify* the experiences and influences that motivated Kunin's politi-
  cal evolution
- *Explain* why what she says leads to political courage and why she
  believes women have been reluctant to take an active part in politics
- *Support* your discussion with specific evidence from the speech
- *Provide* information from the speech that is accurate, relevant, and
  complete
- *Organize* your report in a logical and coherent manner.
- *Use* correct grammar, spelling, and punctuation

Listening Passage

At some gut level, the art of politics—combative, competitive, self-asserting—is sometimes difficult to integrate with our feminine selves. In order for women to achieve political authority in equal numbers with men, we have to overcome that instinctive pause between envisioning change and seeing ourselves as the agents of change.

In my own case, most essential to my political evolution was a strong desire to have an effect on events around me, whether that was a flashing red light at the railroad crossing in my neighborhoods, to protect my children on their walk to school, or whether it was a new environmental law for the state of Vermont. The fact that I succeeded in obtaining the flashing red light, as a private citizen, enabled me to change the environmental laws as governor. Each step builds a new self-image, enabling us to move from the passive to the active voice . . . .

Some of my motivation stems from my background. I came to this country as a child, at the outbreak of World War II, spoke no English, and I was fortunate to have a mother who believed in the American Dream: anything is possible in America. I learned at an early age, observing my mother coping as a widow throughout my childhood, knowing the legacy of the Holocaust, that essentially, one is responsible for one's life. Passivity provides no protection . . . .

Political courage stems from a number of sources: anger, pain, love, hate. There is no lack of political motivation within women. We feel it all. Anger at a world which rushes toward saber-rattling displays of power. Pain at a world which ignores the suffering of its homeless, its elderly, its children. Hatred toward the injustice which occurs daily as the strong overpower the weak. And love for the dream of peace on earth.

All this and so much more are within us to express. That is the first step toward political self-realization. It's back to basics: first you have to want to change the world, then you find a way to do it . . . .

The real pull of political life for me has been the ability to be a voice that articulates a vision, a value system, and provokes a series of actions that affect people's lives for the better . . . .

For too long, women have suppressed that part of themselves, biting the lip, opting for silence, being polite during heated conversations about tough choices . . . .

To live a life where one has an internal personal value system, but to recognize that all those beliefs are in direct opposition to how the world works, is a most frustrating and dangerous experience. That is how we were. Suppressed.

To live a life where one's personal values are reflected from time to time in the society in which one lives, often enough to feel a sense of belonging, is satisfactory, if not ideal. That is where many of us are. Accepted.

To live a life where one transforms one's personal values into public action, where one can see real change take place—a flashing red light at the railroad crossing, better elementary and secondary schools, clean water, welfare reform, a nuclear disarmament treaty—that is truly exciting, that is political equality. That is where we must be.

In the sense, I feel it's a marvelous privilege to be in public life . . . . The time has come to listen to our inner voices, to synthesize those voices with the political structure, and then to act upon our beliefs. We will not accept that there is a permanent dichotomy between being in charge and being feminine. Our goal is to humanize this world by combining both; let us begin.

MULTIPLE-CHOICE QUESTIONS

Directions: Answer the following questions. The questions may help you think about ideas and information you might use in your writing. You may return to these questions anytime you wish.

1 The main reason that the speaker became politically active was
   1 to bring about change in her surroundings
   2 to overcome her quiet nature
   3 to preserve the Earth's environment
   4 to fulfill a personal dream

2 The speaker suggests that political confidence grows from
   1 trying to push for passage of legislation
   2 encouragement from special-interest groups
   3 one small success leading to further action
   4 persuading one's neighbors to support a plan

3 The speaker's expression "move from the passive to the active voice" symbolizes
   1 inaction becoming rhetoric
   2 activity slowing down
   3 desires overcoming obstacles
   4 ideas becoming actions

4   The speaker's reference to the American Dream indicates her belief that
    1   in America there is unlimited opportunity
    2   people need to have dreams
    3   only in America do dreams come true
    4   everything is political in America

5   According to the speaker, the source of political courage and motivation is
    1   noble ideas
    2   strong emotions
    3   national leaders
    4   great ambition

6   According to the speaker, true political equality occurs when women
    1   elect as many women as men to public office
    2   transform personal values into societal changes
    3   make sure to vote in every election
    4   undo the laws men have enacted

7   The speaker's reference to humanizing the world suggests her desire to
    1   accept the political structure
    2   improve the status of the poor
    3   increase feminine influence
    4   organize groups to take action

8   What does the speaker indirectly suggest about the political influence
    of men?
    1   It is totally different from the influence of women.
    2   It has caused women to envy men.
    3   It requires more polish and gentility.
    4   It needs to be balanced by the influence of women.

ANSWERS

| **1.** 1 | **2.** 3 | **3.** 4 | **4.** 1 |
| **5.** 2 | **6.** 2 | **7.** 3 | **8.** 4 |

Review **The Situation** and reread **Your Task** and **Guidelines.** Then write your response.

27

Madeleine Kunin's speech could be seen as a celebration of the privilege to be in public life and as a statement of encouragement to women, especially, to become involved in politics. Write a report for your class in which you discuss the experiences that led Governor Kunin to public life and the ways in which she encourages and reassures women to be active in politics.

Summing Up

The passages selected for listening comprehension measure a number of skills beyond simple recall. They require the listener to interpret, to infer, to sense tone, and to comprehend the author's purpose. The listening passages may include anecdote, persuasive argument, or personal reflection; the arguments may be direct and explicit, or they may be indirect and metaphoric. The good listener, like the good reader, understands and appreciates a variety of expressive methods.

Not all of the written responses in this part of the new Regents exam will require a simple report. The task of writing to inform may include a feature article for publication, a thesis/support paper to endorse a position, or an informational guide. The next chapter, Reading and Writing for Information and Understanding, offers additional examples and review. You may also wish to consult A Glossary of Terms for Writing at the end of Chapter 2.

Chapter 2

READING AND WRITING FOR INFORMATION AND UNDERSTANDING

Much of the work you do in high school or college requires reading for information and understanding and writing to demonstrate your ability to understand, analyze, and organize information and ideas. It is on Part II of the new English Regents exam that your work in subjects other than English—science, social studies, or health, for example—will be especially relevant. It is in those subjects, as well as in writing courses, that you are expected to do many of the following:

- Use both primary and secondary sources of information for research.
- Select and limit topics for informational writing.
- Analyze and integrate data, facts, and ideas to communicate information.
- Take notes and organize information from lectures, documents and texts, video presentations, and on-line sources.
- Synthesize information for different contexts and purposes.
- Use paraphrase and quotation to integrate sources into your own text.
- Understand charts, graphs, and diagrams that support informational text.

These are, of course, skills you use when you do research in any subject, and you will find them in the new Regents Learning Standards for English Language Arts.

WRITING TO INFORM OR PERSUADE: A GENERAL REVIEW

In writing for the first two parts of the new English Regents exam you are directed to:

- Tell your audience what they need to know.
- Use specific, accurate, and relevant information.
- Use a tone and level of language appropriate for the task and audience.
- Organize your ideas in a logical and coherent manner.
- Follow the conventions of standard written English.

These guidelines are also reminders of what your teachers mean when they direct you to compose a "well-written essay" on a given topic.

Here is an example of an essay written in response to a task similar to those you may find on the new Regents exam. It is a good example of what is meant by tone and level of language appropriate for the audience. Also, it is organized in a logical and coherent manner.

Task: A representative of a junior high school in your district has invited you to speak at the junior high [or middle school] graduation ceremonies on the topic "Getting Off to a Good Start in High School." Write a brief speech that you would give to the students, stating your recommendations for a successful start in high school. Use specific reasons, examples, or details to support your recommendations.

Not so long ago, I too was sitting where you are now, thinking and worrying about what my life in high school would be like. Would I stick out? Would I make friends? How should I approach people? Would my classes be too difficult? Would I be able to cope with the stress? These questions kept badgering me throughout the summer before the ninth grade. I was especially nervous about starting school because I had just moved to a new neighborhood and did not know a single person.

By the end of the summer, the thought that especially frustrated me was that I would have no one to eat lunch with on the first day of school. This does not seem like such a big deal but it bothered me a lot. I knew that at the high school people went out to eat with a group of friends. I had no one to go out with. I told myself that I still had a week before school started and did not need to worry.

The first day of school finally arrived. As I neared the school, I felt helpless and lonely. I wanted to plead with Mom to turn the car around and go back home. But I reluctantly got out of the car and slowly approached the front entrance of the school.

Luckily, I found my first class and quickly took a seat in the front. I felt as if all eyes were on me. The new kid. The freak. While everyone was talking and laughing about their summer, I sat in my seat trying to look as though I was busy fiddling with my notebook. I couldn't wait to get out of the classroom. I wanted to run home and hide, for this was one of the most difficult experiences of my life.

Things started to look better around fifth period. I got up the courage and started talking to people. I even went out to lunch with a few girls and had a comfortable time. I was not totally relaxed but knew that I would adapt and soon make more friends.

*I have just finished my junior year in high school. I have many
friends and am very happy in my school. I will be a senior this
coming September and expect to experience new ideas and chal-
lenges. I am now starting to think about what I want to do with
my life and what colleges I might want to attend. Soon I will be
leaving high school and will feel again the nervousness and anxiety which all of you are going through in preparing for high
school. I guess what we are experiencing is not trepidation but
life, and what to expect in the future. You may be scared now, but
be confident that you will overcome those fears and the experiences will only make you stronger.*

Comment

Although this speech is more a personal narrative than a list of recommendations, the writer/speaker clearly understands both the purpose
of the task and her audience: "Not so long ago, I too was sitting where
you are now . . . ." The diction is informal, the tone is conversational, and
the first-person narrative is highly appropriate for the occasion.

The theme is established in the opening sentence, but the speaker's
main point is not stated until the very end: "You may be scared now,
but . . . you will overcome those fears . . . and [be] stronger." She leads
her audience to this conclusion by narrating her own feelings and experiences, starting with a series of "fears" she knows her listeners have.
The narrative covers a period of many weeks, but it is made coherent
by specific references to time: "throughout the summer . . . by the end
of summer . . . on the first day of school . . . my first class . . . around
fifth period . . . lunch." She also uses a reference to time to come back
to the present and bring the speech to a close: "I have just finished my
junior year . . . ."

The ideas are well expressed; and the paragraph in which the writer
describes what it was like to sit in her first class—"The new kid. The
freak"—pretending to be busy with her notebook is especially vivid
and convincing. We also trust the speaker when she tells us that she
had "a comfortable time" at lunch but that she "was not totally relaxed"
either. If she had claimed that after lunch all her fears had disappeared,
we would not believe her. This is a good example of what is meant by
honesty in writing: it rings true in our ears.

This response would be even better if the writer had included more
specific examples of how she overcame her fears.

PERSUASIVE WRITING

Here are two examples of what is called persuasive writing, pieces that develop and support an opinion on a particular topic. Note what makes each a successful argument.

Task: The students in your science class have been invited to submit essays on topics of current interest or controversy for possible publication on the Op-Ed page of the school newspaper.

Using Animals for Scientific Research

The question of whether or not to use animals as subjects for scientific research is a difficult one. Those in opposition claim that using animals in research is inhumane, while those holding a diametrically opposing view maintain that it is a necessary evil whose long-term benefits far outweigh the sacrifice of a handful of animals. I am an ardent supporter of the latter view. I feel that the use of animals is justified by the benefits that are reaped by all of mankind, and that halting the use of animals as subjects would greatly impede advancements in the field of medicine.

One example of the tremendous benefits which animal research can bring about is the discovery of insulin by Dr. William Banting and his assistant, Charles Best. Before this amazing discovery, diabetes mellitus was a devastating and inevitably fatal disease. The extent of treatment that doctors could offer afflicted patients was a starvation diet which prolonged life for only a short time and caused the obviously detrimental and painful effects of virtual starvation.

When Dr. Banting came up with a unique idea that linked the cause of the disease to a hormonal secretion of the pancreas, a potential way to control this deadly disease became apparent. But the idea had to be tested and proven successful before it could be offered to human patients. Dr. Banting proceeded with his experiments, using 15 dogs as his subjects. Although several of the dogs did die as a result of the experiment, the benefits that society gained because of the tests are infinitely greater. If those opposed to utilizing animals in testing had their way, the concept would have died prematurely because there would have been no way to test the idea. Fortunately for the field of science and for the millions of diabetics that have lived in the past few decades, Dr. Banting was able to find this treatment.

32

As a diabetic, I am greatly indebted to the work of Dr. Banting and the studies he conducted using animals as subjects. Today, I am not only alive, but healthy and active. I cannot help but be a supporter of animal testing because I owe my life to it. I understand how one may object to senseless cruelty to animals and the wasting of their lives worthlessly. Using animals strictly for scientific purposes is not "senseless cruelty," however, and it is clearly justified.

Comment

This is a good example of a short essay of opinion because the student has chosen a subject that he could develop with expertise and compelling personal experience; it also demonstrates his skill in organizing and presenting an argument.

One of the most effective ways to approach a controversial topic is to "acknowledge the opposition," that is, to recognize, even respect, the opposing view. This writer agrees that the question "is a difficult one," but goes on to say he is "an ardent supporter" of animal testing. Note that he very skillfully saves his most personal reason for the end, developing first a factual but dramatic example of the benefits of testing for millions of people. Introducing his personal reason earlier would have made the argument less persuasive because he would have appeared less objective. The conclusion is emotionally effective: "I cannot help but be a supporter of animal testing because I owe my life to it." More important, the writer demonstrates skillful argument when he says, "I understand how one may object . . ." and closes with a distinction between scientific experiment and "senseless cruelty." This essay would be a good contribution to an Op-Ed page.

Task: The editor of your local newspaper has proposed that businesses that hire high school graduates pay them salaries in proportion to their grades for the last two years of high school; that is, the higher a graduate's grades for those last two years, the higher the salary. Write a letter to the editor in which you state your opinion of the proposal. Use specific reasons, examples, or details.

I vehemently oppose the proposal that graduates be paid salaries in proportion to their grades for the last two years of high school.

First, grades should not affect the equal opportunity of all workers to receive the same paycheck for the same work. It must be taken into account that many factors influence a student's grades in high school. For example, a student may have a harder course load than another student with higher grades. It is unfair to compare grades from courses that differ in difficulty. Perhaps a student does not do well on tests, but is an excellent student in class. Participation and the ability to speak one's mind are very beneficial in a career, yet these qualities are not reflected by grades. Furthermore, if a student has an inborn proficiency in a subject (and gets good grades), it is unfair to assume that that student works hard to achieve his scores. An average student works harder and may still not get the same scores. Hard work and dedication are important factors in choosing an employee, but these factors cannot always be relayed by report card.

There are other factors besides grades that play a role in whether a student is right for a job. The applicant may have experience in the field of interest, but the proposed system would not take this into account. Perhaps a student has been a volunteer or has been active in clubs and organizations outside of school. By looking at his track record with reference to involvement in organizations, the student's ability to follow through would be noted. This is an important factor to take into account when hiring a worker.

Also, grades do not indicate strength of personal character, an important determinant in the selection of an employee. One must not make the generalization that a student with good grades is also a good person, and that a student with poor grades is not a good person. Only a personal interview can give the employer some sense of personal character of the worker. Positive interactions with other workers are vital to the success of a business.

Finally, by locking-in different salaries and pay rates based on high school grades, the employer is creating unnecessary competition and tension in the workplace. A worker with a lower salary may not work as hard, as a result. The worker with the lower salary might be treated differently, or unfairly by the employer by not being encouraged to work up to potential.

Thank you for your attention to this matter. Perhaps now an employee will be viewed as a person, and not as a report card. Everyone deserves a fair chance.

Comment

This essay would receive a relatively good score on an examination because it expresses a clear and thoughtful opinion, it is well organized, and it is excellent in its development. The essay would not receive the highest score, however, because it is not always focused on the specific topic. The letter begins well, with a clear statement of position, and the first section makes several important points about the limited significance of grades. Note, however, that the argument shifts from a discussion of how workers should be paid to how they should be hired in the first place. The second section makes several good points, but it too refers to *hiring* workers. The writer comes back to the topic of differentiated pay only in the third full paragraph.

If the writer had followed her statement of opinion with a *because* statement and a summary of her main points, she could have established the focus she needs. She clearly took time to gather good examples and reasons, but she did not always show how they related to the topic. The task directed the student to write a letter to an editor and to write *the body of the letter only,* but such letters are really essays of argument and must have focus and coherence to be effective. Composing "letters" of this kind is a very good way to practice writing persuasive essays.

WRITING FROM A PROMPT

On many examinations and in high school or college courses, you will encounter the term *prompt.* This term is used to refer in general to any set of directions or suggestions for what to do in answering a question or composing an essay. In the theater, the prompter gives an actor or singer in danger of forgetting her lines the phrase she needs to remember in order to continue the performance. In writing, a prompt also serves to recall ideas or stimulate discussion. A prompt may be in the form of a task and directions, as on the Regents exam, or in the form of a quote or even a photograph—anything that suggests to the writer a subject and possible direction for discussion of that subject.

Here are two examples of persuasive writing for which the prompt was in the form of a quote only; the writers had to establish controlling ideas and develop examples on their own.

Essay 1. "All the World's a Stage"

> *William Shakespeare once wrote, "All the world's a stage and all [the people] . . . players . . . ." This well-known sentence has stuck in people's minds through time because theater is a prominent medium in society; whether it's an amphitheater in ancient Rome or Broadway in New York City, crowds of people are drawn to the theater every day.*
>
> *The theater appeals to people for many different reasons. Some attend the theater to escape, for a little while, from the harsh realities of life. While sitting in a dark auditorium and watching trials and disputes played by live actors in front of you, it is very easy to forget your own problems. Other people find the*

theater simply entertaining. Plays and musicals involve audiences because they stimulate the senses and the mind. And some people go to the theater as a social event.

But theater is not only something to be watched. For many people, theater is their life. Every day, more and more people are becoming actors and actresses in the hope of becoming rich and famous. And for some people, that dream actually comes true. Many actors join the world of theater because they love to express themselves through their bodies, the tools of the trade. Nothing can compare to that adrenaline rush an actor gets just before stepping on stage in front of hundreds of people who all have their eyes focused on him or her. And the applause of an audience is all the gratitude some actors need to feel appreciated.

Many people don't realize that theater goes beyond the actors, though, and that is where they are deceived. Sometimes the technical aspect of a production is more interesting than the acting is. A Broadway production can have a set with more complicated plans than a skyscraper building. Shows like "Phantom of the Opera" can have over twenty major trap doors and more than ninety minor ones. There are dozens of people in charge of sound, lighting, props, and costumes that no one ever sees or thinks about when they are sitting in the audience. There is just that wonderful feeling that these things just magically happen; no one seems to be responsible.

The theater is an art that will live on for a long time to come, as long as people take the time to support it. The magic of a show that enthralls most viewers, though, is a culmination of the hard work, time, and dedication of many people who never get credit for their contributions. But Shakespeare was right because, for many people in the theater, all the world is a stage.

Essay 2. "All the World's a Stage"

All the world is indeed a stage. And we are the performers. Everything we do in life is a production, and we must constantly perform our best because, in life, there are no rehearsals. Each of us performs on a separate stage, some for a larger audience than others. But each performance, regardless of the size of the audience, is of equal importance, and each performer must meet the standard of life's most important critic—himself.

As a high school student, I often find that there exists much pressure to perform: pressure to perform academically, pressure to perform in sports, pressure to perform in social situations, and countless others. Furthermore, there are many individuals for whom I constantly must perform. At this juncture in life, parents, teachers, friends, and others comprise what I often perceive as an over-whelmingly large audience, which is sometimes overly critical.

As I grow older, I am learning to accept new responsibilities, and I find that my role in life is changing. Often in life, we cannot constantly adhere to a routine performance; sometimes we must improvise. The improvisation, or adjustment to new responsibility, is often difficult, though of critical importance to a successful production. In life, I have come to expect the unexpected and have done my best to deal with new situations. As performers, we must not allow tragedy, depression, and self-doubt to unnerve us. Instead, we must cope, adjust, and continue to perform.

Throughout my performance I have received evaluation from many critics, some of which I have taken better than others. No matter how many critics we have, we should remind ourselves that we are our most important critics, for of life's performance we will make the ultimate evaluation. Even though all the world's a stage, each of us need be concerned with only one performance.

Comment

The first essay stumbles at the beginning: the introduction has a central idea, but it is not well expressed and there is no coherence in the reference to ancient Rome. This essay reads like a first draft, and perhaps the writer was pressed for time. It would be improved not only in revision of the opening paragraph but also in the transitions. This writer begins too many sentences with *and* or *but,* and the language is not always fluent or precise. The writer, however, does establish organization and some unity in the opening of the second paragraph: "The theater appeals to people for many different reasons."

The writer also shows skill in development by moving from the role of theater for audiences to its importance for participants. The concluding sentence works well because it relates the major part of the essay to a fresh meaning of the quote. In this case, a good conclusion rescues an essay with a weak introduction.

The second essay rates a high score because of the exceptional way in which the writer develops the topic as an extended metaphor. The essay is brief, but it is absolutely focused; every detail supports the central idea, the comparison of one's life to a dramatic performance. The writer has maintained a consistent point of view and has developed the topic in a creative way.

EVALUATING COMPOSITION

Every student has seen on a paper or an essay test the comment, "Develop this point more." The Regents rubrics (see Appendix F) for scoring compositions are a reminder that one of the most important criteria in evaluating essays for class or for an exam is the extent to which *the topic has been developed* to achieve the writer's purpose. Simply to announce a subject and say that you have thoughts on that subject is not enough.

For any topic, you must show skill in establishing a central idea and in creating an effective way to develop it. All compositions must be unified and expressed in fluent and precise language, and they must follow the conventions of standard written English. (See A Guide to Standard Written English, Chapter 7.)

PREPARING FOR COMPOSITION EXAMS

All the writing you have done, or studied, constitutes preparation for the writing parts of the English Regents exam. To review, go over the essays and exams you have written in high school; note what is consistently strong and what needs revision; review carefully your teachers' comments. Because this part of the exam assesses your skills in writing from research, be sure to review relevant papers and projects.

Good writers are also readers. Read good writing, observe what makes it effective, and imitate for practice what you admire. In serious magazines and in the editorial pages, letters to the editor, and Op-Ed sections of newspapers you can often find good essays of argument on current topics. (See also Recommended Reading, pages 214–215, for suggested nonfiction works.)

WRITING ON EXAMINATIONS

If you are writing an essay for an examination, you do not have time for extensive preparation; but you can learn to condense the kind of thinking and notetaking you do for course assignments into a process for planning an examination response.

- *First,* be sure you understand the task or the meaning of the topic. One way to do that is to rephrase the question into a topic assertion. You may not actually use such statements in your essay, but the fact that you can express them for yourself means you understand what the question expects or that you have something to say about the topic. If you are creating your own topic, be sure you know what you want to say about it. This may seem obvious, but only when you sketch or outline can you be sure you have sufficient material for an essay.

- *Second,* sketch or outline possible lines of argument. Answer for yourself such questions as these: How can I prove that? What information in the text (if given) can I quote or paraphrase as evidence? How can I persuade someone that what I have to say is true?
- *Third,* outline your reasons, details, examples. All essay writing requires this step. Do not leave it out, even on a timed exam. The outline may consist of only phrases or a brief list to remind you of the points you want to make.
- *Finally,* decide on the order that is best: chronological? sequence of cause and effect? order of importance or intensity? (Common methods of developing ideas in essays are reviewed, with examples, in Reading Nonfiction in Chapter 3.)

USING SYNONYMIES TO ENHANCE YOUR WRITING

Included in the expectations for any well-written essay is the use of language that is vivid and appropriate; the rubrics for scoring Regents essays include "use of original, fluent, and precise language." The term *synonymy* refers to words that can be grouped according to general meaning; that is, they all denote or describe a specific instance of a general concept. Reviewing and creating synonymies will help you develop the vivid and precise language characteristic of good writing. Below are some examples of synonymies for commonly used but often vague or overused expressions.

to cause

bring about	create	effect	engender
excite	generate	give rise to	incite
invent	lead to	originate	persuade
produce	promote	provoke	raise
spawn			

to change

adapt	adjust	alter	amend
become	convert	correct	depart
develop	deviate	differ	digress
diverge	diversify	edit	evolve
grow	mature	metamorphose	modify
modulate	mutate	progress	remake
revise	rework	transform	turn (into)
vary			

to look upon someone/something

analyze	appraise	censure	classify
conclude	condemn	consider	deem
discern	dismiss	distinguish	esteem
evaluate	honor	hypothesize	infer
judge	observe	perceive	ponder
reckon	regard	review	ruminate
scrutinize	stereotype	summarize	typecast
value	view	watch	

to look down upon someone/something

belittle	censure	condescend	condemn
degrade	demote	depreciate	deride
devalue	diminish	discredit	disfavor
disgrace	disparage	disregard	show disrespect
embarrass	find fault with	frown upon	have disdain for
hold inferior	humiliate	ignore	jeer
mock	rebuke	reject	ridicule
scorn	shame	shun	taunt
vilify			

bad

abhorrent	atrocious	awful	base
belittling	blemished	calumnious	catastrophic
contemptible	corrupt	counterfeit	criminal
cruel	damaged	deceptive	defective
defiled	delinquent	depraved	despicable
detrimental	devilish	dirty	disquieting
evil	false	fiendish	foul
fraudulent	grotesque	hateful	heinous
hellish	hideous	horrible	horrid
horrific	immoral	imperfect	impish
inequitable	infamous	inferior	loathsome
malevolent	malign	marred	mean
merciless	monstrous	nefarious	negative
notorious	odious	ominous	perverse

putrid	rotten	ruthless	scabrous
scandalous	scurrilous	shameless	sinful
sinister	slanderous	sour	spiteful
spoiled	squalid	tasteless	terrible
unethical	unscrupulous	vile	villainous
wicked			

effective

capable	cogent	commanding	compelling
convincing	dazzling	dramatic	effectual
efficacious	emotional	forceful	impressive
influential	lively	moving	persuasive
potent	powerful	strong	telling

caring

affectionate	benevolent	bountiful	compassionate
concerned	courteous	devoted	doting
empathetic	empathic	fond	generous
giving	good-hearted	humane	kind
loving	philanthropic	selfless	sympathetic
tender	thoughtful	warm	warm-hearted

due to

as a consequence of	as a result of	because	because of
by reason of	caused by	following from	from
in light of	in view of	induced by	on account of
resulting from			

hard/difficult

arduous	bitter	challenging	complex
daunting	demanding	enigmatic	esoteric
exacting	exhausting	exigent	fatiguing
galling	grievous	grim	harsh
Herculean	impenetrable	impossible	impregnable
inflexible	insurmountable	intricate	labyrinthine
mighty	oppressive	relentless	resistant
rigorous	serious	severe	sharp

strenuous	strong	tiresome	toilsome
tough	unattainable	unbending	uncompromising
unyielding	wearisome		

sad/depressing (depressed)

abject	aching	aggrieved	bereaved
bereft	bleak	blue	cheerless
dark	dejected	desolate	despairing
disconsolate	discontented	distraught	distressing
down	forlorn	forsaken	gloomy
joyless	lugubrious	melancholy	miserable
morose	painful	saddening	somber
sorrowful	tormenting	tragic	unhappy
upset	wretched		

same

akin	alike	allied	analogous
associated	clone	cognate	collective
common	comparable	comparative	compatible
conformable	conforming	congruent	consonant
copy	correspondent	corresponding	duplicate
equal	equivalent	generic	homogeneous
identical	imitation	indiscernible	inseparable
interchangeable	joint	like	matching
mutual	parallel	photocopy	related
replica	same	shared	similar
synonymous	tantamount	twin	

A GLOSSARY OF TERMS FOR WRITING*

anecdote   A brief story or account of a single experience, often biographical, that illustrates something typical or striking about a person. Anecdotes, like parables, are effective as vivid, specific examples of a general observation or quality.

argument   The development of reasons, details, and examples to support a thesis; narrowly, to outline a position on an issue or problem with the intent to clari-

*Many of the terms in this glossary are also discussed in Chapter 3, Reading Prose.

fy or persuade. Argument is also used in a broad sense to refer to the way a writer develops any topic.

audience   For the writer, this term refers to the intended reader. Awareness of an audience determines, for example, the information that the writer may assume a reader already has, the level of diction, and the tone.

coherence   A piece of writing has coherence when the logical relationship of ideas is evident and convincing. In a coherent discussion, statements and sections follow one another in a natural, even inevitable, way. A coherent discussion hangs together; an incoherent one is scattered and disorganized.

description   The expression in words of what is experienced by the senses. Good description recreates what is felt, seen, heard—sensed in any way. We also use the term *describe* to mean *identify, classify, characterize,* even for abstract ideas. Description permits readers to recreate a subject in their own imaginations.

diction   Refers to word choice. Diction may be formal or informal, complex or simple, elegant or modest, depending on the occasion and the audience. The language used in casual conversation is different from the language used in formal writing. The good writer uses language that is varied, precise, and vivid; he or she has resources of language to suit a wide range of purposes.

exposition   The development of a topic through examples, reasons, and details that explain, clarify, show, instruct; the primary purpose of exposition is to convey information. Much of the writing assigned to students is referred to as expository writing: through exposition they can demonstrate what they have learned, discovered, understood, appreciated. (The passage by Sandy Asher on page 2 is a good example of exposition.)

focus   Refers to the way a writer concentrates and directs all the information, examples, ideas, and reasons in an essay on the specific topic.

narrative   Because it tells a story, a narrative has chronological order. The narrative method is commonly used in exposition when examples are offered in a chronological development. (The passage by Annie Dillard on page 11 is a good example.)

prompt   A set of directions for a writing task; may also be a quote or passage meant to stimulate a piece of writing.

tone   In writing, *tone* refers to the attitude of the writer toward the subject and/or toward the reader. Tone may range from *harsh and insistent* to *gentle and reflective;* there is as much variety of tone in writing as there is in human feeling. Some pieces—essays of opinion for example—usually have very distinct tones; other works, especially in fiction or personal expression, may be more subtle and indirect in tone. (See discussion of tone on page 70 in Chapter 3, Reading Prose, and on page 88 in Chapter 4, Reading Poetry.)

transition   Words or phrases used to link ideas and sections in a piece of writing. Common transitions include *first, second . . . in addition . . . finally; on the other hand, moreover, consequently, therefore*. Transitions make the development of an argument clear.

unity   In the narrow sense, *unity* refers to focus: the ideas and examples are clearly related to the topic and to one another. In the larger sense, unity refers to a feature of all good writing: all elements—ideas, form, language, and tone—work together to achieve the effect of a complete and well-made piece.

PART II OF THE NEW EXAM

Sample Text, Task, Questions, and Essay

Directions: Read the text and study the graphs on the following pages, answer the multiple-choice questions, and write a response based on the situation described below. You may use the margins to take notes as you read. You may use scrap paper to plan your response.

The Situation: A community health clinic has invited students in your school to write health-related articles for its newsletter. You decided to write an article discussing factors that influence teenage smoking and the implications of those factors for reducing teenage smoking.

Your Task: Write an article for the community health newsletter. Using relevant information from the text and graphs, discuss the factors that influence teenage smoking and the implications of those factors for reducing teenage smoking.

Guidelines:

- Tell your audience what they need to know about factors that influence teenage smoking
- Discuss the implications of those factors for reducing teenage smoking
- Use specific, accurate, and relevant information from the text and the graphs to develop your discussion
- Use a tone and level of language appropriate for an article for a community health newsletter
- Organize your ideas in a logical and coherent manner
- Be sure to indicate any words taken directly from the article by using quotation marks or referring to the author
- Follow the conventions of standard written English

Passage

Researchers calculate that teenage smoking rates, after declining in the 1970's and leveling off in the 1980's, have climbed sharply over the last five years. Although everything from why the trend began to what might stop it is disputed, it adds up to a huge health problem for the country and a public relations disaster for the tobacco industry.

Teenage smoking rates are still lower than in the 1970's, but they are rapidly increasing. According to the most recent edition of the University of Michigan's Monitoring the Future Survey, last year the percentage of 12th graders who smoked daily was up 20 percent from 1991. This annual study is widely followed by tobacco researchers. The rate among 10th graders jumped 45 percent, and the rate for 8th graders was up 44 percent between 1991 and 1996.

At current smoking rates, five million people now younger than 18 will eventually die of tobacco-related illnesses, according to the most recent projections from the Centers for Disease Control and Prevention in Atlanta.

Rising youth smoking rates have been cited by the Food and Drug Administration and President Clinton as evidence that the industry is marketing its products to youths and should be restricted by the F.D.A. The rates are also fueling demands in many states and nationally for higher taxes on tobacco, based on research showing that price increases typically discourage teenage smokers.

Just what has caused the teenage smoking rate to rise so sharply is hotly debated. The tobacco industry says the increase is due to a broad range of social forces. Industry officials note that other kinds of risk-taking among teenagers, especially the use of marijuana and other drugs, have risen more sharply than tobacco use. The industry also cites teenagers' naturally rebellious reaction to the increasing efforts to stop them from smoking.

Critics of the tobacco industry agree that rebelliousness and other forces are at work. But they say the industry itself is the most important factor. The industry's spending on domestic advertising and promotions soared from $361 million in 1970 to $4.83 billion in 1994, a 250 percent increase after adjusting for inflation, according to the latest data published by the Federal Trade Commission.

Just how that huge pie has been divided is a secret closely guarded not only from critics but even among companies in the industry. Much of the money goes into promotions to encourage retailers to run sales or to display particular brands and signs more prominently. Tobacco companies say they have adopted practices to focus their messages on adults, like requiring that all models be—and look—older than 25.

But critics like John Pierce, head of the Cancer Prevention Center at the University of California at San Diego, say it is most telling that spending rose most rapidly in the 1980's, when the decline in youth smoking was halted. They also point to research showing that children have been strongly attracted to some of the biggest marketing, notably R.J. ReynoldsTobacco's use of the ever-hip Joe Camel and Philip Morris' use of the rugged Marlboro man and the Marlboro Adventure Team, a merchandise promotion.

The surge in teenage smoking in the 1990's coincided with a sharp expansion by both Reynolds and Philip Morris in give-aways of items like T-shirts in return for coupons accumulated by buying their cigarettes. Research showed that the companies had limited success in preventing distribution of the merchandise to children—30 percent of teenage smokers have it—and that the items are just as appealing to teenagers as to adults.

Tobacco companies say critics grossly exaggerate the effects of their marketing. They point out that teenage smoking is also rising in countries where most forms of advertising have been banned. The latest indicator of the distance between the two sides is Philip Morris' creation of a record company—Woman Thing Music—to promote its Virginia Slims brand. The company will be selling bargain-priced compact disks by its female artists along with its cigarettes. Its first artist, Martha Byrne, a nonsmoking actress from the soap opera *As the World Turns,* is on a concert tour. She is appearing in venues where only those older than 21 are allowed.

Making matters worse, some critics say, is that Hollywood's long love affair with smoking seems to be heating up. Cigars are being widely used to symbolize success in movies like *The Associate,* with Whoopi Goldberg. And even though today's stars are not inseparable from their cigarettes the way Humphrey Bogart, Bette Davis, and James Dean were, actors who show up puffing on cigarettes include John Travolta and Uma Thurman as anti-heroes in *Pulp Fiction,* and Winona Ryder as a Generation X drifter in *Reality Bites.* Leonardo DeCaprio went so far as to light up as Romeo in last year's updated *Romeo and Juliet.*

Whether smoking in films contributes to the teenage trend or simply picks up on it is one of many questions. Teenagers say that movie and music stars do shape their sense of what is "cool" and that a desire to be cool is often a reason the youngest smokers first try cigarettes. But many researchers doubt that an effect can be reliably measured.

Moreover, high school students who smoke regularly say it is so common that no one thinks of it as cool. Some concede that they enjoy doing something forbidden, but more often they cite a desire to relieve stress or to stay thin, the taste, or simply the need to fill time as reasons they kept smoking to the point of becoming addicted. Many, like David Bernt of Oak Park, agree with the industry's contention that its marketing had nothing to do with the decision to smoke but that it does influence brand choice.

"If I buy anything but Camel, it feels like I wasted money because I collect Camel cash," he said, referring to the coupons that can be redeemed for Camel merchandise.

The increased smoking rates since 1991 are expected to translate into tens of thousands of additional early deaths because one out of three teenage smokers is expected to develop fatal tobacco-related illnesses. About 46,000 more 8th graders are smoking at least half a pack a day than would have been smoking had the rate remained at its 1991 level, and 250,000 more have smoked within the last 30 days than would have at the 1991 rate, judging from the application of census data to results from the Monitoring the Future surveys. And because of the rising smoking rate since 1991, an extra 110,000 10th graders are half-a-pack-a-day smokers, and nearly 366,000 more of them have smoked in the last 30 days.

—B. Feder

Graph 1

Half a Pack At an Early Age

Percentage in each grade who told surveyors that they smoke at least half a pack of cigarettes a day.

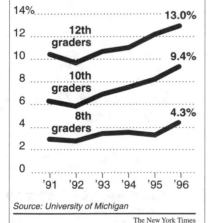

Source: University of Michigan

The New York Times

Graph 2

Teen-Age Smoking Makes a Comeback

The number of 12th graders who try cigarettes has declined over the last two decades, but the number who smoke occasionally and who develop heavier habits has increased sharply in recent years.

Of 12th graders surveyed

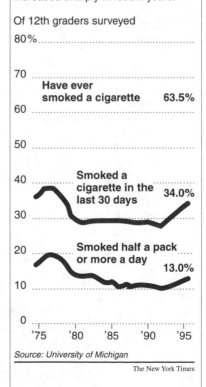

Source: University of Michigan

The New York Times

Directions: Answer the following questions. The questions may help you think about ideas and information you might use in your writing. You may return to these questions anytime you wish.

1   Rising youth smoking rates have led the FDA to propose
    1   a national antismoking campaign
    2   a federal lawsuit against the tobacco industry
    3   restrictions on marketing tobacco products to teenagers
    4   denial of insurance coverage for smokers

2   The text implies that one result of raising taxes on tobacco is that
    1   the FDA will restrict tobacco sales
    2   retailers will lower cigarette prices
    3   tobacco companies will advertise less
    4   teenagers will buy fewer cigarettes

3   Tobacco industry officials imply that a major factor in teenage smok-ing is the tendency of teenagers to
    1   misunderstand cigarette warnings
    2   believe cigarette advertisements
    3   engage in risky behavior
    4   imitate their parents

4   The "secret" mentioned in the first sentence of paragraph 7 refers to the
    1   ways in which advertising money is spent
    2   amount of money spent on advertising
    3   results of increased advertising
    4   reasons for increased advertising

5   According to the text, teenage smoking increased at the same time that the tobacco industry increased its promotion of
    1   long, slim cigarettes
    2   giveaway items
    3   more effective filters
    4   reduced nicotine cigarettes

6   The text mentions Humphrey Bogart and James Dean as examples of movie stars who
    1   died of tobacco-related illnesses
    2   were usually pictured with a cigarette
    3   urged fans not to smoke
    4   refused to smoke on screen

7   The text implies that Hollywood may influence teenagers to smoke by
1   shaping their sense of what is trendy
2   indirectly advertising cigarettes in movies
3   selling cigarettes in movie theaters
4   giving them false information

8   The anecdote about David Bernt implies that marketing techniques influenced Bernt to
1   start smoking
2   buy a certain brand
3   become addicted
4   decide not to smoke

9   What is the main purpose of the text?
1   to criticize the tobacco industry
2   to persuade readers not to smoke
3   to offer solutions to the problem of teenage smoking
4   to report on the increase in teenage smoking

10 Graph 1 shows a steady increase in the
1   age at which teenagers start to smoke
2   number of teenagers who smoke heavily
3   price of tobacco products
4   earnings of tobacco companies

11 What does Graph 2 imply about 12th graders in 1995?
1   About forty percent of them did not smoke at all.
2   About forty percent of them developed tobacco-related illnesses.
3   Twelfth graders smoked primarily on weekends.
4   Twelfth graders started smoking in elementary school.

12 According to Graph 2, the sharpest decrease in teenage smoking occurred during which years?
1   late 1930's
2   late 1960's
3   late 1970's
4   late 1990's

NOTE: The operational examination will include only 8–10 questions on Part II. Additional questions are included here to suggest a fuller range of possible question types.

ANSWERS

1. 3	**2.** 4	**3.** 3	**4.** 1	**5.** 2	**6.** 2
7. 1	**8.** 2	**9.** 4	**10.** 2	**11.** 1	**12.** 3

After you have finished these questions, review **Your Task** and **Guidelines** and write your article. Use scrap paper to plan your response.

Here is one student's article for this task.

Teenage Smoking

There is an epidemic on the rise in the youth of America today. Researchers conclude that teenage smoking rates, after declining and leveling off in the 1970s and 1980s, has increased sharply in the last five years. The tobacco industry, its critics, and teenagers themselves all have ideas about the factors that influence smoking.

The tobacco industry attributes the increase to "a broad range of social forces." The industry says that other drug use and risk-taking procedures by teenagers has risen more sharply than tobacco use. The industry also believes that teenage smoking has increased because of the rebellious attitudes of teens towards increasing efforts to stop them from smoking.

The industry's critics, however, disagree with this hypothesis. The critics believe that the industry's huge increase in spending on domestic advertising and promotions, from $361 million in 1970 to $4.83 billion in 1994, is to blame. Most of the money goes for promotions that encourage stores to run sales or more prominently display particular brands and signs. Spending by the industry increased most rapidly in the 1980s when the decline in youth smoking was halted. Children are also attracted to the advertising campaigns that use Joe Camel or the Marlboro man. The giving-away of items, such as T-shirts for the accumulation of coupons received when buying cigarettes, also attracts teens. Philip Morris even created a record company to promote its Virginia Slims brand that is a draw to teens. Hollywood's use of cigarettes and cigars is also becoming more prevalent and is subliminally encouraging teens to take up smoking because it is trendy and "cool."

Teenagers say that a desire to be cool is often a reason young smokers try cigarettes. Teenagers also say that smoking is a way to relieve stress, stay thin, and fill time. Teenagers also say they were drawn to smoking because of their desire to do something forbidden.

This trend in teenage smoking must end. The increased smoking rates are expected to translate into additional early deaths due to tobacco-related illnesses. The trend can be halted by *increasing the cost of cigarettes, making them too expensive for teens to buy. Hollywood should place a ban on the use of cigarettes and cigars in their films, so as not to project the message that smoking is cool. Teenagers should be made more aware of the effect that smoking will have on their bodies in the future. Also, the tobacco industry should not be allowed to use advertising which is intended to draw teens to their products.*

This epidemic of increased smoking in teens must end, and it takes an effort by all to stop it. Join the battle to end teen smoking!

Comment

This essay meets the Guidelines for the task very well. It gives the audience—readers of a community health newsletter—the information it needs to understand what research indicates is a sharp rise in teenage smoking; the article also reports effectively on the implications of that increase. You will note that the essay is not a simple report; rather, the writer has appropriately interpreted the task and audience to select information from the article and the graphs that supports the controlling idea. The purpose of the piece is to raise concern and urge action, but the writer achieves the effect of a reasoned argument by acknowledging the position of the tobacco industry at the beginning. (The essay on animal testing, page 32, uses the same strategy.) The **tone and level of language** are excellent here, echoing the language of the article in many places, and the **organization** is logical and clear. Any minor errors in the **conventions** do not interfere with the meaning or the effect of the article. According to the rubric in Appendix F, this essay would probably rate a 6 overall.[*]

---

[*]A note on Regents scoring: Final standards for scoring Regents essays will be set in the spring of 1999. The published rubrics, however, have been adopted and reprinted in Appendix F.

Chapter 3

READING PROSE

One of the characters in Moliere's satire *Le Bourgeois Gentilhomme* (*The Bourgeois Gentleman*) makes an astonishing discovery: "For over forty years I have been speaking prose without knowing it!" Prose writing is composed in the rhythms and patterns of spoken discourse. When we read novels and short stories, essays and reports, journals and letters, we are usually reading prose. In our daily lives and as students, we read prose that varies widely in purpose, in method of development, and in tone. Prose serves the purposes of personal expression, persuasion, literary effect, and information.

WHAT WRITERS DO: A LIST OF USEFUL TERMS

A group of high school juniors recently was asked to list all the verbs they could think of to denote what writers *do*. Here is the list they came up with:

address	affirm	alert	amuse	analyze
appraise	argue	assert	assess	capture
caution	censure	cite	clarify	classify
comment	conclude	condemn	conjecture	convey
create	create images	criticize	declare	defend
define	delineate	depict	describe	discern
discover	dramatize	edit	emphasize	enhance
enrich	establish	evaluate	examine	explain
explore	expose	expound	forewarn	formulate
illustrate	imply	infer	influence	inform
inspire	interpret	invent	judge	note
observe	offer	persuade	play	ponder
portray	present	probe	produce	propose
provoke	question	reassure	recreate	refine
reflect	refute	remind	reveal	revise

scrutinize	see	select	shock	show
suggest	summarize	support	symbolize	teach
theorize	uncover	view	work(!)	

As you consider these terms, you will note that they are not separated by categories; many of them denote both purpose and tone, and many suggest a method of development as well. While this list may not include everything writers "do," it is a useful reminder of the great variety in written expression. (Because command of this vocabulary will also help you to express your understanding and appreciation of what you read, you will find examples showing how many of these words are applied to discussions of nonfiction and, in Chapter 5, to writing about literature.)

To read well you must be listening actively to the narrator's voice, thinking with the author. If you are reading a piece for information or direction, ask questions; expect them to be answered. If you are reading a work of argument or persuasion, question it; actively agree or disagree; follow how the argument is developed. If you are reading a piece of personal expression, try to imagine, even share, the experience. If you are reading a piece of vivid description, recreate the images and feelings for yourself. Reading well offers us the entire range of human history and experience expressed in language.

Works of fiction are usually narrative in form. They tell us stories of what *happened* in the lives of the characters and, more important, *why it happened.* Nonfiction takes many forms, and its subjects touch on virtually everything in the human and natural worlds.

READING FICTION

When we speak of fiction, we are generally referring to narrative works—works in which events are recounted, are *told,* and have been imagined and structured by the author. (Although not narrative in form, drama shares many of the essential characteristics of fiction.) The subjects of fiction, however, are no less real than those of history or of what we call the actual or real world. In *Aspects of the Novel,* E. M. Forster shows how "fiction is truer than history." He reminds us that only in narrative fiction and drama can we truly know what is in a character's heart or mind; that is, only in a novel, short story, or play can we fully understand the motives, desires, and reasons for characters' actions. The historian draws conclusions from records of the past; the psychologist interprets interviews and tests; a jury weighs evidence and testimony; and our experience indicates that these are highly reliable ways to understand people and their lives. But only the author of a fictional work can offer an absolutely reliable account of what a character feels, believes, and desires, of why things happen as they do.

Plot and Story

The primary pleasure for most readers of narrative fiction is the story. The reason why we become involved in a novel or short story is that we want to know how it turns out; we want to know what is going to happen to those characters. An author creates a **plot*** when he or she gives order and structure to the action: in a plot, the incidents, or episodes, of the story have meaningful relationships to one another. A story becomes a plot when we understand not only *what happened* but also *why.* In good fiction we are *convinced* of the causal relationship among incidents, and we are convinced by the relationship of characters' motives and feelings to the action.

For most readers of fiction, the first response is to keep track of the plot. We do this spontaneously. If you are preparing a novel or story for class discussion, one of the first things your instructor will expect you to know is, "what happens in . . . ?" This is not a trivial question, because you cannot fully understand the significance of character, theme, or structure if you do not first understand the action as it is presented. Understanding plot, of course, requires memory, and remembering the major incidents of a plot is usually a natural and relatively easy response. The more extensively you read, however, the more skilled you become in remembering and relating the key incidents in a complex plot and in recalling details when their full significance becomes evident—sometimes well after the incidents themselves occur. Keeping notes on the development of a complex plot is very useful, especially for students whose reading of a novel is broken up over days or weeks.

For a class, or as part of your preparation for the Regents exam questions on literature, practice summarizing the plots of works you know or are reading. Be able to tell the story of a novel or play to someone who does not know it in a narrative of your own words, including all the major incidents and their consequences. Be able to tell the story in the same way you would retell a familiar children's story or narrate a significant experience of your own.

Plot and Conflict

At the end of any meaningful story, something has *happened;* something is significantly different in the world and lives of the characters from what it was at the beginning. **Conflict** in the most general sense refers to the forces that move the action in a plot. Conflict in plot may be generated from a search or pursuit, from a discovery, from a deception or misunderstanding, from opportunities to make significant choices, or from unexpected consequences of an action. Although the term *conflict* connotes an active struggle

*Terms in bold are featured in A Glossary of Literary Terms and Techniques at the end of the chapter.

between opposing or hostile forces, conflict in fiction may refer to any progression, change, or discovery. The resolution of conflict in a plot may be subtle and confined to the inner life of a character or it may be dramatic and involve irreversible change, violent destruction, or death.

This term may identify an actual struggle between characters, anything from dominance or revenge to simple recognition or understanding. A plot may also focus on conflict between characters and the forces of nature or society. These are essentially **external conflicts**. A work may also center on **internal conflicts**, characters' struggle to know or change themselves and their lives. Most works of fiction and drama contain more than one aspect of conflict.

In Shakespeare's *Romeo and Juliet*, the most dramatic conflicts are external, vivid, and literal: the street brawls between followers of the rival Capulets and Montagues, the fatal fight with Tybalt that leads to Romeo's banishment, and the tragic deaths of the young lovers. In *Macbeth,* however, the primary interest is in the internal conflict between Macbeth's ambitious desires and his understanding of the moral consequences of the actions he takes to achieve those desires. The action in Edith Wharton's most famous story, "Roman Fever," is ironically serene and pleasant: two middle-aged women, long-time friends now both widowed, sit on a terrace overlooking the splendors of Rome and reflect on their common experiences and lifelong friendship. At the end of the conversation—and the story—their actual feelings of rivalry have surfaced, and one of the two learns something that reveals how little she truly knew her husband or understood her marriage or the life of her friend. The conflict between the two women emerges almost imperceptibly, and its meaning is fully understood only in the completely unexpected revelation of the last line.

Plot and Chronology

Narrative is not necessarily presented in chronological order, but it does have a chronology. In other words, incidents may be presented out of the order in which they actually occurred, but by the end of the work the reader understands their order and relationship and appreciates why the story was structured as it was. Plots that are narrated in flashback or from different points of view are common examples.

The Great Gatsby, by F. Scott Fitzgerald, and *Ethan Frome,* by Edith Wharton, are novels in which the narrators first introduce themselves and their interest in the story, then tell the story in a narrative flashback whose full significance to the narrator (and reader) is revealed only at the end. Tennessee Williams's play *The Glass Menagerie* has a similar structure, in which the character of Tom serves both as a narrator in the present and as a principal character in the series of memory scenes that make up the drama. The memory scenes in Arthur Miller's play *Death of a Salesman,* however, are not flashbacks in the same way. Willy Loman relives incidents from the past while the other characters and the action of the play continue in the present. As the play progresses, the shifts in time occur only within Willy's mind.

Shakespeare's tragedies are dramas in which normal chronology is preserved, as it is in such familiar novels as William Golding's *Lord of the Flies* and Mark Twain's *Huckleberry Finn.*

Plot and Time

Related to understanding of chronology is appreciation of how an author creates understanding of *elapsed time.* In the several hours required to read a novel, the two to three hours for a full-length play, and the half-hour to an hour for a one-act play or short story, how much time in the lives of the characters has been accounted for? In one-act plays and many short stories, the time covered by the action is equal to the time to read them. In Wharton's "Roman Fever," for example, the action of the story is contained in a few hours of one afternoon—little more time than it takes to read the story. That conversation, however, completely transforms the women's, and the reader's, understanding of their lives over twenty-five years. The time required for the action in Shirley Jackson's widely read story "The Lottery" is also roughly equal to the time required to read it, yet the plot accounts indirectly for events that have taken place for longer than anyone in the story can even remember. Miller's play *Death of a Salesman* takes place over a period of only twenty-four hours, but the plot and Willy's memories tell us the story of an entire lifetime. Awareness of how an author uses and accounts for time adds considerably to the reader's appreciation of a work.

Narrative Point of View

The **narrator** of a work is the character or author's **persona** that tells a story. **Point of view** is the standpoint, perspective, and degree of understanding from which the narrator speaks. For many students and scholars, how a story is told is one of the most interesting questions. What is the narrative point of view? Is the narration **omniscient**, essentially the point of view of the author? If not, who is the narrator? What is the narrator's relationship to the story? What is the narrator's understanding of the story? How much does the narrator really know? Appreciating how, or by whom, a story is told is often essential to understanding its meaning.

One of the most easily discerned narrative points of view is the first person (*I*), in which either the central character or another directly involved in the action tells the story. J. D. Salinger's novel *Catcher in the Rye* is a vivid and popular example of such narration. Fitzgerald's *The Great Gatsby* is also told in the first person. In each of these works, the fundamental meaning of the novel becomes apparent only when the reader understands the character of the narrator. In each of these works, what the narrator experiences and what he learns about himself and the world are the novel's most important themes.

In first-person narration, the incidents of the plot are limited to those that the narrator himself experiences. First-person narrators can, however, report what they learn from others. In Wharton's *Ethan Frome,* the engineer who narrates tells us that he has "pieced together the story" from the little he has been able to learn in the town of Starkfield, from his limited conversations with Frome himself, and from his brief visit to the Frome house. Wharton's method, of course, dramatizes Frome's inability to express or fulfill the desires of his heart and reveals the reluctance of the people of Starkfield to fully understand the lives of those around them.

Authors may also use first-person narration to achieve an ironic or satiric effect. In Ring Lardner's well-known story "Haircut," a barber in a small midwestern town narrates a story about a local fellow who kept the town entertained with his practical jokes on people. As the story progresses, the reader understands how cruel and destructive the fellow's pranks were, but the barber does not. The narrative method in this story reveals, indirectly, a story of painful ignorance and insensitivity in the "decent" citizens of a small town. Mark Twain's masterpiece, *Huckleberry Finn*, is told by Huck himself. Through the morally naive observations of Huck, Twain satirizes the evils of slavery, fraud, hypocrisy, and virtually every other kind of corrupt human behavior. Edgar Allan Poe's story "The Tell-Tale Heart" is the confession of a cunning madman.

In third-person narration (*he, she, it, they*) a story is reported. The narrative voice may be *omniscient* and, therefore, able to report everything from everywhere in the story; this voice can also report on the innermost thoughts and feelings of the characters themselves. In many novels of the eighteenth and nineteenth centuries, the omniscient narrator even speaks directly to the reader, as if taking him or her into the storyteller's confidence. In Nathaniel Hawthorne's *The Scarlet Letter,* the narrator pauses from time to time to share personal feelings with the reader, as does Nick Carraway, the narrator of *The Great Gatsby.* The method is not common, however, in contemporary fiction.

A widely used narrative method is the **limited omniscient** point of view. The narrative is in the third person but is focused on and even may represent the point of view of a central character. The actions and feelings of other characters are presented from the perspective of that character. Hawthorne's short story "Young Goodman Brown" is an excellent example.

Some third-person narration is dramatically **objective** and detached; it simply reports the incidents of the plot as they unfold. This narrative method, too, can be used for intensely **ironic** effect. Jackson's "The Lottery" is one of the best examples. The real horror of the story is achieved through the utterly detached, nonjudgmental unfolding of the plot.

In some plays, too, there is a character who serves a narrative role: the Chorus in Shakespeare's *Henry V*, the character of Tom in Williams's *The Glass Menagerie,* and the Stage Manager in Thornton Wilder's *Our Town* are familiar examples.

In each of the works discussed here, the narrative method is not simply a literary device; it is an intrinsic part of the meaning of the work.

Setting

The setting of a work includes the time and places in which the action is played out; setting may also include a significant historical context. In drama, setting may be presented directly in the set, costumes, and lighting. In narrative fiction, it is usually presented directly through description. In some works, the physical setting is central to the plot and developed in great detail; in other works, only those details necessary to anchor the plot in a time or place will be developed. Regardless of detail, responsive readers recreate images of setting as they read.

In addition to the physical and natural details of the fictional world, setting also includes mood and **atmosphere**. In some works, social or political realities constitute part of the setting. *The Scarlet Letter* is not only set in Puritan Boston, it is also *about* that society; and *The Great Gatsby* presents a vivid picture of life in New York during Prohibition and the roaring twenties.

For some works, the author may create specific details of setting to highlight a theme. In Golding's novel *Lord of the Flies*, the island on which the story takes place has everything essential for basic survival: food and water are available, and the climate is temperate. In order to explore the moral questions of the boys' regression into savagery, Golding carefully establishes a setting in which survival itself is not a primary issue. In *Ethan Frome,* details of the harsh winter and of the isolation of a town "bypassed by the railroad" intensify the story of a man's desperately cold and isolated life.

Character

We understand characters in fiction and drama, as we do the people in our own lives, by what they say and do and by what others say about them. Because characters are imagined and created by an author, we can even understand them more reliably and fully than we can many of the people around us. Many students find their greatest satisfaction in reading works about characters to whom they can relate, characters whose struggles are recognizable and whose feelings are familiar.

Understanding character in fiction means understanding a person's values and **motivation**, beliefs and principles, moral qualities, strengths and weaknesses, and degree of self-knowledge and understanding. To fully appreciate a work, the reader must understand what characters are searching for and devoting their lives to.

Literature also seeks to account for the forces outside individuals that influence the directions and outcomes of their lives. These "forces" range from those of nature and history to the demands of family, community, and society. The response of characters to inner and outer forces is what literature depicts and makes comprehensible.

When you review the questions for the literature part of the New Regents exam, you will see that questions about character in literature are the most common. (See Chapter 5 for a detailed review.) The reason is that any meaningful or convincing plot stems from human thought, motive, and action. Depending on the narrative point of view (see page 57), a character's thoughts and feelings may be presented directly through omniscient narrative or first-person commentary. In "Young Goodman Brown," the narrator tells us directly what the title character is thinking and feeling; in "Roman Fever," the reader discovers the most important revelations of character simultaneously with the two central characters. Character in drama is revealed directly in dialogue and action, but it may be expanded through soliloquies and asides. In Shakespeare's *Othello,* for example, the full extent of Iago's evil is revealed through the variety of methods Iago uses to manipulate different characters and through his **soliloquies**.

In some works, the author's primary purpose is to reveal character gradually through plot; in others, the author establishes understanding of character from the beginning in order to account for what happens. In the opening pages of *The Great Gatsby,* the narrator, Nick, who is also a character in the novel, introduces himself and declares his judgment of the moral quality of the people and events he is about to narrate. With Nick's own character and motives clearly established, the reader then shares his *gradual* discovery of the truth about Gatsby and his life.

Theme

The subjects of literature may come from any aspect of human experience: love, friendship, growing up, ambition, family relationships, conflicts with society, survival, war, evil, death, and so on. **Theme** in a work of literature is the understanding, insight, observation, and presentation of such subjects. Theme is what a work *says about* a subject. Themes are the central ideas of literary works.

One way to think about theme is to consider it roughly analogous to the topic or thesis of an expository essay. If the author of a novel, story, or play had chosen to examine the subjects of the work in an essay, what might be the topic assertions of such an essay? The student is cautioned, however, not to overinterpret the analogy. Themes in literature are rarely "morals," such as those found at the end of a fable, but neither are they are "hidden meanings." Although scholars and critics often express thematic ideas in phrases, students are often required to state themes in full sentences. In the next paragraph are some examples of statements about theme.

Macbeth is a play about the temptation to embrace evil forces and about the power of ambition to corrupt; Macbeth himself makes one of the most important statements of theme in the play when he says, "I do all that becomes a man/who does more is none." *Ethan Frome* and Lardner's "Haircut" both illustrate that people in small towns do not truly understand the innermost needs and desires of other people they *think* they know. William Golding's novel *Lord of the Flies* illustrates the bleak view that human beings' savage nature will prevail without external forces of authority, that human beings are not civilized in their fundamental natures. In contrast, in *Adventures of Huckleberry Finn,* Twain presents civilization as the source of corruption and finds truly moral behavior only in the runaway slave, Jim, and the ignorant boy, Huck.

In Chapter 5 you will find an extensive list of Regents literature questions, many of which are expressed in terms of theme.

READING NONFICTION

Fiction and nonfiction share many common elements; they also make similar demands and offer comparable rewards to the thoughtful reader. In broad contrast to fiction, where characters and plot are imaginative creations of the author, nonfiction is about actual persons, experiences, and phenomena. Nonfiction also speculates on abstract and philosophical questions of history and politics, ethics and religion, culture and society, as well as the natural world. In biography and autobiography, the writer focuses on what is meaningful and interesting in the life of an individual. The purpose of this section is to review some of the distinctive features of formal and informal essays and to illustrate some of the methods authors use to develop arguments in persuasive writing. The glossary at the end of the chapter also features extended definitions and examples of many important terms.

Questions for the Critical Reader

Here are the questions you are urged to keep in mind as you prepare for the listening and reading tasks on the Regents exam:

What is the purpose of this piece? its tone or mood? its overall effect?

What does the author say? believe? recall? value? assert?

What does the author mean? imply? suggest? agree with? disagree with?

How are language and imagery used?

What conclusions or inferences is the reader led to?

What experience is meant to be shared and understood?

Purpose

In speaking of fiction, the central ideas of a work are identified as its themes. In essays, purpose refers both to the central ideas and to their intended effect on the reader. For example, many authors of essays develop a thesis with a view to influencing opinion or urging action. We encounter such writing daily on the editorial and Op-Ed pages of a newspaper. Many of the verbs on the list of "what writers do" (page 53) identify such purposes: *affirm, alert, argue, assert, caution, censure, condemn, criticize, declare, defend, evaluate, expose, forewarn, imply, inspire, judge, persuade, propose, provoke, reveal, scrutinize, support.*

Much nonfiction, of course, has as its purpose to explain and inform. The verbs used to identify informative writing include *analyze, assess, clarify, define, describe, explore, formulate, illustrate, interpret, recreate, summarize.*

Other purposes may be likened to conversations between the author and the reader; these "conversations" may be about anything from the most personal experiences to reflections on the nature of life and the universe. Some useful verbs here might be *address, amuse, capture, comment, conjecture, depict, discover, enhance, enrich, examine, explore, invent, observe, offer, ponder, probe, propose, question, recreate, reflect, shock.*

Methods of Development and Patterns of Organization

The ability to use a variety of methods to organize and express ideas is one of the most important skills a student writer learns. The thoughtful reader should also be able to appreciate how a writer develops material. Here is a review of some of the most common patterns of organization. (Page references are to excerpts from the comprehension passages.)

FROM ABSTRACT TO CONCRETE/FROM GENERAL TO SPECIFIC

Going from the general to the specific is the most common and natural pattern for explanation, illustration, and reasoning. A passage by Sandy Asher is an especially good example:

> **As a child, I sensed there was something I desperately needed from books. As a writer for young readers, I've tried to figure out what that something was. It turned out to be a combination of three things: companionship, a sense of control, and magic.**

In her essay, Asher goes on to develop a paragraph about each of the three things that make up the "something" she is explaining. (See page 2.)

Here is how Ernie Pyle begins his explanation of what "The awful waste and destruction of war" really means:

> **I walked for a mile and a half along the water's edge of our many-miled invasion beach. I walked slowly, for the detail on the beach was infinite.**
>
> **The wreckage was vast and startling. The awful waste and destruction of war, even aside from the loss of human life, has always been one of its outstanding features to those who are in it. Anything and everything is expendable. And we did expend on our beachhead in Normandy during those first few hours.**
>
> **For a mile out from the beach there were scores of tanks and trucks and boats that were not visible, for they were at the bottom of the water—swamped by overloading, or hit by shells, or sunk by mines.**

His description of a Normandy beach following the D-Day invasion in 1944 is developed in a series of vivid images and poignant details that make the waste and destruction of war comprehensible to those who have not experienced it.

FROM CONCRETE TO ABSTRACT/FROM SPECIFIC TO GENERAL

Reversing the more common pattern, going from the specific to the general can also be a very effective way to develop understanding of a general concept. This is the pattern William Kittredge uses in the **anecdote** about his boyhood encounter with a sage grouse. The passage recounts a specific experience, which leads to the closing general observation:

> **For that childhood moment I believed the world to be absolutely inhabited by an otherness which was utterly demonic and natural, not of my own making. But soon as that bird was enclosed in a story which defined it as a common-place prairie chicken, I was no longer frightened. It is a skill we learn early, the art of inventing stories to explain away the fearful sacred strangeness of the world. Storytelling and make-believe, like war and agriculture, are among the arts of self-defense, and all of them are ways of enclosing otherness and claiming ownership.**

FROM QUESTION TO ANSWER

Another method of developing **argument** and explanation is to pose a question, which the paragraph or essay then answers. Here is an example from the conclusion of Thoreau's *Walden:*

> **Why should we be in such desperate haste to succeed, in such desperate enterprises? If a man does not keep pace with his companions, perhaps it is because he hears a different drummer. Let him step to the music which he hears, however measured or far away.**

And here is a passage from "The Almost Perfect State," an essay by Don Marquis:

> **You have seen the tall towers of Manhattan, wonderful under the stars. How did it come about that such growths come from such soil—that a breed lawless and prosaic has written such a mighty hieroglyphic against the sky? How is it that this hideous, half-brute city is also beautiful and a fit habitation for demi-gods? How come? . . . It comes about because the wise and subtle deities permit nothing worthy to be lost. It was with no thought of beauty that the builders labored . . . the baffled dreams and broken visions and the ruined hopes and the secret desires of**

each one labored with him . . . the rejected beauty, the strangled appreciation, the inchoate art, the sub-merged spirit—these groped and found each other and gathered themselves together and worked them-selves into the tiles and mortar of the edifice and made a town that is a worthy fellow of the sunrise and the sea winds.

The passage by Sandy Asher (see page 2) is also an example of this method; the final paragraph reveals that the essay is an answer to the question, "Why do I write for children?"

Magic, companionship, a sense of control. The won-der of ourselves, of each other, and of life—this is the true subject matter of all novels. The best children's literature speaks not only to children but to the human condition. Writing for children simply means writing for human beings in the beginning, when you can still take part in creation, before habit, cynicism and despair have set in, and while there is still hope and energy, a willingness to learn, and a healthy sense of humor. These qualities I find irresistible in the young people I write about and for, qualities I want to hang onto and to cultivate in myself. So I write for children, not just for their sakes—but for my own.

CHRONOLOGICAL ORDER/NARRATION

Although narration is the primary mode of development for fiction, it is also widely used in **exposition** and argument. The historian uses narration and chronology in recounting significant events; the scientific writer may use narration to explain a process. Narration is also an essential part of biography and the personal essay. Annie Dillard uses narration to explain what she means by the "unwrapped gifts and free surprises" of Nature (see page 11):

I walked up to a tree, an Osage orange, and a hun-dred birds flew away. They simply materialized out of the tree. I saw a tree, then a whisk of color, then a tree again. I walked closer and another hundred black-birds took flight. Not a branch, not a twig budged:

the birds were apparently weightless as well as invisible. Or, it was as if the leaves of the Osage orange had been freed from a spell in the form of red-winged blackbirds; they flew from the tree, caught my eye in the sky, and vanished. When I looked again at the tree, the leaves had reassembled as if nothing had happened. Finally I walked directly to the trunk of the tree and a final hundred, the real diehards, appeared, spread, and vanished. How could so many hide in the tree without my seeing them? The Osage orange, unruffled, looked just as it had looked from the house, when three hundred red-winged blackbirds cried from its crown. I looked upstream where they flew, and they were gone. Searching, I couldn't spot one. I wandered upstream to force them to play their hand, but they'd crossed the creek and scattered. One show to customer. These appearances catch at my throat; they are the free gifts, the bright coppers at the roots of trees.

CAUSE AND EFFECT

Formal development of cause and effect arguments is essential to the historian, the scientist, and the lawyer. It also serves as a basic method for much of the expository writing students do. This paragraph from the speech by Madeleine Kunin (page 25) offers a good example of explanation through cause and effect:

In my own case, most essential to my political evolution was a strong desire to have an effect on events around me, whether that was a flashing red light at the railroad crossing in my neighborhood, to protect my children on their way to school, or whether it was a new environmental law for the state of Vermont. The fact that I succeeded in obtaining the flashing red light, as a private citizen, enabled me to change the environmental laws as governor. Each step builds a new self-image, enabling us to move from the passive to the active voice.

COMPARISON AND CONTRAST

In these paragraphs, historian Bruce Catton in "Lee and Grant: A Study in Constrasts," brings to a close his extended discussion of the contrasts between Ulysses S. Grant and Robert E. Lee and introduces the discussion of how the two men were alike:

> **So Grant and Lee were in complete contrast, representing two diametrically opposed elements in American life. Grant was the modern man emerging; beyond him, ready to come on the stage, was the great age of steel and machinery, of crowded cities and a restless burgeoning vitality. Lee might have ridden down from the old age of chivalry, lance in hand, silken banner fluttering over his head. Each man was the perfect champion of his cause, drawing both his strengths and his weaknesses from the people he led.**
>
> **Yet it was not all contrast, after all. Different as they were—in background, in personality, in underlying aspiration—these two great soldiers had much in common. Under everything else, they were marvelous fighters. Furthermore, their fighting qualities were really very much alike.**

Here, from *Life on the Mississippi* (1883), is Mark Twain's comparison of how the North and South treated the Civil War as a topic of conversation, years after it ended:

> **In the North one hears the war mentioned, in social conversations, once a month; sometimes as often as once a week; but as a distinct subject for talk, it has long ago been relieved of duty. There are sufficient reasons for this. Given a dinner company of six gentlemen to-day, it can easily happen that four of them—and possibly five—were not in the field at all. So the chances are four to two, or five to one, that the war will at no time during the evening become the topic of conversation; and the chances are still greater that if it become the topic it will remain so but a little while. If you add six ladies to the company, you have added six people who saw so little of the**

dread realities of the war that they ran out of talk concerning them years ago, and now would soon weary of the topic if you brought it up.

The case is very different in the South. There, every man you meet was in the war; and every lady you meet saw the war. The war is the great chief topic of conversation. The interest in it is vivid and constant; the interest in other topics is fleeting. Mention of the war will wake up a dull company and set their tongues going, when nearly any other topic would fail. In the South, the war is what A.D. is elsewhere: they date from it . . . . It shows how intimately every individual was visited, in his own person, by the tremendous episode. It gives the inexperienced stranger a better idea of what a vast and comprehensive calamity invasion is than he can ever get by reading books at the fireside.

DEVELOPMENT THROUGH EXTENDED METAPHOR

An extended metaphor or **analogy** is a very effective way to develop an argument or illustrate a concept. It uses the known and familiar to explain the unfamiliar. Here is the introduction to an essay written by a student on the topic "All the World's a Stage." (See Chapter 2 for the complete essay and analysis.)

All the world is indeed a stage. And we are the performers. Everything we do in life is a production, and we must constantly perform our best because, in life, there are no rehearsals. Each of us performs on a separate stage, some for a larger audience than others. But each performance, regardless of the size of the audience, is of equal importance, and each performer must meet the standard of life's most important critic—himself.

Here is a passage from Stephen Crane's novel *The Red Badge of Courage:*

The ground was cluttered with vines and bushes, and the trees grew close and spread out like bouquets. The creepers, catching against his legs, cried out harshly as their sprays were torn from the barks of trees. The swishing saplings tried to make known his presence to the world. He could not conciliate the forest. As he made his way, it was always calling out protestations. When he separated embraces of trees and vines the disturbed foliage waved their arms and turned their face leaves toward him.

DEFINITION OR CLASSIFICATION

In this paragraph from the speech by Madeleine Kunin (page 25), she develops a key term by classifying its component parts:

Political courage stems from a number of sources: anger, pain, love, hate. There is no lack of political motivation within women. We feel it all. Anger at a world which rushes toward saber-rattling displays of power. Pain at a world which ignores the suffering of its homeless, its elderly, its children. Hatred toward the injustice which occurs daily as the strong overpower the weak. And love for the dream of peace on earth.

The essay by Sandy Asher (page 2) employs the same method, developing each part of the definition in a full paragraph.

EXAMPLES IN ORDER OF IMPORTANCE

The most persuasive arguments are those in which the reasoning has a cumulative effect. The skilled writer does not present the supporting details of a thesis in random order; rather, the skilled writer presents details in an order that stresses importance and significance. Here is the closing argument from a piece by Robert Finch:

To consume whales solely for their nourishment of human values is only a step from consuming them for meat. It is not only presumptuous and patronizing, but it is misleading and does both whales and men a grave disservice. Whales have an inalienable right to exist, not because they resemble man or because they

> **are useful to him, but simply because they do exist, because they have a proven fitness to the exactitudes of being on a global scale matched by few other species. If they deserve our admiration and respect, it is because, as Henry Beston put it, "They are other nations, caught with ourselves in the net of life and time, fellow prisoners of the splendor and travail of life."**

These models offer examples of only some of the ways in which writers develop ideas. As you read more widely, you will appreciate the extent to which every writer, especially the writer of essays, creates a form best suited to the subject and purpose. When you find a piece of writing you especially admire or find convincing, note how the author developed the ideas.

Tone

When we speak of **tone** in writing we are referring to the attitude of the writer toward the subject and/or toward the reader. Tone may range from *harsh* and *insistent* to *gentle* and *reflective*. There is as much variety of tone in writing as there is in human feeling. Some pieces—essays of opinion, for example—usually have a very distinct tone; other works, especially in fiction or personal expression, may have a more subtle and indirect tone.

Here is a list of adjectives to help you identify the tone or mood of a prose passage. Many have been gathered by students in their reading of Op-Ed page essays; most have appeared in the comprehension questions of the Regents English exam in recent years. Each reflects a distinctive feeling; be sure to look up in a dictionary any that you are not sure about.

admiring	advisory	affectionate	alarmed
amused	anguished	appalled	apprehensive
argumentative	arrogant	assured	(with) awe
bewildered	bitter	boastful	candid
cautionary	cautious	challenging	concerned
credible	critical	curious	cynical
defensive	disappointed	dismayed	eerie
frank	grateful	haughty	humorous
indifferent	indignant	informed	inquiring
instructive	intense	ironic	knowledgeable

melancholy	mocking	mysterious	nonchalant
nostalgic	objective	offended	optimistic
outraged	peaceful	probing	provocative
questioning	reasoned	reflective	sad
sarcastic	satirical	sentimental	skeptical
surprised	thoughtful	troubled	understanding
whimsical	wondering		

The Op-Ed pages of most newspapers offer daily examples of essays on current topics, representing widely varied methods of argument, style, and tone. Many national magazines, such as *Harper's Magazine, Atlantic Monthly, Natural History, The New Yorker,* and *The New York Review of Books* feature excellent selections of essays and other nonfiction, as do many university review and literary journals. The list of Recommended Reading on page 214 also offers titles of books of nonfiction available in paperback.

A GLOSSARY OF LITERARY TERMS AND TECHNIQUES

abstract In contrast to the *concrete,* abstract language expresses general ideas and concepts apart from specific examples or instances. Very formal writing is characterized by abstract expression. An *abstract* (n.) is a brief summary of the key ideas in a scientific, legal, or scholarly piece of writing.

analogy An expression of the similarities between things that are not wholly alike or related. (See, for example, the student essay on page 68.) See *metaphor* in A Glossary of Poetic Terms and Techniques, Chapter 4.

anecdote A very brief, usually vivid, story or episode. Often humorous, anecdotes offer examples of typical behavior or illustrate the personality of a character. Writers of biography and autobiography make extensive use of anecdote to reveal the lives of their subjects.

antithesis In formal argument, a statement that opposes or contrasts with a *thesis* statement. Informally, we use the term to refer to any expression or point of view completely opposed to another. In literature, even an experience or feeling may be expressed as the *antithesis* of another. See also *thesis.*

argument In persuasive writing or speaking, the development of reasons to support the writer's position; also the method of reasoning used to persuade. Informally, we may use the term to describe the development of a topic in any piece of exposition. Historically, it has also denoted a summary of a literary work's plot or main ideas.

atmosphere Closely related to *tone* or mood, it refers to a pervasive feeling in a work. Atmosphere often stems from setting and from distinctive characters or actions. For example, the atmosphere in many of Poe's stories is mysterious, troubling, even sinister, and Hawthorne's "Young Goodman Brown" reflects the threatening and ambiguous world of its Puritan setting.

autobiography A formally composed account of a person's life, written by that person. While we must trust, or be skeptical of, the reliability of the account, we often appreciate the firsthand narration of experience. Autobiography is also a rich source of information and insight into an historical period or into literary or artistic worlds. Autobiography, like the novel, has *narrative* and chronology. (See also *journal.*) We describe literary works that are closely based on the author's life as "autobiographical." Eugene O'Neill's *Long Day's Journey into Night* and Tennessee Williams's *The Glass Menagerie* are plays that reflect many details of their authors' lives.

biography A narrative, historical account of the life, character, and significance of its subject. Contemporary biography is usually researched in detail and may not always paint an admiring portrait of its subject. A critical biography of a literary figure includes discussion of the writer's works to show the writer's artistic development and career. Biographies of figures significant in history or public affairs also offer commentary on periods and events of historical importance.

character Characters are the imagined persons, created figures, who inhabit the worlds of fiction and drama. E. M. Forster distinguished between *flat* and *round* characters: flat are those, like stereotypes, who represent a single and exaggerated human characteristic; round are those whose aspects are complex and convincing, and who change or develop in the course of a work. In good fiction, plot must develop out of character. The desires, values, and motives of characters account for the action and conflict in a plot.

characterization The method by which an author establishes character; the means by which personality, manner, and appearance are created. It is achieved directly through description and dialogue and indirectly through observations and reactions of other characters.

concrete Refers to the particular, the specific, in expression and imagery. That which is concrete can be perceived by the senses. Concrete also refers to that which is tangible, real, or actual, in contrast to the *abstract,* which is intangible and conceptual.

conflict In the most general sense, it identifies the forces that give rise to a plot. This term may identify an actual struggle between characters, anything from revenge to simple recognition or understanding. A plot may focus on conflict between characters and the forces of nature or society. These are essentially **external conflicts**. A work may also center on **internal conflicts**, characters' struggles to know or change themselves and their lives. Most works of fiction and drama contain more than one aspect of conflict. (See the discussion on page 55.)

denouement A French term meaning "untying a knot," it refers to the way the complications or conflict of a plot are finally resolved. It also refers to what is called the "falling action" in a drama, that part of the play that follows the dramatic climax and reveals the consequences of the main action for minor characters; it also accounts briefly for what happens in the world of the play after the principal drama is resolved. In Arthur Miller's *Death of a Salesman*, the "Requiem" may be considered a denouement; it accounts for the response to Willy's death by his wife, sons, and only friend. In Shakespeare's *Macbeth,* the climax is in the scene following the death of Lady Macbeth in which Macbeth understands that he has destroyed all capacity for feeling and has rendered his life meaningless; the denouement includes the battle in which Macbeth comprehends the treachery of the witches and is killed by MacDuff, thus restoring the throne to the rightful heir, Malcolm.

determinism The philosophical view that human existence is determined by forces over which humans have little or no control. The concept that fate predestines the course of a character's life or a tragic figure's downfall is a form of determinism.

episode A series of actions or incidents that make up a self-contained part of a larger narrative. Some novels are structured so that each chapter is a significant episode. Fitzgerald's *The Great Gatsby* and Mark Twain's *Huckleberry Finn* are good examples of this structure. A *scene* in a play is often analogous to an episode in a narrative. Many television series are presented in weekly episodes.

essay A general term (from French *essai,* meaning an attempt, a trying out of something) to denote an extended composition, usually expository, devoted to a single topic. Essays may be composed to persuade, to reflect on philosophical questions, to analyze a subject, to express an opinion, or to entertain. As a literary form, the essay dates from the sixteenth century and remains a popular and widely practiced form. See *formal/informal* essay.

exposition Writing whose purpose is to inform, illustrate, and explain. In literature, exposition refers to those passages or speeches in which setting, offstage or prior action, or a character's background is revealed. In *The Great Gatsby,* Nick Carraway pauses in the narrative to give the reader additional information about Gatsby's background. The prologue to Shakespeare's *Romeo and Juliet* is an example of exposition.

flashback A presentation of incidents or episodes that occurred prior to the beginning of the narrative itself. When an author or filmmaker uses flashback, the "present" or forward motion of the plot is suspended. Flashback may be introduced through the device of a character's memory or through the narrative voice itself. William Faulkner's "Barn Burning" and *Light in August* include vivid passages of memory and narrative flashback. Jack Burden's recounting of the Cass Mastern story in Robert Penn Warren's *All the King's Men* is also a form of flashback.

foreshadowing A technique in which an author establishes details or mood that will become more significant as the plot of a work progresses. Thoughtful readers usually sense such details and accumulate them in their memories. In one of the opening scenes of *Ethan Frome*, Ethan and Mattie talk about the dangers of sledding down Starkfield's steepest hill; and, in the second paragraph of "The Lottery," the boys are stuffing their pockets with stones or making piles of them on the edge of the square.

form The organization, shape, and structure of a work. Concretely, form may refer to *genre* (see below), for example, the sonnet form, the tragic form. More abstractly, form also refers to the way we sense inherent structure and shape.

formal/informal essay The formal essay emphasizes organization, logic, and explanation of ideas, whereas the informal essay emphasizes the voice and perspective of the writer. In the latter, also called a *personal essay*, the reader is aware of the author's *persona* and is asked to share the author's interest in the subject. The passage by Annie Dillard in Chapter 1 is an excellent example of an informal essay.

genre A type or form of literature. Examples include *novel, short story, epic poem, essay, sonnet, tragedy*.

image Although the term suggests something that is visualized, an image is an evocation through language of *any* experience perceived directly through the senses. See also A Glossary of Poetic Terms and Techniques, Chapter 4.

irony In general, a tone or figure of speech in which there is a discrepancy (a striking difference or contradiction) between what is expressed and what is meant or expected. Irony achieves its powerful effect indirectly: in satire, for example, which often uses *understatement* or *hyperbole* to express serious criticism of human behavior and social institutions. We also speak of *dramatic irony* when the narrator or reader understands more than the characters do.

journal A diary or notebook of personal observations. Many writers use journals to compose personal reflection and to collect ideas for their works; the journals of many writers have been published. Students are often urged to keep journals as a way to reflect on their reading, compose personal pieces, and practice writing free of concern for evaluation.

melodrama A plot in which incidents are sensational and designed to provoke immediate emotional responses. In such a plot, the "good" characters are pure and innocent and victims of the "bad" ones, who are thoroughly evil. The term refers to a particular kind of drama popular in the late nineteenth century and, later, in silent films and early Westerns. A work becomes melodramatic when it relies on improbable incidents and unconvincing characters for strong emotional effect.

memoir A form of autobiographical writing that reflects on the significant events the writer has observed and on the interesting and important personalities the writer has known.

monologue In a play, an extended expression or speech by a single speaker that is uninterrupted by response from other characters. A monologue is addressed to a particular person or persons, who may or may not actually hear it. Ring Lardner's short story "Haircut" is an example of monologue as a method of narration. In it, a barber tells the story to a customer (the reader) who is present but does not respond. See also *dramatic monologue* in A Glossary of Poetic Terms and Techniques, Chapter 4.

motivation The desires, values, needs, or impulses that move characters to act as they do. In good fiction the reader understands, appreciates, and is convinced that a character's motivation accounts for the significant incidents and the outcome of a plot.

narrative point of view The standpoint, perspective, and degree of understanding from which a work of narrative fiction is told. See *omniscient point of view, objective point of view.*

narrator The character or author's *persona* that tells a story. It is through the perspective and understanding of the narrator that the reader experiences the work. In some works, the narrator may inhabit the world of the story or be a character in it. In other works, the narrator is a detached but knowledgeable observer.

naturalism Closely related to *determinism,* naturalism depicts characters who are driven not by personal will or moral principles but by natural forces that they do not fully understand or control. In contrast to other views of human experience, the naturalistic view makes no moral judgments on the lives of the characters. Their lives, often bleak or defeating, simply *are* as they are, determined by social, environmental, instinctive, and hereditary forces. Naturalism was in part a reaction by writers against the nineteenth century Romantic view of man as master of his own fate. It is important to note, however, that none of the Naturalistic writers in America (Crane, Dreiser, London, Anderson, and Norris chief among them) presented a genuinely deterministic vision. Several of these authors began their careers in journalism and were drawn to the Naturalistic view of life as a result of their own experience and observation of life in the United States. See also *realism.*

objective point of view In fiction or nonfiction, this voice presents a story or information, respectively, without expressed judgment or qualification. A fundamental principle of journalism is that news *reports* should be objective. Ernest Hemingway's short story "The Killers" is an example of fiction rendered in a completely detached, objective point of view.

omniscient point of view Spoken in third person (*she, he, it, they*), this is the broadest narrative perspective. The omniscient narrator speaks from outside the story and sees and knows everything about the characters and incidents. Omniscient narration is not limited by time or place. In **limited omniscient** point of view, the author may choose to reveal the story through full understanding of only one character and limit the action to those incidents in which this character is present.

persona A term from the Greek meaning "mask," it refers in literature to a narrative voice created by an author and through which the author speaks. A narrative persona usually has a perceptible, even distinctive, personality that contributes to our understanding of the story. In Nathaniel Hawthorne's *The Scarlet Letter,* the omniscient narrator has a distinctive persona whose attitudes toward Puritan society and the characters' lives are revealed throughout the novel.

plot The incidents and experiences of characters selected and arranged by the author to create a meaningful narrative. A good plot is convincing in terms of what happens and why.

poetic justice The concept that life's rewards and punishments should be perfectly appropriate and distributed in just proportions. In Ring Lardner's short story "Haircut," Jim Kendall's ironic fate is an example of poetic justice: he is a victim of one of his own crude and insensitive practical jokes.

point of view In nonfiction, this denotes the attitudes or opinions of the writer. In narrative fiction, it refers to how and by whom a story is told: the perspective of the narrator and the narrator's relationship to the story. Point of view may be *omniscient,* where the narrator knows everything about the characters and their lives; or it may be *limited* to the understanding of a particular character or speaker. Point of view may also be described as *objective* or *subjective. Third-person* narrative refers to characters as "he, she, it, they." *First-person* narrative is from the "I" point of view. J. D. Salinger's *Catcher in the Rye* and Twain's *Huckleberry Finn* are told in the first person. *Second-person* narrative, the "you" form, is rare but is found in sermons addressed to a congregation or in essays of opinion addressed directly to a leader or public figure: "You, Mr. Mayor (Madame President), should do the following . . ." Russell Baker and William Safire occasionally write pieces in the second-person voice for the Op-Ed page of *The New York Times.*

prologue An introductory statement of the dramatic situation of a play or story. Shakespeare's *Romeo and Juliet* begins with a brief prologue. The first two pages of Fitzgerald's *The Great Gatsby* are a prologue to the story Nick Carraway will tell.

prose Most of what we write is prose, the expression in sentences and phrases that reflect the natural rhythms of speech. Prose is organized by paragraphs and is characterized by variety in sentence length and rhythm.

protagonist A term from Ancient Greek drama, it refers to the central character, the hero or heroine, in a literary work.

realism The literary period in the United States following the Civil War is usually called the Age of Realism. Realism depicts the directly observable in everyday life. Realistic writers seek to *present* characters and situations as they would appear to a careful observer, not as they are imagined or created by the author. After 1865, American writers became increasingly interested in the sources of power and force, and in the means to survival and success, in an increasingly materialistic society. For writers of this period, realism was a literary mode to express a *naturalistic* philosophy. See also *naturalism, verisimilitude*.

rhetoric From Ancient Greece, the art of persuasion in speech or writing achieved through logical thought and skillful use of language.

rhetorical question A question posed in the course of an *argument* to provoke thought or to introduce a line of reasoning.

romance A novel or tale that includes elements of the supernatural, heroic adventure, or romantic passion. Hawthorne's *The Scarlet Letter* is a romance, not because it is a love story but because it goes beyond *verisimilitude* in dramatizing elements of demonic and mystical forces in the characters and their lives.

satire A form or style that uses elements of irony, ridicule, exaggeration, understatement, sarcasm, humor, or absurdity to criticize human behavior or a society. All satire is **ironic** (see above) in that meaning or theme is conveyed in the discrepancy between what is said and what is meant, between what is and what should be, between what appears and what truly is. While satire is often entertaining, its purpose is serious and meant to provoke thought or judgment. The verses of Alexander Pope are often extended satire, and many poems by e. e. cummings are satiric. In prose, much of the writing of Mark Twain is satire; *Huckleberry Finn* is the most striking example. Other American writers of satire include Sinclair Lewis, Dorothy Parker, Edith Wharton, Joseph Heller, Veronica Geng, and Tom Wolfe. Newspaper columnists Russell Baker, Herb Caen, Art Buchwald, and Jack Anderson are best known for their satirical pieces.

short story This form is distinguished from most novels not simply by length but by its focus on few characters and on a central, revealing incident. In short stories, however, there is as much variety in narrative point of view, subject, and technique as there is in novels. Edgar Allan Poe characterized the short story as "a short prose narrative, requiring from a half-hour to one or two hours in its perusal."

soliloquy A form of *monologue* in which a character expresses thoughts and feelings aloud but does not address them to anyone else or intend other characters in the work to hear them. In essence, the audience for a play is secretly listening in on a character's innermost thoughts. Macbeth's reflection on "Tomorrow, and tomorrow, and tomorrow . . ." is the best-known soliloquy in the play.

speaker   The narrative voice in a literary work (see *persona*). Also, the character who speaks in a *dramatic monologue*.

symbol   Most generally, anything that stands for or suggests something else. Language itself is symbolic; sounds and abstract written forms may be arranged to stand for virtually any human thought or experience. In literature, symbols are not Easter eggs or mushrooms—they are not "hidden meanings." Symbols are real objects and *concrete* images that lead us to *think about* what is suggested. They organize a wide variety of ideas into single acts of understanding. They embody not single "meanings" but suggest whole areas of meaning.

theme   Roughly analogous to thesis in an essay, this is an observation about human experience or an idea central to a work of literature. The *subject* of a work is in the specific setting, characters, and plot. Theme in a work of fiction is what is meaningful and significant to human experience generally; themes are the ideas and truths that transcend the specific characters and plot. Shakespeare's *Macbeth* is about an ambitious nobleman who, encouraged by his equally ambitious wife, murders the king of Scotland in order to become king himself. The themes in *Macbeth* include the power of ambition to corrupt even those who are worthy and the mortal consequences of denying what is fundamental to one's nature.

thesis   The central point, a statement of position in a formal or logical argument. Also used to refer to the topic, or controlling, idea of an essay. Use of the term *thesis* implies elaboration by reasons and examples. See *antithesis*.

tone   The attitude of the writer toward the subject and the reader. See also A Glossary of Poetic Terms and Techniques, Chapter 4.

transition   A transition is a link between ideas or sections in a work. In prose arguments, single words such as *first, second . . . moreover,* and *therefore* or phrases such as *in addition, on the other hand,* and *in conclusion* serve as transitions. In fiction, a brief passage or chapter may serve as a transition. In *The Great Gatsby,* the narrator pauses from time to time to "fill in" the reader and to account for the passage of time between the dramatic episodes that make up the novel's main plot.

turning point   In drama and fiction, the moment or episode in a plot when the action is moved toward its inevitable conclusion.

verisimilitude   A quality in fiction and drama of being "true to life," of representing that which is real or actual. Verisimilitude in fiction is often achieved through specific, vivid description and dialogue; first-person narration also creates the effect of verisimilitude. In drama it may be enhanced through means of set, costumes, and lighting that are realistic in all their details.

See also, in Chapter 4, A Glossary of Poetic Terms and Techniques.

Chapter 4

READING POETRY

INTRODUCTION

How should you read a poem? Aloud. Several times. And never quickly. Here is a short poem about baseball. As you read, pay attention first to what the poem by Robert Francis says.

Pitcher

His art is eccentricity, his aim
How not to hit the mark he seems to aim at,
His passion how to avoid the obvious,
His technique how to vary the avoidance.
The others throw to be comprehended. He
Throws to be a moment misunderstood.
Yet not too much. Not errant, arrant, wild,
But every seeming aberration willed.
Not to, yet still, still to communicate
Making the batter understand too late.

Now, read the poem again, with particular attention to the varied length of the statements; read from comma to comma or period to period as you would in prose. When you reach the end of the first and fifth lines, for example, pause very slightly—but do not stop. After several readings, you will not only appreciate what Robert Francis undertands about the art of pitching but also feel the way in which the rhythm of the poem is also the rhythm of pitching.

In poetry we are meant to sense a structure and to feel the rhythm. (See **meter*** and **rhythm**.) The structure and rhythm of poetry may be formal, informal, even "free." Poetry is also characterized by its directness of effect and by its concentration—ideas and feelings are expressed in relatively few words. Karl Shapiro says, "Poems are what ideas *feel like*." Robert Francis's poem is about what good pitching *feels like*.

---

*Terms in bold type are defined in A Glossary of Poetic Terms and Techniques at the end of the chapter.

This poem, by Emily Dickinson (1830–1886), recalls the feeling of mourning:

> **After great pain, a formal feeling comes—**
> **The nerves sit ceremonious, like Tombs—**
> **The stiff Heart questions was it He, that bore,**
> **and Yesterday, or Centuries before?**
>
> **The Feet, mechanical, go round—**
> **Of Ground, or Air or Ought—**
> **A Wooden way**
> **Regardless grown,**
> **A Quartz contentment, like a stone—**
>
> **This is the Hour of Lead—**
> **Remembered, if outlived,**
> **As Freezing persons, recollect the Snow—**
> **First—Chill—then Stupor—then the letting go—**

In this poem, Dickinson recreates what it feels like suddenly to encounter a snake in the grass:

> **A narrow Fellow in the Grass**
> **Occasionally rides—**
> **You may have met Him—did you not**
> **His notice sudden is—**
> **The Grass divides as with a Comb—**
> **A spotted shaft is seen—**
> **And then it closes at your feet**
> **And opens further on—**
>
> **He likes a Boggy Acre**
> **A Floor too cool for corn—**
> **Yet when a boy, and Barefoot—**
> **I more than once at Noon**
> **Have passed, I thought, a Whip lash**
> **Unbraiding in the Sun**
> **When stooping to secure it**
> **It wrinkled, and was gone—**
>
> **Several of Nature's People**
> **I know, and they know me—**

I feel for them a transport
Of cordiality—

But never met this Fellow
Attended, or alone
Without a tighter breathing
And Zero at the Bone—

Where the writer of prose may seek immediate clarity of meaning above all, the poet often seeks **ambiguity**, not to create "confusion," but to offer multiplicity of meaning, in single words, in images, in the meaning of the poem itself. Look again at "Pitcher." Might this poem also be a reflection on the art of poetry itself? It is because of such richness in meaning that poems often require several readings.

The experience of poetry is conveyed in vivid **imagery**, which appeals to the mind and to the senses. It is often expressed in **figurative language**, that is, words and comparions that are not literal but that imaginatively create original, vivid, and often unexpected images and associations. (See **metaphor** and **simile**.) Finally, in poetry there is particular significance in the way words and lines sound. The story or experience is enhanced through musical effects. A poem must be felt and heard!

STRUCTURE AND LANGUAGE IN POETRY

All the traditional poetic forms stem from an oral tradition, in which poetry was sung or recited. The **epic** and the **ballad** are the oldest forms of **narrative poetry**, but modern poets also tell stories in narrative verse. (Robert Frost's "Out, Out—" is a well-known example.) Most of the poetry we read today, however, is **lyric** poetry.

Think of the lyric poem as a song; in the Ancient Greek tradition, the lyric poem was meant to be sung to the accompaniment of a lyre, a small harplike instrument. Indeed, we speak of the words for a song as its lyrics. The ancient form is evident in the songs for Shakespeare's plays, in the tradition of the nineteenth-century art song, and in the twentieth-century ballads and songs you associate, for example, with Rogers and Hart, Cole Porter, and Jerome Kern as sung by Ella Fitzgerald, Tony Bennett, Frank Sinatra, and Barbra Streisand, among others.

Lyric poems are relatively brief and are expressed in the voice (that is, from the point of view) of a single speaker. They express a powerful emotion, usually captured in a significant experience or dramatic situation. A lyric poem, like a song, often tells a story, but it does so in nonnarrative form. The **speaker** (or "poet") may recall an experience, or render it directly, in order to understand its meaning and then reveal it to the reader. Thus, many lyric poems are *meditations, reflections,* or *recollections* of experience that lead to a *discovery,* to an emotionally powerful *recognition* of the meaning of the experiences. The effect of the poem is to convey that meaning directly, to engage readers in such a way that they share the experience, feel the emotion, with the speaker. The poems by Robert Francis and Emily Dickinson on the previous pages are examples of lyrics.

This poem by Robert Penn Warren appeared on the June 1993 New York State Regents exam.

Old Photograph of the Future

That center of attention—an infantile face
That long years ago showed, no doubt, pink and white—
Now faded, and in the photograph only a trace
Of grays, not much expression in sight.

(5) That center of attention, swathed in a sort of white dress,
Is precious to the woman who, pretty and young,
Leans with a look of surprised blessedness
At the mysterious miracle forth-sprung.

In the background somewhat, the masculine figure
(10) Looms, face agleam with achievement and pride.
In black coat, derby at breast, he is quick to assure
You the world's in good hands—lay your worries aside.

The picture is badly faded. Why not?
Most things show wear around seventy-five,
(15) And that's the age this picture has got.
The man and woman no longer, of course, live.

They lie side by side in whatever love survives
Under green turf, or snow, and that child, years later,
    stands there
While old landscapes blur and he in guilt grieves
(20) Over nameless promises unkept, in undefinable despair.

In this poem, the speaker expresses the profound feelings of guilt and despair he feels in looking at an old photograph of himself and his parents when he was an infant. The **tone** of the poem is reflective, that of an elegy. The mood at the end is one of regret and loss as the speaker recalls his dead parents, confronts his own age, "the age this picture has got," and grieves at the "nameless promises unkept." Although the narrator speaks of "that child, years later" who "stands there . . . and . . . in guilt grieves," the intensity and privacy of feeling at the end indicate that the speaker <u>is</u> that child. The narrative voice and the lack of specific identification of the characters serve to emphasize the passage of time and underscore the fact that looking at the photograph leads the "child," now old, to reflect on his entire life.

The structure is simple and easy to observe: five **quatrains** with alternating **rhyme**; each quatrain is self-contained—ends with a period—and tells a part of the story. The first fifteen lines of the poem describe the picture and the "characters" in it. Note that the final section of the poem begins with the last line of the fourth quatrain, the description having concluded in line 15. Line 16 both ends the narrator's rendering of the photograph and also begins the "conclusion," which is the significance of the experience of looking at the photograph.

The rhythm within lines is varied and often broken by dashes or other pauses; this rhythm allows us to share the speaker's questions and reflections. The rhythm of the fourth stanza slows as each line completes a thought. In contrast, the final stanza should be heard as a single, long gesture of recognition and regret.

The experience of looking at the picture—in which he is the "center of attention"—leads the speaker to reflect on whether he has satisfied the "promises" that the "mysterious miracle" of his birth meant to his awed and proud parents. The photograph also leads the speaker to reflect on the unfulfilled promises of his own life.

There is little in the way of figurative language in this poem. The imagery, however, reveals more than a description of a photograph, and the paradox in the title reveals one of the poem's central **themes**, the cycle of birth, life, and death. On rereading Warren's poem, with our appreciation of the poet's experience in mind, we see how the third and fourth lines are more than a description of the photograph—they also suggest the speaker's age. He sees himself (in the photo and metaphorically) as "faded . . . only a trace of grays, not much expression in sight." The repetition of the fact that he was the "center of attention" (in the photograph and in his parents' lives) makes more poignant the grief over "promises unkept" at the end.

The poet offers only a few details of the photograph, but they are the details we all recognize from our own photographs of grandparents and great-grandparents: the father "In the background somewhat" and in formal pose—"in black coat, derby at breast"—the child (girl or boy) in "a sort of white dress." It is, of course, such widely shared experience that is both the poem's form and its theme.

In this poem by Theodore Roethke, the speaker recalls a significant experience from childhood:

Child on Top of a Greenhouse

The wind billowing out of the seat of my britches,
My feet crackling splinters of glass and dried putty,
The half-grown chrysanthemums staring up like accusers,
Up through the streaked glass, flashing with sunlight,
A few white clouds all rushing eastward,
A line of elms plunging and tossing like horses,
And everyone, everyone pointing up and shouting!

Try repeating just the verbs of this poem, feeling their dramatic energy. The repetition of "-ing" forms also creates what is called **internal rhyme**, while the words "like," "sunlight," "white," "line" form the pattern of sound called **assonance**.

In this poem by Donald Hall the speaker also recalls an important childhood experiece:

The Sleeping Giant
(A Hill, So Named, in Hamden, Connecticut)

The whole day long, under the walking sun
That poised an eye on me from its high floor,
Holding my toy beside the clapboard house
I looked for him, the summer I was four.

I was afraid the waking arm would break
From the loose earth and rub against his eyes
A fist of trees, and the whole country tremble
In the exultant labor of his rise;

Then he with giant steps in the small streets
Would stagger, cutting off the sky, to seize
The roofs from house and home because we had
Covered his shape with dirt and planted trees;

And then kneel down and rip with fingernails
A trench to pour the enemy Atlantic
Into our basin, and the water rush,
With the streets full and the voices frantic.

That was the summer I expected him.
Later the high and watchful sun instead
Walked low behind the house, and school began,
And winter pulled a sheet over his head.

In this poem, a child's fearful and vivid imagination is sparked by **personification** of the hill near his house. This poem is particularly effective because it recalls for us the fact that small children are literal and that they tend to give names and human character to inanimate things. This child actually sees—and fears—the sleeping giant. Note too how the images of the sun in the first and last stanzas both unify the poem and denote the passage of time. Finally, there is a gentle **irony** in the final line that suggests that the child, no longer fearful, can now "play" with the metaphor of the sleeping giant, as "winter pulled a sheet over his head."

Shakespeare's Sonnet 30 illustrates several of the formal aspects of verse:

When to the sessions of sweet silent thought

When to the sessions of sweet silent thought
I summon up remembrance of things past
I sigh the lack of many a thing I sought
And with old woes new wail my dear time's waste:

(5) Then can I drown an eye, unused to flow,
For precious friends hid in death's dateless night,
And weep afresh love's long-since-canceled woe,
And moan th'expense of many a vanished sight;

Then can I grieve at grievances forgone,
(10) And heavily from woe to woe tell o'er
The sad account of fore-bemoaned moan,
Which I new pay as if not paid before.
  But if the while I think on thee, dear friend,
  All losses are restored and sorrows end.

The structure of the Shakespearean **sonnet** is three **quatrains** and a closing **couplet**. The **rhyme scheme** is *abab/cdcd/efef/gg*. This pattern allows us to hear the structure of the poem, to hear the development of the ideas. The couplet, with its similar end rhyme and self-contained thought, contrasts the feelings expressed in the previous 12 lines and concludes the poem.

We find in this Shakespearean sonnet, as well, examples of **alliteration** and assonance: In the first quatrain, we hear alliteration in the many words that begin with "s." In lines 7 through 12 we hear assonance in the repetition of "oh" sounds, which are also examples of **onomatopoeia**—that is, the sounds reflect the meanings of the words. Lines 4 and 10 also illustrate what is called internal rhyme.

THEME IN POETRY

Some lyric poems may assert a belief. Others may be a comment on the nature of human experience—love, death, loss or triumph, mystery and confusion, conflict and peace, on the humorous and the ironic, on the imagined and the unexpected in all its forms. Some poems reflect on the nature of time, of existence. Many lyrics are about poetry itself. These aspects of human experience are what we refer to as the themes of poetry.

In this well-known sonnet, Number 55, Shakespeare asserts that poetry confers immortality, that it can prevail over the most powerful forces of time. Note how the central idea is developed in the three quatrains and how the couplet—in its thought and its rhyme—concludes the development of that idea.

Not marble, nor the gilded monuments

Not marble, nor the gilded monuments
Of princes, shall outlive this pow'rful rhyme;
But you shall shine more bright in these contents
Than unswept stone besmeared with sluttish time.

When wasteful war shall statues overturn,
And broils root out the work of masonry,
Nor Mars his sword nor war's quick fire shall burn
The living record of your memory.

'Gainst death and all-oblivious enmity
Shall you pace forth; your praise shall still find room

Even in the eyes of all posterity
That wear this world out to the ending doom.
  So, till the judgment that yourself arise,
  You live in this, and dwell in lovers' eyes.

The best known lyrics, however, are probably love poems—Sonnet 116 of Shakespeare, for example:

Let me not to the marriage of true minds

Let me not to the marriage of true minds
Admit impediments. Love is not love
which alters when it alteration finds,
Or bends with the remover to remove.

O, no, it is an ever-fixed mark
That looks on tempests and is never shaken;
It is the star to every wand'ring bark,
Whose worth's unknown, although his height be taken.

Love's not Time's fool, though rosy lips and cheeks
Within his bending sickle's compass come;
Love alters not with his brief hours and weeks,
But bears it out even to the edge of doom.
  If this be error and upon me proved,
  I never writ, nor no man ever loved.

This modern lyric by Langston Hughes is also a love poem.

Juke Box Love Song

I could take the Harlem night
and wrap around you,
Take the neon lights and make a crown,
Take the Lenox Avenue buses,
Taxis, subways,
And for your love song tone their rumble down.
Take Harlem's heartbeat,
Make a drumbeat,
Put it on a record, let it whirl,

And while we listen to it play,
Dance with you till day—
Dance with you, my sweet brown Harlem girl.

TONE

Tone in poetry, as in prose and all forms of human communication, expresses the *attitude* of the speaker toward the reader or listener and toward the subject. Tone in literature is as varied as the range of human experience and feeling it reflects. When we speak of the *mood* of a piece of writing, we are also speaking of tone, of an overall feeling generated by the work.

Here are some terms to help you recognize and articulate tone or mood:

ambiguous*	amused	angry	bitter
celebratory	elegiac (from elegy*)	grateful	harsh
humorous	insistent	ironic*	melancholy
mournful	mysterious	nostalgic	optimistic
paradoxical*	questioning	reconciled	reflective
regretful	reminiscent	satiric*	sorrowful
thoughtful	understated*		

WRITING ABOUT POETRY/EXPLICATION

When you are asked to *explicate* a poem, you are being asked to look closely at it and "unfold" its meaning, line by line, idea by idea. Explication combines paraphrase with close reading of form. You are explaining both the content *and* the form: the ideas and meaning as well as the structure and poetic elements.

To begin an explication, read the poem several times to discover what it says. Who is the speaker? What is the subject? the dramatic situation? What theme or experience is central to the poem? What is the tone or mood? Try to summarize or paraphrase the poem as a whole. Then note the formal details: What is the pattern of organization? What is the movement of ideas and feeling? of images and metaphors? How do stanzas or arrangement of lines reveal that? How do rhyme, meter, and rhythm contribute to the experience, to the meaning of the poem? (The commentary that follows Robert Penn Warren's "Old Photograph of the Future" on page 82 is an example of explication.)

---

*These terms are defined in A Glossary of Poetic Terms and Techniques.

POETRY ON EXAMINATIONS

On examinations, such as the new English Regents exam and the AP Literature and Composition exam, the multiple-choice questions are designed to measure your skill at close reading and *explication.* You are expected to recognize and identify the elements of poetry. (See A Glossary of Poetic Terms and Techniques.) Part III of the new English Regents exam may include a poem for close reading and discussion as well as a prose passage. In addition, you are usually required to compose an essay/explication of a poem on the AP Literature and Composition exam, and such essays are commonly assigned in high school and college literature courses. *Analysis,* which requires detailed examination of particular elements of a poem or passage, is usually reserved for course assignments. The thoughtful student will, of course, develop skill in both explication and analysis.

A HANDFUL OF POEMS FOR FURTHER READING

In this **prose poem**, Karl Shapiro offers a definition of the poet and the power of poetry.

As You Say (Not Without Sadness), Poets Don't See, They Feel

As you say, (not without sadness), poets don't see, they feel.
And that's why people who have turned to feelers seem
like poets. Why children seem poetic. Why when the
sap rises in the adolescent heart the young write poetry.
Why great catastrophes are stated in verse. Why lunatics
are named for the moon. Yet poetry isn't feeling with
the hands. A poem is not a kiss. Poems are what ideas
feel like. Ideas on Sunday, thoughts on vacation.

Poets don't see, they feel. They are conductors of the senses
of men, as teachers and preachers are the insulators.
The poets go up and feel the insulators. Now and again
they feel the wrong thing and are thrown through a wall
by a million-volt shock. All insulation makes the poet
anxious. Clothes, strait jackets, iambic five. He pulls at
the seams like a boy whose trousers are cutting him in
half. Poets think along the electric currents. The words

are constantly not making sense when he reads. He
flunks economics, logic, history. Then he describes what
it feels like to flunk economics, logic, history. After
that he feels better.

People say: it is sad to see a grown man feeling his way, sad
to see a man so naked, desireless of any defenses. The
people walk back into their boxes and triple-lock the
doors. When their children begin to read poetry the
parents watch them from the corner of their eye. It's
only a phase, they aver. Parents like the word "aver"
though they don't use it.

In this excerpt from an extended essay in verse, Alexander Pope reflects
on how poets express meaning through sound and rhythm.

An Essay on Criticism

True ease in writing comes from art, not chance,
As those move easiest who have learned to dance.
'Tis not enough no harshness gives offense,
The sound must seem an echo to the sense:
Soft is the strain when Zephyr gently blows,
And the smooth stream in smoother numbers flows;
But when loud surges lash the sounding shore,
The hoarse, rough verse should like the torrent roar.

The horror and loss of war are often expressed through irony. Here is
Stephen Crane's reflection on war:

Do Not Weep, Maiden, for War Is Kind

Do not weep, maiden, for war is kind.
Because your lover threw wild hands against the sky
And the affrighted steed ran on alone,
Do not weep.
War is kind.

Hoarse, booming drums of the regiment
Little souls who thirst for fight
These men were born to drill and die.

The unexplained glory flies above them,
Great is the battle-god, great, and his kingdom—
A field where a thousand corpses lie.

Do not weep, babe, for war is kind.
Because your father tumbled in the yellow trenches,
Raged at his breast, gulped and died,
Do not weep.
War is kind.

Swift blazing flag of the regiment,
Eagle with crest of red and gold,
These men were born to drill and die.
Point for them the virtue of slaughter,
Make plain to them the excellence of killing
And a field where a thousand corpses lie.

Mother whose heart hung humble as a button
On the bright splendid shroud of your son,
Do not weep.
War is kind.

In this poem, by Walt Whitman (1819–1892), the speaker moves from the observation of a spider to a reflection on the soul's search to understand all existence.

A Noiseless Patient Spider

A noiseless patient spider,
I mark'd where on a little promontory it stood isolated,
Mark'd how to explore the vacant vast surrounding,
It launch'd forth filament, filament, filament, out of itself,
Ever unreeling them, ever tirelessly speeding them.

And you O my soul where you stand,
Surrounded, detached, in measureless oceans of space,
Ceaselessly musing, venturing, throwing, seeking the spheres
        to connect them,

Till the bridge you will need be form'd, till the ductile
    anchor hold,
Till the gossamer thread you fling catch somewhere,
    O my soul.

In this brief poem by Alfred, Lord Tennyson (1809–1892) the language and imagery convey the experience of both the observer and of the eagle itself.

The Eagle

He clasps the crag with crooked hands;
Close to the sun in lonely lands,
Ringed with the azure world, he stands.

The wrinkled sea beneath him crawls;
He watches from his mountain walls,
And like a thunderbolt he falls.

Here, in free verse, is Whitman's vision of eagles:

The Dalliance of Eagles

Skirting the river road, (my forenoon walk, my rest,)
Skyward in air a sudden muffled sound, the dalliance
    of the eagles,
The rushing amorous contact high in space together,
The clinching interlocking claws, a living, fierce,
    gyrating wheel,
Four beating wings, two beaks, a swirling mass tight
    grappling,
In tumbling turning clustering loops, straight downward
    falling.
Till o'er the river pois'd, the twain yet one, a moment's
    lull,
A motionless still balance in the air, then parting, talons
    loosing,
Upward again on slow-firm pinions slanting, their
    separate diverse flight,
She hers, he his, pursuing.

Observe how Gwendolyn Brooks uses rhyme with varied line lengths to create this portrait.

The Bean Eaters

They eat beans mostly, this old yellow pair.
Dinner is a casual affair.
Plain chipware on a plain and creaking wood,
Tin flatware.

Two who are Mostly Good.
Two who have lived their day,
But keep on putting on their clothes
And putting things away.

And remembering . . .
Remembering, with twinklings and twinges,
As they lean over the beans in their rented back room that
        is full of
beads and receipts and dolls and cloths, tobacco crumbs,
vases and fringes.

In the first of these two poems by Robert Browning (1812–1889) the rich and varied imagery recreates the journey of a lover to his beloved and, in the second, his return to the "world of men."

Meeting at Night

The grey sea and the long black land;
And the yellow half-moon large and low;
And the startled little waves that leap
In fiery ringlets from their sleep,
As I gain the cove with pushing prow,
And quench its speed i' the slushy sand.

Then a mile of warm sea-scented beach;
Three fields to cross till a farm appears;
A tap at the pane, the quick sharp scratch
And spurt of a lighted match,
And a voice less loud, through its joys and fears,
Than the two hearts beating each to each.

Parting at Morning

Round the cape of a sudden came the sea,
And the sun looked over the mountain's rim:
And straight was a path of gold for him,
And the need of a world of men for me.

In this sonnet, George Meredith (1828–1909) imagines the desire of this fallen angel, now Satan, to return to the heavens he once inhabited.

Lucifer in Starlight

On a starred night Prince Lucifer uprose.
Tired of his dark dominion swung the fiend
Above the rolling ball in cloud part screened,
Where sinners hugged their spectre of repose.
Poor prey to his hot fit of pride were those.
And now upon his western wing he leaned,
Now his huge bulk o'er Afric's sands careened,
Now the black planet shadowed Arctic snows.
Soaring through wider zones that pricked his scars
With memory of the old revolt from Awe,
He reached a middle height, and at the stars,
Which are the brain of heaven, he looked, and sank.
Around the ancient track marched, rank on rank,
The army of unalterable law.

In this well-known sonnet by Percy Bysshe Shelley (1792–1822) we experience the ironic fate of a once proud and arrogant king.

Ozymandias

I met a traveler from an antique land
Who said: Two vast and trunkless legs of stone
Stand in the desert. Near them, on the sand,
Half sunk a shattered visage lies, whose frown,
And wrinkled lip, and sneer of cold command,
Tell that its sculptor well those passions read
Which yet survive, stamped on these lifeless things,
The hand that mocked them and the heart that fed;

And on the pedestal these words appear:
"My name is Ozymandias, king of kings:
Look on my works, ye Mighty, and despair!"
Nothing beside remains. Round the decay
Of that colossal wreck, boundless and bare,
The lone and level sands stretch far away.

These poems represent only a few examples of the great variety of expression in verse. Your own textbooks and anthologies offer many more examples; and the list of Recommended Reading at the end of the book includes titles of collections readily available in paperback. Your library, of course, offers collections of poetry by individual authors, and many national monthly magazines, such as *The New Yorker* and *Atlantic Monthly* publish contemporary verse. You should read as widely as possible, and always aloud!

A GLOSSARY OF POETIC TERMS AND TECHNIQUES

allegory A narrative, in prose or verse, in which abstract ideas, principles, human values or states of mind, are *personified.* The purpose of the allegory is to illustrate the signficance of the ideas by dramatizing them. *Parable* and *fable* are particular kinds of allegory, in which a moral is illustrated in the form of a story.

alliteration The repetition of initial consonant sounds in words and syllables. This is one of the first patterns of sound a child creates; (for instance "ma-ma," "pa-pa.") The children's stories of Dr. Seuss use alliteration and assonance. Poets use alliteration for its rich musical effect: "Fish, flesh, and fowl commend all summer long/Whatever is begotten, born, and dies." (Yeats); for humor: "Where at, with blade, with bloody, blameful blade/He bravely broached his boiling bloody breast" (Shakespeare); and to echo the sense of the lines: "The iron tongue of midnight hath told twelve." (Shakespeare).

allusion A reference to an historical event, to Biblical, mythological, or literary characters and incidents with which the reader is assumed to be familiar. Allusion may, with few words, enrich or extend the meaning of a phrase, idea, or image. Allusion may also be used for ironic effect. In his poem "Out, out . . ." Robert Frost expects the reader to recall from Macbeth's final soliloquy the line, "Out, out brief candle!" Such expressions as "a Herculean task" or "Achilles heel" are also forms of allusion.

ambiguity Denotes uncertainty of meaning. In literature, however, especially in poetry, we speak of *intentional* ambiguity, the use of language and images to suggest more than one meaning at the same time.

assonance The repetition of vowel sounds among words that begin or end with different consonants. Sonnet 30 of Shakespeare (page 85) and "Child on Top of a Greenhouse" by Theodore Roethke (page 84), for example, are rich in assonance. Some poets may vary end rhymes with assonance; for example, Emily Dickinson (page 80) does it here: "The Feet, mechanical, go round—Of Ground, or Air, or Ought—".

ballad Narrative poem, sometimes sung, that tells a dramatic story.

blank verse Unrhymed *iambic pentameter,* usually in "paragraphs" of verse instead of stanzas. Shakespeare's plays are composed primarily in blank verse. For example, from *Macbeth* (Act I, Scene 5):

> **Your face, my Thane, is as a book where men**
> **May read strange matters. To beguile the time,**
> **Look like the time; bear welcome in your eye,**
> **Your hand, your tongue; look like the innocent flower,**
> **But be the serpent under't . . .**

connotation The feelings, attitudes, images, and associations of a word or expression. Connotations are usually said to be "positive" or "negative." See also discussion on page 172 in Chapter 9, Vocabulary.

couplet Two lines of verse with similar meter and end rhyme. Couplets generally have self-contained ideas as well, so they may function as stanzas within a poem. In the English (Shakespearean) *sonnet,* the couplet concludes the poem. (See the sonnets on pages 86–87). Also many scenes in Shakespeare's plays end with rhymed couplets: "Away, and mock the time with fairest show/False face must hide what the false heart doth know." (*Macbeth* Act I, Scene 7).

denotation That which a word actually names, identifies, or "points to." Denotation is sometimes referred to as "the dictionary definition" of a word.

dramatic monologue A poem in which a fictional character, at a critical or dramatic point in life, addresses a particular "audience," which is identifiable but silent. In the course of the monologue, we learn a great deal, often ironically, about the character, who is speaking and the circumstances that have led to the speech. Robert Browning is the best-known nineteenth-century poet to compose dramatic monologues; "My Last Duchess" is a famous example. In the twentieth century, such poets as Kenneth Fearing, E.A. Robinson, T.S. Eliot ("The Love Song of J. Alfred Prufrock"), Robert Frost, and Amy Lowell have composed well-known dramatic monologues.

elegy A meditative poem mourning the death of an individual.

epic A long narrative poem often centering on a heroic figure who represents the fate of a great nation or people. *The Iliad* and *The Odyssey* of Homer, *The Aeneid* of Vergil, and the Anglo-Saxon *Beowulf* are well-known epics. Milton's *Paradise Lost* and Dante's *Divine Comedy* are examples of epic narratives in which subjects of great human significance are dramatized. *Omeros,* by Derek Walcott, is a contemporary example of an epic poem.

figurative language The intentional and imaginative use of words and comparisons that are not literal but that create original, vivid, and often unexpected images and associations. Figurative language is also called *metaphorical language.* See *metaphor* and *simile.*

free verse A poem written in free verse develops images and ideas in patterns of lines without specific metrical arrangements or formal rhyme. Free verse is distinguished from prose, however, because it retains such poetic elements as assonance, alliteration, and figurative language. The poetry of Walt Whitman offers striking examples.

hyperbole An exaggerated expression (also called overstatement) for a particular effect, which may be humorous, satirical, or intensely emotional. Hyperbole is the expression of folk tales and legends and, of course, of lovers: Romeo says to Juliet, "there lies more peril in thine eye/Than twenty of their swords." Hyperbole is often the expression of any overwhelming feeling. After he murders King Duncan, Macbeth looks with horror at his bloody hands: "Will all great Neptune's ocean wash this blood/Clean from my hand . . . ?" In her sleepwalking scene, Lady Macbeth despairs that "All the perfumes of Arabia will not sweeten this little hand." And everyone of us has felt, "I have mountains of work to do!"

iambic pentameter The basic meter of English speech: "I think I know exactly what you need/and yet at times I know that I do not." Formally, it identifies verse of ten syllables to the line, with the second, fourth, sixth, eight, and tenth syllables accented. There is, however, variation in the stresses within lines to reflect natural speech—and to avoid a "sing-song" or nursery rhyme effect. Most of the dialogue in Shakespeare's plays is composed in this meter. See *blank verse.*

image Images and imagery are the heart of poetry. Although the term suggests only something that is visualized, an image is the recreation through language of *any* experience perceived directly through the senses. For example, Tennyson's "The Eagle" (page 91) is composed of striking visual images. The feelings of fear and of mourning in Emily Dickinson's poems are also images. In "Juke Box Love Song" (page 87) we hear and feel music; and in "Pitcher" (page 79) we feel the motion of pitching.

internal rhyme A pattern in which a word or words within a line rhyme with the word that ends it. Poets may also employ internal rhyme at irregular intervals over many lines. The verbs in Theodore Roethke's poem "Child on Top of a Greenhouse" (page 84) create the effect of internal rhyme.

irony In general, a tone or figure of speech in which there is a discrepancy—(a striking difference or contradiction)—between what is expressed and what is meant or expected. Irony may be used to achieve a powerful effect indirectly. In satire, for example, it may be used to ridicule or criticize. Stephen Crane's poem "Do Not Weep, Maiden, for War is Kind" (page 90) is intensely ironic, both in the stanzas apparently seeking to comfort those whose lovers, fathers and sons have died and in the contrasting stanzas of apparent celebration of the glories of war. We also speak of *dramatic irony* in fiction in which the reader understands more than the characters do. Ring Lardner's short story "Haircut" is an excellent example.

lyric A general term used to describe poems that are relatively brief and expressed in the voice of a single *speaker* (narrative voice). Lyric poems express a powerful emotion revealed in a significant experience or observation. (See discussion on page 81).

metaphor A form of analogy. Through metaphor, a poet discovers and expresses a similarity between dissimilar things. The poet use metaphors to imaginatively find common qualities between things we would not normally or literally compare. As a figure of speech, metaphor is said to be implicit or indirect. This contrasts to *simile* (see page 99), where the comparison is expressed directly. In his final soliloquy, Macbeth uses a series of metaphors to express the meaninglessness of his own life: "Life's but a walking shadow, a poor player . . . it is a tale told by an idiot . . . ."

meter and rhythm Rhythm refers to the pattern of movement in a poem. As music has rhythm, so does poetry. Meter refers to specific patterns of stressed and unstressed syllables. See *iambic pentameter.*

ode A meditation or celebration of a specific subject. Traditional odes addressed "elevated" ideas and were composed in elaborate stanza forms. Keats's "Ode to a Nightingale" and "Ode to Autum" are particularly fine examples. Modern odes may address subjects either serious or personal. One well-known contemporary ode is Pablo Neruda's "Ode to My Socks."

onomatopoeia The use of words whose sound reflects their sense. "Buzz," "hiss," and "moan" are common examples. Shakespeare's Sonnet 30 shows how the sounds and rhythm of whole lines may be onomatopoetic.

oxymoron Closely related to *paradox,* oxymoron is a figure of speech in which two contradictory or sharply contrasting terms are paired for emphasis or ironic effect. Among students' favorite examples are "jumbo shrimp" and "army intelligence." Poets have written of the "wise fool," a "joyful sadness," or an "eloquent silence."

paradox An expression, concept, or situation whose literal statement is contradictory, yet which makes a truthful and meaningful observation. Consider the widely used expression, "less is more," for example. Shakespeare's play *Macbeth* opens with a series of paradoxes to establish the moral atmosphere in which "foul is fair." John Donne's famous poem "Death Be Not Proud" ends with the paradox, "Death thou shalt die," and the title of Robert Penn Warren's poem "Old Photograph of the Future" is a paradox.

personification A form of metaphor or simile in which nonhuman things—objects, plants and animals, forces of nature, abstract ideas—are given human qualities; for example, "The half-grown chrysanthemums staring up like accusers" (Roethke, page 84), "the walking sun/that poised an eye on me from its high floor" (Hall, page 84); "Time . . . the thief of youth" (Milton), and "Blow winds, and crack your cheeks! Blow! Rage!" (Shakespeare).

prose poem   This form appears on the page in the sentences and paragraphs of prose yet its effect is achieved through rhythm, images, and patterns of sound associated with poetry. Karl Shapiro's poem on page 89 is an example.

quatrain   Stanza of four lines. The quatrain is the most commonly used stanza form in English poetry. Quatrains may be rhymed, *abab, aabb, abba,* for example, or they may be unrhymed. The sonnets of Shakespeare (pages 85–87), "Old Photograph of the Future" (page 82), and "The Sleeping Giant" (page 84) are also composed in quatrains.

rhyme   In general, any repetition of identical or similar sounds among words that are close enough together to form an audible pattern. Rhyme is most evident when it occurs at the ends of lines of metrical verse. The *quatrains* of Shakespeare's Sonnet 55 (page 86) have alternating rhyme as do those of Robert Penn Warren's poem "Old Photograph of the Future" (page 82).

rhyme scheme   A regular pattern of end rhyme in a poem. The rhyme scheme in Shakespeare's sonnets, for example, is *abab/cdcd/efef/gg.*

satire   A form or style that uses elements of irony, ridicule, exaggeration, understatement, sarcasm, humor, or absurdity to criticize human behavior or a society. All satire is *ironic* (see page 97) in that meaning or theme is conveyed in the discrepancy between what is said and what is meant, between what is and what should be, between what appears and what truly is. While satire is often entertaining, its purpose is serious and meant to provoke thought or judgment. The verse of Alexander Pope is often extended satire, and many poems by e. e. cummings are satiric.

simile   An expression that is a direct comparison of two things. It uses such words as *like, as, as if, seems, appears.* For instance: "A line of elms plunging and tossing like horses" (Theodore Roethke); "Mind in its purest play is like some bat" (Richard Wilbur); "I wandered lonely as a cloud" (William Wordsworth).

soliloquy   A form of monologue found most often in drama. It differs from a dramatic monologue in that the speaker is alone, revealing thoughts and feelings to or for oneself that are intentionally unheard by other characters. In Shakespeare's plays, for example, the principal characters' reflections on how to act or questions of conscience are revealed in their soliloquies. Hamlet's "To be, or not to be . . ." is probably the most famous dramatic soliloquy in English.

sonnet   A poem of fourteen lines in *iambic pentameter* that may be composed of different patterns of stanzas and rhyme schemes. The most common forms are the English, or Shakespearean, sonnet, which consists of three quatrains and a closing couplet, and the Italian sonnet, which consists of an *octave* of eight lines and a *sestet* of six lines.

speaker The narrative voice in a poem. Also, the character who speaks in a *dramatic monologue.* The poems "The Sleeping Giant" and "Old Photograph of the Future" have distinctive speakers who are also the central characters in the dramatic experience of the poem.

stanza The grouping of lines within a poem. A stanza provides the basic organization and development of ideas, much as a paragraph does in an essay. Many stanza patterns have a fixed number of lines and a regular pattern of rhyme; the poems of Robert Penn Warren (page 82) and Donald Hall (page 84) are good examples. Poets, however, often create stanzas of varying length and form within a single poem. A stanza that ends with a period, completing an idea or image, is considered "closed," while a stanza that ends with a comma or with no punctuation, is called "open," indicating that there should be very little pause in the movement from one stanza to another. Roethke's poem "Child on Top of a Greenhouse" (page 84) is an example of a poem composed in a single stanza.

symbol Most generally, anything that stands for or suggests something else. Language itself is symbolic; sounds and abstract written forms may stand for virtually any human thought or experience. Symbols are real objects and *concrete* images that lead us to think about what is suggested. Symbols organize a wide variety of ideas into single acts of understanding. They embody not single "meanings" but suggest whole areas of meaning.

tone The attitude or feeling of the speaker toward the subject. Tone may also refer to the dominant mood of a poem. (See discussion of *tone* on page 88).

understatement Expression in which something is presented as less important or significant than it really is. The first and third stanzas of Stephen Crane's "Do Not Weep, Maiden" (page 90) ironically understate the horror of death in battle and the loss for those who mourn. Understatement is often used for humorous, *satiric,* or *ironic* effect. Much of the satire in *Huckleberry Finn* stems from Huck's naive and understated observations. One particular form of understatement, actually a double negative, includes such expressions as "I was not uninterested," which really means "I was interested," or "He was not without imagination," which really means "He had some imagination."

Chapter 5

WRITING ABOUT LITERATURE: A GENERAL REVIEW

For most students, writing papers and responding to essay questions on exams are the most challenging aspects of their course work. Writing requires that you articulate and focus your understanding of what you read. Like all good writing, writing about literature not only demonstrates to others what you understand and think but also obliges you to clarify *for yourself* what you truly know. That process is sometimes hard, but it is worthwhile. Writing is essential to developing your critical reading and thinking skills.

TOPICS FOR LITERARY ESSAYS

Much of your writing about literature is done in response to assignments and exam questions. Students are also urged to maintain notes and journals. For essays, instructors may assign very specific topics, or they may offer general subjects that require you to develop your own topic and controlling idea.

In your literature courses and exams you will find that the majority of the questions focus on **character.** Because essay topics may apply to many works of nonfiction you read—personal essay, memoir, and autobiography in particular—the term *character* should be understood to refer to any persons, not exclusively to those of fiction and drama.

As you think about characters in the literature you read, keep the following questions in mind: What are a character's values and motives? beliefs and principles? moral qualities? strengths and weaknesses? illusions or delusions? For what is a character searching? striving? devoting his or her life? What significant decisions and actions does a character take? What are the consequences of those decisions and actions? To what extent does a character "succeed" or "fail"? understand or fail to understand?

Literature also seeks to account for the forces outside individuals, that is, the external forces that influence the direction and outcome of their lives. These "forces" range from those of nature and history to the demands of family, community, and society. The response of individuals to inner and outer forces is what literature considers and dramatizes. (See Chapters 3 and 4 for discussions of reading literature and for glossaries of important terms and techniques.)

101

TOPIC AND FOCUS

As any essay must, your paper must have a clear purpose, a controlling idea; moreover, the development of the purpose must be convincing to the reader. *Focus* means in writing, as it does in a photograph, that the subject is clear! We can see it, even recognize it. And, if the photographer/writer has "framed" the material properly, we see the relationship of the background details to the principal subject. When you take a picture of your best friend at camp, or of the place you most want to remember from a vacation trip, you keep the lens of your camera directed at what is most important—not at the tree next to your friend, not at the bus that took you to Niagara Falls.

SELECTION OF SIGNIFICANT DETAILS

One of the most widely observed characteristics of short stories is that they are very selective in detail. The author of a short story includes only those elements of setting, character, and plot that reveal the significance of the central incident. In "The Lottery," for example, we do not know when the story takes place, we do not even know the name of the town or where it is located, and we know little about the lives of individual characters. Those details are not *significant*—they do not matter —to the story Shirley Jackson tells; comparable details *are* significant in "Haircut," and, therefore, Ring Lardner includes them.

To achieve focus in your essays about works of literature, you must exercise the same rigorous process of selection. However interesting you may find a particular incident or aspect of a character, do not include those details if they do not directly explain or clarify your topic.

DEVELOPING THE TOPIC

Many of the common methods of developing arguments are discussed in Chapter 3, Reading Prose. Here are some of those methods as they might be used to develop essays on works of literature:

Comparison/Contrast

Although *compare* means to identify similarities, and *contrast* means to identify differences, the term *comparison* is often used for a discussion that examines both similarities and differences among the items being compared. This is one of the most useful approaches, and one of the most commonly used, because the process of comparing helps sharpen thought. To compose a meaningful comparison, the writer must understand the objects of comparison in detail.

Any literary aspect found in two or more works may serve as a basis for comparison. For example, one could compare the effective use of first-person narration in *The Great Gatsby* and *Ethan Frome,* or in *The Catcher in the Rye* and *Huckleberry Finn.* Although the circumstances of their lives are vastly different, the fact that both Ethan Frome and Jay Gatsby fail to achieve what they most desire—a life with the women they love—offers a rich possibility for comparison and contrast. "Haircut" and "The Lottery" share common elements of setting and irony. *Othello* and *Romeo and Juliet* have a common theme—the tragic destruction of great love.

Comparison may, of course, focus on much narrower topics and be confined to a single work. The best way to develop notes for a comparison is first to list the aspects common to the items under comparison, then to list for each all the specific details that differentiate them. Finally, as you do in preparation for any essay, you select those that are most significant.

The essay on Part III of the new Regents exam is a form of comparison/contrast because it requires discussion of two works of different genres.

Analysis

Analysis requires detailed examination of a particular aspect of a literary work. The purpose of an analytic paper is to show the significance of that aspect to the meaning of the work as a whole. Examples of analytic topics include the use of time in Miller's *Death of a Salesman,* the imagery of light and dark in *Othello,* and the extended metaphor in Emily Dickinson's poem "I Taste a Liquor Never Brewed."

Classification

Classification organizes objects, people, and other living things into categories; it is a process of identifying and relating. In discussions of literature, classification may be an important part of an essay, or it may constitute a topic in its own right. An essay in which the writer shows how a particular work exemplifies a **genre** is considered classification: *The Scarlet Letter* as a **romance;** Shakespeare's *Macbeth* as Elizabethan **tragedy;** Dreiser's *Sister Carrie* as **naturalism.**

Cause and Effect

Many of the topics for writing and discussion of literature may be developed by showing how circumstances or actions have direct and observable consequences. Demonstrating actual cause and effect, however, requires careful thinking and attention to detail. Cause and effect are more easily demonstrated in logic and chemistry than in human experience.

Literary topics that focus on **plot** often lend themselves to cause and effect development because virtually any plot is built on cause and effect:

specific circumstances, actions, or decisions lead to others and have conse-quences in the lives of the characters. Plot summary alone does *not* estab-lish cause and effect; it simply relates "what happened." Cause-and-effect argument requires the writer to show how and why incidents are related.

Exemplification

Whenever you cite specific details to support a thesis, and when you choose the works you will use to answer the Part IV Regents literature ques-tion, you are using exemplification. *To exemplify* means to illustrate the meaning of a general concept through use of specific examples. This method is fundamental to the development of nearly any essay or literary topic.

LOOKING AT KEY TERMS IN LITERATURE QUESTIONS

identify   To name and also to characterize and to place in context; sometimes you may be required to state the significance of what you are identifying. Often identification includes linking characters to the theme or
experience that serves as the topic.
describe   To give the essential characteristics of a person, object, or experience. If you are asked to describe, your choice of details or characteristics must reveal your understanding of a larger question. Why are these
details relevant to the topic? Description alone will not be the focus of a
literature topic.
explain/show/discuss   These terms indicate the most important parts of a
question, which will be developed in the body of an essay. Once you
have identified and described your subject, you must interpret and
demonstrate the significance of your examples and details; you must
offer evidence, using specific references, to support your argument.

USING FLUENT AND PRECISE LANGUAGE

Effective writing is characterized by interesting and vivid language, and "use of precise and engaging language" is among the criteria for evaluation of Regents essays. From the list of what writers *do,* here are some terms to help you articulate your observations about creation of plot:

convey, create, delineate, depict, describe, dramatize, foreshadow, illustrate, invent, portray, present, recreate, reveal, select, shock, show, symbolize

The following terms offer precision and variety in discussing details of a plot:

> *affair, circumstance, climax, development, episode, event, experience, incident, instance, juncture, moment, occasion, occurrence, opportunity, scene, situation*

Terms useful in referring to *character* include:

> *disposition, identity, individuality, makeup, mettle, nature, persona, personality, self, spirit, temperament*

Finally, here is a list of adjectives collected by students to describe some of the many relationships and attitudes among characters in literature (and in our own lives!):

> *admiring, affectionate, bitter, cautious, compassionate, curious, deceitful, disapproving, disdainful, dishonest, distant, envious, false, fearful, generous, hostile, indifferent, loving, optimistic, reluctant, resentful, reserved, respectful, scornful, sincere, skeptical, stern, suspicious, sympathetic, treacherous, watchful*

(See also Using Synonymies to Enhance Your Writing in Chapter 2, Reading and Writing for Information and Understanding.)

CHOOSING YOUR OWN TOPIC: REPRESENTATIVE LITERARY SUBJECTS AND THEMES

In many high school and college literature courses, students must select their own topics for writing. The subjects of literature are as varied as human experience itself, and below are some of the many themes authors dramatize. You will encounter these as topics in class discussion and as topics for essays and examination questions. These topics may, of course, serve for discussion of more than one work in an essay.

Topics That Focus on Character

- In many works of literature, an important theme is an **individual's achievement of self-knowledge as a result of undergoing an ordeal.** This self-knowledge may be a recognition of the individual's own strengths, weaknesses, values, prejudices, aspirations, or fears. Identify the individual and the self-knowledge he or she achieves. Using specific references from the work, explain how the ordeal led the individual to the self-knowledge.
- **Nature** can have different effects on different people. It can defeat someone with its power; it can inspire someone with its beauty. Identify the character; using specific references, show how he or she was either defeated or inspired by nature.
- It has been said that to live with **fear** and not be overcome by it is the final **test of maturity.** Explain what fear a character lives with; show how the character "passes" or "fails" the test of maturity on the basis of his or her response to that fear.
- A commonly held belief is that **suffering strengthens an individual's character.** The suffering can be physical, mental, or emotional. Identify the individual; describe the nature of the suffering; explain how the suffering did or did not strengthen the individual's character.
- Sometimes a person **struggles to achieve a goal** only to discover that, once the goal is achieved, the results are not what was expected.
- In many works of literature there are characters who are **troubled by injustice** in society, such as poverty, discrimination, or lawlessness, and **who try to correct** the injustice. Identify the character and the injustice, explain what actions the character takes; discuss whether or not the efforts are successful.
- In many works, characters who love one another or share a special friendship often face **obstacles to their relationship.** Sometimes characters overcome the obstacle; sometimes they are defeated by it. Identify the characters and the obstacle; explain how the characters overcome or are defeated by the obstacle; discuss the effect this outcome (the success or failure, not the obstacle) has on the relationship.
- In many works of literature, **a character sacrifices something of value** in order to achieve something of greater value.
- Sometimes a character faces a **conflict between his or her conscience** and the standards of behavior expected by others. Identify the character; explain the specific nature of the conflict; discuss how the character was affected by this conflict.
- In many works of literature, a character reaches a **major turning point** in his or her life. From that point onward, the character undergoes a significant change.
- Characters in works of literature frequently **learn about life or themselves** by taking risks.

106

- The phrase **"rite of passage"** describes a situation in which a young person is faced with an experience that results in his or her becoming mature. Explain the experience; discuss how the young person matures as a result of the way in which he or she deals with the experience.
- In many works of literature, characters are **challenged by unfamiliar environments.** Show how the character was or was not successful in meeting the challenge.
- Some individuals in literature **try to do what they believe is right,** even though they face opposition.
- In some works of literature, an important character **makes a mistake that advances the reader's understanding of that individual.**
- Confusion, danger, or tragedy sometimes results when **one character misunderstands the words or actions of another character.**
- In many works of literature, a character **struggles against circumstances that seem to be beyond his or her control.** Sometimes the character is victorious, sometimes not.

Topics That Focus on Literary Elements and Techniques

Questions about character are the most common on Regents and other exams, but essay questions may require discussion of the literary aspects of a work. The following topics have appeared on recent Regents exams and are widely used in high school and college courses:

- Some authors are especially successful at creating **a memorable visual image** that contributes to the reader's understanding of a work. Identify the image and its importance; show how the image contributes to the meaning of the work.
- In many works of literature, the **setting** contributes to the reader's understanding of the central conflict in the plot. Describe the setting; show how it contributes to the reader's understanding of the conflict on which the plot hinges.
- Authors often create a **predominant mood** in a work of literature. Using specific references, discuss incidents that convey that mood and explain the importance of mood to the work.
- Authors sometimes use **foreshadowing** to help develop the plot of a work. Foreshadowing usually takes the form of incidents that seem to be unimportant at first, but take on added significance later. Discuss examples of foreshadowing and show how they contribute to the overall effect and meaning of the work.
- A work of literature may be defined as **a classic** because it promotes deep insight into human behavior, presents a universal theme, or

uses language in an exceptional way. Show how a particular work meets the above definition of the term *classic*.

- Through their work, some **authors reveal their acceptance or rejection of values** held by society. Identify the value; state whether the author accepts or rejects it; using specific references, show how the author reveals his or her attitude toward that value.
- In literature, **symbols** are used to reinforce the central idea or to represent characters. Using specific references, explain how the symbol in a particular work enriches the reader's understanding of either the central idea or a character.
- The **narrative point of view** is significant to the effect and meaning of a literary work. Illustrate the truth of this statement by specific references to a work of literature.

AUDIENCE AND LITERATURE ESSAYS

Most teachers mention audience in the assignments they give; if it is not clear for whom you are writing, it is a good idea to ask before you complete an assignment. For most outside examinations, including the new Regents, assume that you are writing the essay for a reader who is familiar with the works of literature but who has not considered the topic; background discussion and *detailed* explanation of plot are not needed.

A NOTE ON CONCLUSIONS

No essay, however brief, should simply stop. Even if you run out of time or things to say, try not to telegraph that information to the reader. A conclusion must come back to the topic, must complete the discussion, in a way that leaves the reader feeling convinced by what you have written. On examinations, most students close with a brief, summative conclusion that highlights the relationship of the literary work or works to the topic or restates the thesis of the essay. Even if the reader of a short essay does not really *need* the conclusion to appreciate your argument, the obligation to compose a conclusion keeps you focused on the topic.

Student writers are urged to avoid the following in their conclusions: the expression "what this paper has shown . . ." or "As you can see . . ."; a reminder that Shakespeare was a great playwright or that Mark Twain was an important figure in American literature; a confession that the reader *really* liked or did not like a particular work. Above all, the conclusion is not the place to introduce a new topic or tack on an idea that properly belongs in the body of the essay.

Chapter 6

WRITING ABOUT LITERATURE ON THE NEW REGENTS EXAM

The new Regents exam requires you to compose two essays on aspects of literature. Part III requires an essay that discusses the ways in which two given passages of different literary genres reveal a common subject and that shows how specific literary elements (theme, characterization, structure, point of view) and techniques (figurative language, irony, symbolism) convey the meanings of the selected passages. This task expects you to be able to identify the distinguishing features of different literary genres and to recognize and understand the significance of a wide range of literary elements and techniques in order to interpret the works. Chapter 3 of *Let's Review* offers a detailed review of the literary elements you are expected to know and illustrates them with references to works widely read in high school. Be sure to refer also to the Glossary of Literary Terms and Techniques at the end of that chapter.

Part IV of the new Regents exam allows you to choose the works on which you will write and does not limit the genres: you may write on fiction, on nonfiction, on works of book length, or on single poems, essays, or short stories. Your essay, however, must discuss "works of literature you have read . . ."; this specification does not include films. This essay gives you the opportunity to demonstrate that you recognize and appreciate the significant themes in literature and that you understand the range and complexity of literary expression. The literature essay requires you to go beyond plot summary or character description. The essay must show why and how the works chosen illustrate your interpretation of a "critical lens" (see page 117), and it must do so through clear organization and effective language. You will have three hours on the second day of the Regents examination to complete the two tasks in Parts III and IV.

PART III OF THE NEW EXAM: READING AND WRITING FOR LITERARY RESPONSE

In this part of the exam you are given two passages to read and respond to. The passages will be of different literary genres, such as poetry, drama, and fiction; passages may also be selected from nonfiction, such as memoir, journal, or reflective essay. Your task is to appreciate how these two passages develop a common theme using different literary styles and techniques. After answering 8–10 multiple-choice questions on the passages, you will compose "a unified essay . . . in which you use evidence from both passages to develop your controlling idea, and show how each author uses specific literary elements or techniques to convey ideas." Below is a sample Part III task with texts, questions, and a sample essay.

Sample Texts, Task, Questions, and Essay

Directions: Read the passages (a poem and an excerpt from a story) on the following pages and answer the multiple-choice questions. Then write the essay described in "Your Task." You may use the margins to take notes as you read and scrap paper to plan your response.

Your Task: After you have read the passages and answered the multiple-choice questions, write a unified essay about the effects of war on the soldiers who do the fighting as revealed in the passages. In your essay, use ideas from both passages to establish a controlling idea about the effects of war on the soldiers, cite evidence from both passages to develop your controlling idea, and show how each author uses specific literary elements or techniques to convey ideas.

Guidelines:

- Use ideas from both passages to establish a controlling idea about the effects of war on the soldiers who do the fighting, as revealed in the passages
- Use specific and relevant evidence from both passages to develop your controlling idea
- Show how each author uses specific literary elements (for example, theme, characterization, structure, point of view) or techniques (for example, symbolism, irony, figurative language) to portray the effects of war on the soldiers who do the fighting
- Organize your ideas in a logical and coherent manner
- Use language that communicates ideas effectively
- Follow the conventions of standard written English

Passage I

Our brains ache, in the merciless iced east winds that knive us . . .
Wearied we keep awake because the night is silent . . .
Low, drooping flares confuse our memory of the salient . . .
Worried by silence, sentries whisper, curious, nervous,
(5)   But nothing happens.

Watching, we hear the mad gusts tugging on the wire,
Like twitching agonies of men among its brambles.
Northward, incessantly, the flickering gunnery rumbles,
Far off, like a dull rumour of some other war.
(10)   What are we doing here?

The poignant misery of dawn begins to grow . . .
We only know war lasts, rain soaks, and clouds sag stormy.
Dawn massing in the east her melancholy army
Attacks once more in ranks on shivering ranks of gray,
(15)   But nothing happens.

Sudden successive flights of bullets streak the silence.
Less deadly than the air that shudders black with snow,
With sidelong flowing flakes that flock, pause and renew,
We watch them wandering up and down the wind's nonchalance,
(20)   But nothing happens.

Pale flakes with fingering stealth come feeling for our faces—
We cringe in holes, back on forgotten dreams, and stare, snow-dazed.
Deep into grassier ditches. So we drowse, sun-dozed,
Littered with blossoms trickling where the blackbird fusses.
(25)   Is it that we are dying?

Slowly our ghosts drag home: glimpsing the sunk fires, glozed*
With crusted dark-red jewels; crickets jingle there;
For hours the innocent mice rejoice: the house is theirs;
Shutters and doors, all closed: on us the doors are closed,—
(30)   We turn back to our dying.

Since we believe not otherwise can kind fires burn;
Nor ever suns smile true on child, or field, or fruit.
For God's invincible spring our love is made afraid;
Therefore, not loath, we lie out here; therefore were born,
(35)   For love of God seems dying.

---

*glazed over

Tonight, His frost will fasten on this mud and us,
Shriveling many hands, puckering foreheads crisp.
The burying-party, picks and shovels in their shaking grasp,
Pause over half-known faces. All their eyes are ice,
(40)   But nothing happens.

—Wilfred Owen

Passage II

They carried USO stationery and pencils and pens. They carried Sterno, safety pins, trip flares, signal flares, spools of wire, razor blades, chewing tobacco, statuettes of the smiling Buddha, candles, grease pencils, *The Stars and Stripes,* fingernail clippers, bush hats, bolos, and much more. Twice a week, when the resupply choppers came in, they carried hot chow in green mermite cans and large canvas bags filled with iced beer and soda pop. They carried plastic water containers, each with a two gallon capacity. Mitchell Sanders carried a set of starched tiger fatigues for special occasions. Henry Dobbins carried Black Flag insecticide. Dave 10 Jensen carried empty sandbags that could be filled at night for added protection. Lee Strunk carried tanning lotion. Some things they carried in common. Taking turns, they carried the big PRC-77 scrambler radio which weighed 30 pounds with its battery. They shared the weight of memory. They took up what others could no longer bear. Often, they carried each other, the wounded or weak. They carried infections. They carried chess sets, basketballs, Vietnamese-English dictionaries, insignia of rank, Bronze Stars and Purple Hearts, plastic cards imprinted with the Code of Conduct. They carried diseases, among them malaria and dysentery. They carried lice and ringworm and leeches and paddy algae and various rots and molds. They carried the land itself—Vietnam, the place, the soil . . . dust that covered their boots and fatigues and faces. They carried the sky . . . the stink of fungus, and decay, all of it, they carried gravity.

—Tim O'Brien

Directions: Answer the following questions. The questions may help you think about the ideas you might want to use in your essay. You may return to these questions anytime you wish.

Passage I (the poem)—Questions 1–7 refer to Passage I.
1   The mood conveyed in the first stanza is one of
    1   mystery
    2   foreboding
    3   peacefulness
    4   confusion

2   Lines 13 and 14 (Dawn . . . gray) refer to
    1   storm clouds
    2   advancing soldiers
    3   hungry rats
    4   enemy tanks

3   In stanza 4 of the poem the dominant figure of speech is
    1   onomatopoeia
    2   personification
    3   oxymoron
    4   alliteration

4   In lines 6 through 20, the soldiers are bombarded by
    1   overwhelming hunger
    2   merciless weather
    3   painful memories
    4   paralyzing fear

5   Lines 17 through 19 suggest that the action of the snowflakes is
    1   puzzling
    2   noisy
    3   erratic
    4   threatening

6   The statement "Slowly our ghosts drag home" (line 26) refers to dead comrades as well as
    1   injured animals
    2   living relatives
    3   suffering survivors
    4   absent soldiers

7   The repetition of the phrase "But nothing happens" underscores the soldiers' feelings of
   1   fear
   2   hopelessness
   3   anger
   4   indifference

Passage II (the excerpt from a story)—Questions 8–12 refer to Passage II.
8   Throughout Passage II, "they" refers to
   1   soldiers
   2   trains
   3   civilians
   4   ambulances

9   The variety of items the men carried reflects their desire to
   1   make friends
   2   bribe villagers
   3   sell products
   4   maintain morale

10   The repetition of the expression "they carried" helps establish a feeling of
   1   relentlessness
   2   monotony
   3   suspense
   4   disappointment

11   The word "gravity" (line 23) is used to mean
   1   earthly delights
   2   fond memories
   3   weighty matters
   4   unexplained forces

12   The organization of this passage is characterized by a movement from
   1   literal to figurative
   2   past to present
   3   emotion to reason
   4   far to near

NOTE: The operational examination will include only 8–10 questions on Part III. Additional questions are included here to suggest a fuller range of possible question types.

ANSWERS

1. 2	**2.** 1	**3.** 4	**4.** 2	**5.** 3	**6.** 3
7. 2	**8.** 1	**9.** 4	**10.** 1	**11.** 3	**12.** 1

Review **Your Task** and **Guidelines** and write your response to Part III. You may use scrap paper to plan your essay.

Here is an essay one student wrote in response to this task:

Sample Essay Response

The effects of war on soldiers are terrible. The description of pain, disease, stress, and unhappiness are present in both passages. Feelings of dread surround each work of literature.

In passage I, the soldiers' pain is shown in poetic form. Each stanza poses the fact that these people are unhappy, and frightened. At the beginning of the poem it states "Our brains ache," and "Wearied we keep awake." The poem describes the weather, and how dark, cold and silent the night is. At the end of most of the stanzas is a statement: "But nothing happens." This statement describes how the soldiers are waiting for the war, but nothing happens. This language tells the reader how expectant the soldiers are. The dread is incessant throughout this work. In stanza two the speaker speaks of the wind and how they hear "the mad gusts tugging on the wire." He goes on to state that it's like "twitching agonies of men among its brambles." This image of death is a horrid one, and these soldiers must deal with it day after day. The effect of war upon these people is great. We know this by the way in which the speaker thinks of everything in terms of war. He only knows "war lasts," and refers to dawn with "her melancholy army" which are storm clouds. Also, the speaker personifies snow flakes as "bullets." This imagery caused by the use of language is truly effective for getting across the author's point of how horrible war can be.

The second passage however takes a different form. This paragraph states the effects of war in an entirely different manner, but poses the same answer. Throughout the paragraph the author uses monotonous language, and often repetition. He states the things that soldiers from Vietnam carried during the war. He begins by stating reasonable things that a soldier would be expected to carry: "They carried Sterno, safety pins, trip flares, signal flares . . ." and many other reasonable items. This language and even the fact that the work is a paragraph tells the reader how monotonous and scary a soldier's life was. The effect of war on a fighting soldier is harsh, as portrayed in this paragraph. They had many things to "carry" and not all of them were inanimate objects. The author states: "They carried each other, the wounded or weak. They carried infections." The author also states that even through all this the soldiers still maintained their pride. They held purple hearts and codes of conduct. This use of language gives the reader the feeling that these were good men; they didn't give up their pride. The author concludes by using figurative language, stating the soldiers also held "gravity." This is symbolic of the weight the soldiers had on their shoulders.

Indeed, both of these works of literature provide insight to the reader on the effect of war. By using personification, verse form, and the successful use of language the reader understood these atrocities.

Comment

This is quite a good response, primarily because the writer reveals excellent understanding of the central theme of the passages and of the literary techniques in each. There is also a clear sense of organization and a worthy effort to compose a conclusion that captures the common elements of the two passages. The introduction establishes an excellent controlling idea in the concept of "dread" surrounding each work; the essay would be even better if the writer had emphasized how the cumulative effect of O'Brien's list, moving from everyday, practical items to "gravity," is one of increasing dread over the fate of these men. This piece had several spelling errors in key terms (corrected here), and some other errors in the conventions. The student's own language is not always as vivid or precise as the ideas deserve, so the essay would probably rate a 5 on the Regents rubric. Overall, this is a very thoughtful response to a challenging task.

Preparing for this part of the new Regents exam means reviewing the important literary terms and techniques (see Chapters 3 and 4) and, more important, reviewing carefully the essays on literary topics you have written and revised throughout high school.

PART IV OF THE NEW EXAM: READING AND WRITING FOR CRITICAL ANALYSIS AND EVALUATION

This part of the new Regents also assesses your ability to show how literary elements and techniques reveal theme, but it requires that you first interpret and respond to what is called a "critical lens." You will then choose from works you have read and use those works to support the critical position you have established. For most students, this will be the most challenging part of the exam. A closer look at the different parts of this task, however, will show you that much of the reading, discussion, and writing about literature you have done in high school has prepared you for it.

What Is a *Critical Lens*?

A *critical lens* does much of what the lenses in a pair of glasses or the lens in a camera does: it allows us to bring what we are looking at into focus—and, like the lens of a camera, it directs our attention to something worth looking at. We can pursue the metaphor further: some lenses may alter or color what we are looking at; in literary terms, a critical lens expresses and shapes a point of view about how to evaluate literature.

For the Regents exam, the purpose of the critical lens is to give you the opportunity to respond to a critical point of view as a prompt for discussion of works you know and appreciate. The critical lens statements are likely to focus on what literature "is about" and how authors convey the meanings and achieve the effects of their works.

Here is a familiar example, which the developers of the new Regents exam have offered as a model:

Sample Tasks

Your Task: Write a position paper in which you explain what the statement below means to you, agree or disagree with the statement, and support your opinion using two works from the literature you have studied.

Critical Lens: According to author Joseph Conrad, the task of a writer is "by the power of the written word, to make you hear, to make you feel—it is, before all, to make you see."

Note that there are three parts to this task: first, you must *interpret* the statement, say what it means to you; then, you must tell whether you agree or disagree with the statement; finally, you must choose two literary works for a discussion that supports your position.

To interpret what Conrad means here, you must first look at the key terms. He is talking about the *power* of the written word to make us recreate the experience of hearing, feeling, and seeing, and the power to make us understand—*to see* in the figurative sense. Remember: to interpret means to state what you think Conrad means; then you must state your response to the quote.

To agree with Conrad's statement, you might choose works of literature that are particularly vivid in imagery and show how they are effective in recreating experience for the reader. This would be a literal but perfectly valid interpretation of the quote. A more subtle discussion would emphasize Conrad's final point—the power of literature to make us understand character and theme in new and powerful ways.

To disagree with Conrad's statement, if you consider that the greatest power of literature is to make us feel, for example, you would choose works of literature whose effect on the reader is primarily emotional or affecting. This too would be a valid response to the task.

Here is another example of a critical lens as a prompt, followed by the Guidelines for completing the essay described in Your Task on the preceding page:

Critical Lens: "The best literature is about the old universal truths, such as love, honor, pride, compassion, and sacrifice."—William Faulkner (adapted)

Guidelines:

- Explain what Faulkner's statement means to you
- State whether you agree or disagree with the statement as you have interpreted it
- Choose two works you have read that you believe best support your opinion
- Specify the titles and authors of the works you choose
- For each work, use specific references to appropriate literary elements (for example, theme, characterization, structure, language, point of view) to show how the work supports your opinion
- Organize your ideas in a unified and coherent manner
- Follow the conventions of standard written English

Summing Up

The new Standards for English Language Arts are expressed in terms of "the knowledge, skills, and understandings that individuals can and do habitually demonstrate . . . ." The emphasis here is on the word *habitually;* that is why the tasks on the new Regents exam, including Parts III and IV, engage the reading, thinking, and writing skills students develop, in English courses and in many other subjects, throughout secondary school. Keep this fact in mind as you prepare for the exam.

You may wish to review the ELA Standards (Appendix C) and the rubrics for scoring (Appendix F). They express widely shared goals for the education of all students.

Chapter 7

GRAMMAR AND USAGE FOR THE CAREFUL WRITER: A GUIDE TO STANDARD WRITTEN ENGLISH

The grammar of a language is its logic. We observe the conventions of standard usage in order to write and speak clearly, in order to communicate precisely what we mean. This section reviews those aspects of grammar and usage you are expected to know and to apply.

The New New York State Regents Comprehensive Examination in English evaluates your mastery of standard written English by how well you write in your essays. The SAT II/Writing exam tests your mastery through both multiple-choice error recognition and revision questions and a brief essay.

Neither of these exams requires you to identify errors in usage by name, but a review of the essential terms and structures will help you to recognize errors and to understand how to correct them. What are the essentials?

REVIEWING THE FUNDAMENTALS

The Parts of Speech

Below are the parts of speech that you should review. These include the noun, pronoun, adjective, verb, and adverb, as well as conjunction preposition, and interjection.

NOUN

Names or identifies persons, creatures, objects, ideas. The articles *the, a, an* usually precede and signal a noun. For example:

woman	child	book	happiness
climate	history	English	politics
education			

PRONOUN

Replaces or "stands in for" nouns or other pronouns already stated; the noun or pronoun referred to (replaced) is the **antecedent**.

Subject Forms: I, you, he/she/it, we, you, they
Object Forms: me, you, him/her/it, us, you, them
Possessive Forms: mine, yours, his/hers/its, ours, yours, theirs
Relatives: that, which, who, whom, whose, whoever, whomever

ADJECTIVE

Modifies nouns, that is, it describes, limits, specifies, what a noun names. For instance:

tall woman	*young* child	*illustrated* book
temperate climate	*American* history	*public* education

VERB

Denotes any *action*: run, talk, think, intend, suggest, play, strike, have, do; or *state of being*: appear, seem, be, feel. The principal parts of a verb are as follows:

Infinitive: to run, to talk, to think, to intend, to appear, to seem
Simple past: ran, talked, thought, intended, appeared, seemed
Present participle: running, talking, thinking, intending, appearing, seeming
Past participle: (has) run, (has) talked, (has) thought, intended, appeared, seemed

ADVERB

Modifies verbs; it indicates the manner, quality, or degree of an *action*.

run *swiftly*	talk *loudly*	think *clearly*
play *well*	strike *suddenly*	

Adverbs also function as *intensifiers*; that is, they indicate the degree or intensity of modifiers, both adjectives and adverbs.

rather tall woman	*very* young child
talk *too* loudly	*nearly* complete project

CONJUNCTION

A word that connects two or more words or groups of words.

Coordinating conjunctions:	and, but, yet, so, for
Subordinating conjunctions:	because, although, since, while, if, until, when, unless, before, after

There are a tall woman *and* a young child.

We will stay home *if* it rains.

Because he trains regularly, he plays well.

PREPOSITION

Expresses relationships of time, space, or position.

above	across	after	at
before	behind	beside	between
except	for	in	into
on	over	to	under
within	without		

INTERJECTION

An expression that begins or interrupts a sentence to express a particular feeling.

Ouch!, that hurts.	*Oh,* how interesting!	*Bravo!*

Phrases, Clauses, and Sentences

While we may express feelings and give commands with single words, our most useful expression is in words grouped in phrases, clauses, and sentences.

PHRASE

A meaningful group of words. There are many kinds of phrases in English. Here are some common examples:

A noun and its modifiers:	the large brick building
	the tall young woman

A verb and its auxiliaries:	has run
(to show different tenses):	will arrive
	should have been done

A preposition and its object:	across the room
	down the hill
	on the roof
	in the final chapter

A participle and its object or modifiers:	walking slowly
	opening the door carefully
	sensing danger
	returning after many years*

CLAUSE

A meaningful group of words that contains a verb and its subject.

Clauses are *dependent* when they form only part of a complex sentence of more than one clause:

Because he was late, . . .	If it rains tomorrow, . . .
. . . when the plane arrives	. . . that you requested

Each of these expressions contains a verb and *its* subject, but you can see that the sentence will not be complete—that is, the assertion will not be fully expressed or understood—until at least one additional clause is added.

---

* Note that prepositional phrases, which are modifiers because they function as adjectives and adverbs do, may be part of a larger participial phrase.

In these examples, one *independent* clause has been added to form a *complete sentence:*

[Because he was late], his appointment was canceled.

I will call you [when the plane arrives].

The book [that you requested] is now available.

A *sentence,* then, may be made up of a few words—a subject, and a predicate verb that establishes the action or state of being of the subject, and modifiers:

She ran.

The dog barked.

He was late.

The crowd cheered enthusiastically.

Or a sentence may be made up of more than one clause and contain several phrases as modifiers.

Because he was late, his appointment was canceled and had to be rescheduled for the following week.

The large crowd in the bleachers cheered enthusiastically as the home team took the field in the last inning.

Tests of standard usage are tests of how well you understand and can compose the many relationships of words, phrases, clauses, and sentences that make up standard written English.

Most of the problems in grammar and usage you are expected to recognize and be able to correct are considered "errors" because they result in a lack of clarity, even confusion, in the writer's expression.

Although writing that contains minor errors in standard usage may still be understood, careful writers seek expression that is precise and clear—even elegant—and that demonstrates their ability to use variety in language and structure. It is only through mastery of a wide range of expression that students may fully reveal their ideas, insights, and feelings.

AVOIDING COMMON ERRORS IN WRITING

When we refer to errors in writing, we are referring to expressions that are illogical, inconsistent, vague, or imprecise. The elements of usage reviewed here are those that high school students should be able to recognize.

Agreement of Subject and Verb

Agreement is a form of consistency and is one of the most basic elements of grammar. When you learn to conjugate verbs, for example, you are applying the concept of agreement. Singular subjects take singular verbs; plural subjects take plural verbs.

He speaks/they speak; One is/many are

Errors in agreement commonly occur in sentences where the subject follows the verb:

On the desk *are* my notebook, a few pencils, and the assignments for tomorrow.

"Desk" is not the subject of the verb; "notebook, pencils, assignments" is the subject, *they* are on the desk. In such inverted word order, the writer must hear and think ahead to choose the correct form of the verb. Similarly:

There *seems* to be only *one answer*.

There *seem* to be *several ideas* worth considering.

Here *are* the *pieces* you have been looking for.

Agreement errors may also occur when a subject followed by a phrase precedes the verb:

New York with its many historical sites and tourist attractions *is* a fascinating city to visit.

His *many talents* in sports, academics, and student leadership *make* him a popular candidate.

Subjects may be expanded by such prepositional phrases as *along with, in addition to, as well as, together with*. These phrases, however, do not form part of the *grammatical* subject; they modify the subject:

English, as well as math, science, and social studies, *is* a required subject for most high school students.

Evan, along with several of his friends, *is* planning to visit colleges in the fall.

In some sentences, the subject may be modified by one or more clauses before the predicate verb is stated. In such sentences the writer must "remember" the actual subject before composing the correct form of the verb:

The *fact* that Americans must now compete in a global economy and must recognize the necessity for higher standards in our schools *has led* to educational reform in many states.

Many common pronouns are singular and must take a singular verb:

Each one of these books *is* worth reading.

Every one of us *is* prepared to contribute.

None of these solutions *is* acceptable. (No *one* is)

Note how agreement with correlatives *either/or, neither/nor* is achieved:

Either Susan or her brother *is* home now.

(Either Susan is . . . or her brother is)

Neither rain, nor sleet, nor snow *deters* us . . . .

When the correlative contains both a singular and plural expression, the verb agrees with the one closest:

Neither Susan nor her sisters *are* at home.

Either the members of the legislature or the governor *is* authorized to submit a budget.

Do not be confused when the predicate is completed with a plural expression:

His most reliable *source* of encouragement *is* friends and family.

To avoid the correct but awkward-sounding expression above, rewrite as follows:

His *friends and family are* his most reliable source of encouragement.

Collective nouns take singular verbs because all the "members" are understood to act as a single unit:

The *jury was* unanimous in its decision to acquit.

A school *board has* extensive responsibilities.

Our *family has agreed* on plans for the vacation.

The *team practices* for two hours every day.

When there is not such unity of action, you may use a plural verb:

The *jury are* not in unanimous agreement.

The *family are* expected to arrive at different times.

It is better, however, to avoid such awkward sounding expressions by rewriting to make the plural idea clear:

The members of the jury are not in agreement.

Players on the team are required to keep their uniforms and equipment in good order.

Family members are expected to arrive at different times.

Agreement of Pronoun and Antecedent

Because pronouns replace nouns or other pronouns, they must agree with their singular or plural antecedents.

Evelyn is very grateful to *her parents* for *their* constant support and encouragement.

Most pronoun/antecedent errors arise when we use the indefinite pronouns *anyone, anybody, everyone, everybody, someone, somebody, no one,* and so on. These pronouns are singular because they refer to *individuals:*

Everybody is responsible for *his* own work.

Someone has left *her* books on the floor.

If *anyone* calls while I am out, please tell *him* or *her* I will call back after lunch.

The common practice of replacing *him/her* with *them,* or *her/his* with *their,* solves the problem of choosing gender, but it is ungrammatical and illogical. The careful writer (and speaker) avoids these errors or rewrites:

Please tell *anyone who calls* that I will return at noon.

Someone's books have been left on the floor.

Everyone has individual responsibility for the assignments.

Form of Pronouns

Use the subject forms when pronouns are *subjects* of verbs or identify the subject after a linking verb:

> *He and I* received the information we needed.
>
> *She* is the favorite candidate of the party.
>
> *He* is the head baseball coach.
>
> The head baseball coach is *he.*
>
> (Think of the verb *is* as an = sign.)

It is easy to avoid the awkward sound of the last sentence by choosing the preceding expression, which uses the pronoun first.

Pronouns as *objects* of verbs or prepositions must be in the object form:

> Please give *him* the information.
>
> Give the information to *them.*
>
> *Whom* did you see yesterday?

Errors often occur when we have pronouns preceded by a noun; the writer no longer "hears" the preposition and is reluctant to use the object form. But,

> Please give the information to Ellen and *him.* (to Ellen . . . to him)
>
> The host was very gracious to Ellen and *me.*
> (to Ellen . . . to me; *not* to Ellen and I)
>
> Just between you and me, this is simple.

We also use the object form with infinitives:

> We understand *her to be* the favorite candidate.
>
> We understand the favorite candidate *to be her.*

Remember to use the possessive form with *gerunds* ("-ing" verb forms that function as nouns):

> I do not approve of *your staying* out so late.
> (of your "late hours")
>
> She was concerned about *his working* too hard.
> (about his excessive work)

Note the following:

Mark's mother saw *him* [*running* after the bus].

Mark's mother encouraged [*his running* on the cross-country team].

In the first example, *running* is a participle describing *him,* which is the object of the verb *saw.* In the second example, *running* is a noun; it is the object of the verb *encouraged.*

Parallelism

Parallelism is used for consistency and clarity. Parallel ideas and expressions in a series should be composed in the same form:

He wants to spend the summer *reading, sleeping, and traveling.*

He plans *to read, to sleep, and to travel.*

Use parallel phrases and clauses:

She is known *for* her talent and *for* her generosity.

We expect our presidents to be skilled *not only in* domestic affairs *but also in* foreign policy.

Our state senator was reelected *because* she is honest, *because* she works hard for the district, *and because* she has an important leadership position in the senate.

Use parallel construction when you use correlatives: *either, or; not only, but also:*

Either you will complete the work now, *or* he will complete it in the morning.

We will *either take* a train this afternoon *or take* a plane this evening.

Consistency of active and passive voice is also a form of parallelism:

The research team *formulated* its ideas and *developed* its proposal.

Ideas *were formulated* and a proposal *was developed* by the research team.

Verbs: Using the Correct Tense

Use the simple past tense for actions completed in the past:

> The train *arrived* at 6:30.
> He *retired* in 1993.
> The Nobel prizes *were announced* in January.

Use the present perfect tense to establish facts, to assert that something *has occurred, has happened, has been done*, without reference to a specific time.

> *Have you done* your homework yet?
> The renovation of our house *has been completed.*
> I *have read* Macbeth several times.

Note the correct *sequence of tenses* in the following:

> The novelist *completed* the book in 1993, two years after he *had begun* it.
> She *recorded* the names of everyone who *had called* the day before.

> In the Middle Ages, most people *believed* that the earth *is* round.
> Copernicus *demonstrated* that the earth *orbits* the sun.

> If I *were* you, I *would accept* the offer.
> If the congressman *were indicted,* he *would* lose the support of many constituents.

> If we *had taken* more time to plan, our trip *would have been* more pleasant.
> If you *had trained* harder, you *would have* made the team.

If you would have called earlier is sometimes heard but this is not an acceptable construction in standard English.

Finally, you are generally expected to write about works of literature in the *present tense.*

> Macbeth *is driven* by ambition.
> Jay Gatsby *believes* he can recreate the past.
> Willy Loman *dies* believing his son will achieve great success.

Aspects of character, themes, plot, and setting remain constant—they *are* what they are—regardless of how the plot concludes or when we finish reading the work.

Logical Comparisons

My sister is *taller* than I [am].

She is *more* clever than he [is].

Josh is the *tallest* member of the team.

Among all of Miller's plays, *Death of a Salesman* is the *best* known.

Avoid incomplete comparisons in your writing:

Dreiser's novels are *more* popular now [than they were when they were first published].

Shakespeare's plays are *harder* to read [than modern works are].

The passages in brackets should be fully stated.
In informal speech we may use *so* as an intensifier:

I was *so* tired. He was *so* angry.

In writing, however, be sure every *so* is followed by a *that,* every *more* by a *than.*
Comparisons must be parallel and logical:

The paintings of Monet are more popular than Goya **should read**:

The paintings of Monet are more popular than *the paintings* of Goya.

You must compare paintings to paintings, not inadvertently compare paintings to a man.
And,

Anne is a better player than anyone on her team. **should read**:

Anne is a *better* player *than any other* [player] on her team.

or,

Anne is the *best player* on the team.

It is illogical to suggest Anne is better than she herself is.

Clear and Logical Modification

The careful writer must also be aware of errors in modification and in the logical relationships of ideas. Many such errors are corrected simply, with commas; others may require revision or reorganization of sentences.

Introductory subordinate (dependent) clauses must be set off by a comma:

> *After the lights had come back on,* the children were no longer frightened by the thunderstorm.
>
> *When it rains,* cats and dogs prefer not to go outside.

Without the comma, such sentences would be ambiguous.

Nonrestrictive (nonessential) phrases and clauses are set off by commas:

> My aunt, *who lives in Milwaukee,* will be flying in for a weekend visit to New York.
>
> Several stranded passengers, *feeling restless and impatient,* demanded flights on another airline.

When such phrases or clauses are restrictive* (essential to the meaning of the sentence), do not set them off with commas:

> Passengers *traveling with small children* will be permitted to board the plane first.
>
> My cousin *who lives in Milwaukee* will have to fly, but the cousins *who live in the New York area* will be able to drive to my brother's wedding.

A common error occurs when we begin a sentence with a participial phrase:

> Feeling restless and impatient, seats were demanded on other airlines' flights [by many travelers].
> (The seats are not restless . . .)
>
> *Barking loudly,* we were afraid the dog would wake our neighbors.
> (We are not barking, the dog is . . .)
>
> *Tired and hungry,* even cold leftovers looked good to us.
> (The leftovers are not hungry, we are . . .)

(*For additional examples, see *which/that/who* on page 140.)

The *subject* of the participle must also be stated as the subject of the clause that follows:

> *Feeling restless and impatient, many stranded travelers* sought seats on other airlines' flights.
>
> *Barking loudly, the dog* wakened our neighbors.
>
> *Tired and hungry, we* were satisfied with the cold leftovers.

You may also recompose sentences to make the modification clear:

> We were afraid our dog, *barking loudly,* would wake the neighbors.
>
> *Because we were tired and hungry,* even cold leftovers looked good to us.

EXPRESSIONS OFTEN CONFUSED, MISUSED, AND OVERUSED*

accept/except

> To **accept** is to receive, take willingly, agree to:
>
> I **accept** your offer, apology, invitation
>
> To **except** is to exclude, to separate out:
>
> I will **except** you from the requirement.
>
> **Except** is also a preposition:
>
> Everyone **except** him will be leaving on Tuesday.

affect/effect

> To **affect** (vb.) means to move, influence, or change. It also means to put on an artificial quality of personality or character; such an exaggerated or artificial person may be called **affected**.
>
> An **effect** (n.) is a consequence or result.
>
> To **effect** (vb.) means to put into action, to complete—a plan or a change, for example.

---

*See also Words Commonly Confused/Misspelled in Chapter 10, Spelling.

134

aggravate

To **aggravate** means to make worse. Do not use it when you really mean to irritate or annoy.

allusion/illusion

An **allusion** is a reference (see Glossary of Poetic Terms and Techniques, Chapter 4); an **illusion** is a false or deceptive idea or vision.

among/between

Use **between** for two, **among** for three or more:

between you and me

among all the members of the family

amount/number

One has an **amount** of something (the quantity as a whole) and a **number** of things (that can be counted):

an **amount** of time/a **number** of hours, days

a large **amount** of work/a **number** of tasks

See also **fewer/less** for the same distinction.

as far as . . . is/are concerned

The expression **as far as** used by itself creates an incomplete and illogical statement; it must be completed with **is/are concerned.** The expression as **far as . . . goes/go** is also widely used and correct as completed.

Faulty: **As far as** plans for school construction in the future, we expect the legislature to take action in the next session.

As far as the weather, it will be sunny and pleasant tomorrow.

Correct: **As far as** plans for school construction in the future are concerned, we expect the legislature to take action in the next session

As far as the weather goes, it will be sunny and pleasant.

bad/badly, good/well

Use **bad** and **good** (adjectives) to describe how one feels; use **badly** and **well** (adverbs) to describe how one does something.

He felt **bad** (sorry, regretful) because he caused the team to lose.

The team lost the game because he played so **badly**.

She feels **good** (in good spirits, positive) when her work is going **well.**

She is feeling **well** (no longer ill) now after a long bout with the flu.

The team lost because he did not play **well**.

being as, being that

These expressions are not standard speech. Use *because* or *since* instead.

compare to, compare with

Use **compare to** when you are expressing an analogy or similarity; use **compare with** when you are showing similarities and differences between two things.

He compared his small room **to** a closet.

The critics compared the movie **with** the book.

could of/ should of

Do not make this unfortunate confusion in the way words sound! You mean **could have/should have**.

different from (not **than**)

You should use the preposition **from** with **different** because you are making a distinction, a separation. Use **than** for comparisons, to show degrees of the same quality:

She is only slightly older **than** her sister, but her personality is very different **from** her sister's.

due to

This expression is popularly used for almost any cause and effect relationship. Avoid its overuse in your writing:

Absence **due to** illness is excused.

Delays **due to** bad weather are common in winter.

It is more precise to say:

The road was closed **because of** an accident.

The defendant was acquitted **by reason of** insanity.

There were many landslides **caused by** the heavy rains.

everybody, somebody, someone, nobody

These are *singular* forms; they may refer to many people, but they refer to *each one individually.* Singular antecedents take singular pronouns:

Everybody has *his/her* books, lunch, opinions.

Someone, a person has *his/her* opinions.

farther/further

In general, you may use **farther** or **further** for actual or figurative distance:

The nearest town is ten miles **farther** from here.

The latest agreements move us **further** toward a full peace.

Use **further** when you mean more:

We have nothing **further** to discuss.

A final agreement requires **further** negotiations.

fewer/less

One has **fewer** things and **less** something.

fewer hours/**less** time

fewer dollars/**less** money

fewer ideas/**less** content

first, second, . . .

To show transition and to enumerate examples, use these terms instead of *firstly, secondly,* . . .

hang/hanged/hung

When we use this verb in the past tense to denote an execution, we use **hanged**; for such things as clothes and pictures, we use **hung.**

The condemned man was **hanged** at dawn.

We **hung** our winter coats in the hall closet.

hopefully

This expression is popularly used to mean we hope, it is hoped, and so on. The careful writer should use it only as an adverb:

The cat looked **hopefully** at the leftover chicken.

But:

We **hope** the situation will improve.

It is hoped that research will lead to a cure.

however

Along with its cousins *therefore, moreover,* and *consequently,* **however** should be placed *within the sentence,* close to the verb it modifies; think of it as a conjunction, not as a transition at the beginning of a sentence.

if/whether

Use **if** to introduce conditional expressions; use **whether** (or not) for choices, decisions, questions:

If it rains, our game will be postponed.

If you work hard, you will succeed.

I do not know **whether** we will play or not.

infer/imply

To **infer** is to conclude, to draw an inference from evidence; to **imply** is to suggest or hint.

We can **infer** from his comments that he is pleased.

She **implied** in her speech that she is planning to run for public office.

its/it's

it's = a contraction* for it is.

its = a possessive form; do not add an apostrophe.

if . . . were/if . . . was

Use the **if . . . were** construction for *hypothetical* conditions and situations:

If you were President, what would you do?

If I were you, I would accept the offer.

---

*Contractions should be avoided in formal writing, unless you are quoting someone. Contractions are features of spoken language.

Use **if . . . was** for situations that *were possible*:

> **If** that really **was** Linda who called yesterday, she should have left a message.

incredible/incredulous

Incredible means unbelievable, beyond belief or understanding. In formal writing, avoid using it as *hyperbole.* Use instead such terms as *astonishing* or *extraordinary.*

A person is **incredulous** when he/she utterly cannot believe what is being said.

kind of/sort of/type of

Avoid using *a* or *an* with these expressions:

> **That type of** character is popular in children's books.

> **Those types of** characters are . . .

> **This kind of** fabric is best for the new sofa.

Also avoid using **kind of** or **sort of** when you mean *a little, rather, somewhat.*

lie/lay

These verbs are often confused. Note their principal parts and distinctions in meaning: to **lie (down)** means to recline, be situated, rest:

> You **lie** on your bed to take a nap.

> The mail **has lain** on your desk since yesterday.

> Last winter the snow **lay** on the ground for weeks.

Note that to **lay** means to put or place something. (It is a transitive verb and always takes a direct object.):

> You can **lay** your hat and gloves on the hall table.

> Masons **lay bricks** and hens **lay eggs**.

> He cannot remember where he **laid** his car keys.

like/as/as if

Use **like** as a preposition, use **as** and **as if** as conjunctions:

> He looks just **like** his father.

> A talent **like** hers is rare.

139

It looks **as if** it will rain this afternoon.

You should do the assignments **as** you were instructed to.

"Do **as** I say, not **as** I do!"

only/just

These modifiers should be placed as close as possible to the expressions they actually limit:

I have **only** two dollars for lunch.

He has time for **only** a brief conversation.

I have **just** one thing to say.

presently

This should be used to denote the immediate future; it means right *away* or in *a little while:*

I will answer your question **presently**.

He is expected to arrive **presently**.

The meeting will begin **presently**.

For current time, use **at present** or **currently**:

He is **currently** a junior at North High.

At present, she is working on her master's degree.

toward/towards

Either is acceptable; **toward** is more formal.

when/where

These are terms of time and place; do not use them to introduce definitions.

which/that/who

These relative *pronouns* introduce *clauses* that describe or define. Use **that** for clauses that are *restrictive* (defining, limiting):

The books **that** you ordered will arrive tomorrow; the ones **that** Sam ordered will come next week. (those particular books . . .)

He likes the car **that** he bought last year better than any other he has owned. (that particular car)

Basketball is the game **that** he plays best.

140

Use **which** for clauses that are *nonrestrictive* (descriptive):

> The house on the corner, **which** was built in the 1880s, will be restored to its original design.

> Shakespeare's plays, **which** were written nearly 400 years ago, remain popular in theaters and movies as well as in English courses.

Use **who** for persons. (**That** is sometimes used when the identification is distant or impersonal.) Do not use **which** for persons:

> Lady Macbeth is a character **that** (**who**) remains fascinating to many students.

Use **whom** when the pronoun is an object:

> To **whom** should I give the information? (obj. of prep.)

> **Whom** did you ask? (obj. of verb)

who/whom/whoever/whomever

When these *pronouns* introduce *clauses,* their form is determined *solely* by their function in the clause:

> The new coach, **who** led the team to a county title, gave all the credit to her players.
> (**Who** is the subject of the verb *led;* therefore, it is in the subject form.)

> Please give the information to (**whoever** needs it.)
> (**Whoever** is the subject in the clause; the *entire* clause is the object of *give to.*)

> Please give the award to (**whomever** you choose.)
> (**Whomever** is the object of the verb *choose;* the *entire* clause is the object of *give to.*)

Careful attention to the conventions of usage and style outlined in this chapter will enhance your ability to express ideas and discuss information clearly and persuasively. When you have command of the language you use, you have command of the relationship between thought and expression.

Chapter 8

PUNCTUATION: GUIDELINES AND REMINDERS

When is the semicolon or colon used? Are there any rules for commas? Do I underline titles of books and poems or put them in quotation marks? Where do I put the period when a sentence ends with quotation marks? Even experienced writers need to consult a usage handbook for the answers to some of these questions.

In conversation we use pauses, stresses, and tone of voice to make our meaning clear. The printed page, however, does not readily show what voice and gesture can reveal, so the writer uses punctuation to achieve absolute clarity. Below, you will find a review of the elements of punctuation high school students should know and use in their own writing. Featured are answers to those questions most often raised about how to punctuate. (Many of the examples from the writing of specific authors come from the passages reprinted elsewhere in the book.)

END PUNCTUATION

The period, exclamation mark, and question mark bring statements and expressions to a close; they signal a full stop.

The Period

Use a **period** to indicate the end of a sentence or of a group of words having the emphasis of a sentence.

Declarative sentences (make a statement):

Good writers are also good readers.

"The guns squatted in a row like savage chiefs." (Stephen Crane, *The Red Badge of Courage*)

Imperative sentences (give an order or direction):

Be sure to proofread.

Come to practice on time or leave the team.

Tell me how much I owe you.

Fragments for emphasis:

"No doubt my younger brother and sister were in the house and warm.

Eating cookies." (William Kittredge)

"Much of their [whales'] behavior seems to be recreational: they sing, they play. *And so on.*" (Robert Finch)

The Exclamation Mark

Use an **exclamation mark** to show intensity and emphasis in sentences or fragments.

Come to practice!

Be sure to proofread!

Look out!

Congratulations!

CAUTION: *Do not overuse the* **exclamation mark** *in expository writing; use effective language and sentence structure to achieve emphasis.*

The Question Mark

Use a **question mark** to signal interrogative forms in complete sentences, fragments, or series.

Can you explain how to do this?

Do you understand what he said?

Can you recommend a good restaurant in the theater district?

What was that all about? a joke? a mistake?

Where should we meet? at home? at school?

Ask questions as you read an essay: What is the author's purpose? tone? conclusion? Do you agree? disagree? feel convinced?

Question marks may also be used with single words or phrases as needed:

When?

Leave the team?

You did?

What homework?

SPECIAL CONSIDERATIONS

Periods are used in many abbreviations. For example:

U.S. government	Dipl. B.A. M.A. Ph.D.
U.N. Security Council	D.D.S. M.D. Esq.
N.Y.S. Board of Regents	A.M. P.M.

Some abbreviations take no periods:

CIA	mph
MTV	rpm
WCBS	

A sentence may end with more than one kind of punctuation. If it ends with an abbreviation using a period, do not add a second period.

Please report to my office promptly at 10:00 a.m.

In order to apply for a teaching position, you must have completed your M.A.

If it ends with a quotation or expression in quotation marks, place the final period *inside* the quotation marks.

Most high school students have read Poe's short story, "The Cask of Amontillado."

When told his wife is dead, Macbeth remarks, "She should have died hereafter."

If the **entire sentence** requires a question mark, place it outside the quotation marks:

Have you read Poe's story "The Cask of Amontillado"?

Why does Macbeth say, "She should have died hereafter"?

If the quotation at the end of a sentence requires a question mark, keep it within the quotes. (Do not add an additional period.)

> The title of a recent editorial in *The New York Times* was "Where do we go from here?"

If a statement within the quotes is a question, the question mark within the quote is sufficient.

> Did you read the editorial entitled "Where do we go from here?"

Similarly, if an exclamation point is part of a quoted expression, place it within the quote. An additional period is not required.

> One of my favorite pieces by James Thurber is called "Excelsior!"

To make the above into a question, however:

> Have you read Thurber's story "Excelsior!"?

If a sentence ends with a passage in parentheses, put the period outside the closing parenthesis:

> We did not leave on time because Sally was late (as usual).

Even if the expression is a complete sentence, do not punctuate within the parentheses:

> We did not leave on time because Sally was late (she always is).

If, however, the expression within the parentheses requires quotation marks, a question mark, or an exclamation point, include them:

> We did not leave on time because Sally was late (isn't she always?).

In such cases, a better solution would be to separate the parenthetical statement:

> We did not leave because Sally was late. (Isn't she always?)

What is the logic to all this? When sentences or passages are made up of a variety of elements, punctuation should make the structure of each element clear. If the end of a sentence becomes cluttered by the need to bring several individual pieces to a close at the same time, punctuate from the inside out—smaller pieces first, then larger. But do not double the end punctuation unless it is required for accuracy. If you have a question within a question, one question mark will do. If a closing quotation ends with a "strong" piece of punctuation, don't add a modest and redundant period to the whole sentence. Close with the strength of the quote.

INTERNAL PUNCTUATION

Internal punctuation includes the comma, the semicolon, the colon, and the dash. The single purpose of internal punctuation is to prevent confusion; to achieve clarity. The comma indicates brief pauses between separate elements in a sentence; the semicolon establishes a direct connection between two independent statements to form a single sentence; the colon serves to introduce things; and the dash permits you to digress or emphasize.

The Comma

Use the comma in compound sentences with coordinating conjunctions *and, but, yet, so, or, for.* A compound sentence joins two or more independent clauses that could be expressed separately as simple sentences. *Note that the comma precedes the conjunction:*

> "I walked slowly, *for* the detail on the beach was infinite." (Ernie Pyle)
>
> "The luncheon hour was long past; *and* the two had their end of the vast terrace to themselves." (Edith Wharton, "Roman Fever")
>
> "I was not going to talk about Whitewater today, *but* then I thought that if I didn't you'd think I know something about it, *and* the only way for me to prove that I don't is to talk about it at length, *so* I will." (Garrison Keillor)

In sentences where the clauses are short and the meaning is clear, you may omit a comma:

> The team tied the score in the last seconds of the game and the crowd cheered wildly.

If there is any possibility of misreading, you must use a comma:

> I went to the movies with Roger and Sally stayed home.
>
> I went to the movies with Roger, and Sally stayed home.

WHAT IS A COMMA SPLICE?

One of the most common errors in writing is the use of a comma alone to join independent clauses. This is the error familiar to students as the "run-on" sentence.

Run on: The crowd cheered wildly, the game was tied in the last few seconds.

            I went to the movies with Roger, Sally stayed home.

            The novel was riveting, I did not want it to end.

Correct: The crowd cheered wildly when the game was tied in the final seconds.

            I went to the movies with Roger, and Sally stayed home.

            The novel was riveting, so I did not want it to end.

DO I USE A COMMA BEFORE THE LAST ITEM IN A SERIES?

Some editors and instructors insist that all items in a series be set off by a comma; others prefer that you omit the last one, especially in a series of single words:

You can find models of style in books, newspapers, and magazines.

You can find models of style in books, newspapers and magazines.

SUGGESTION: For sentences like the one above, the second comma needlessly slows down the sentence and makes no contribution to clarity. In a series of longer expressions, however, or in a series without a conjunction, set off each with a comma.

For class you are expected to bring a notebook, a pen or pencil, and the text we are reading.

"He was white-headed as a mountain, bowed in the shoulders, and faded in general aspect." (Thomas Hardy)

Writing has many purposes: personal expression, persuasion, literary effect, information.

Use a Comma After Introductory Clauses

As the crowd cheered them on, the home team scored the winning touchdown.

If you are hungry, please help yourself to a sandwich.

"As the bell sounded the hour, there came a knocking at the street door." (Edgar Allan Poe)

Do not use a comma if the main clause is followed by a dependent clause:

Please help yourself to a sandwich whenever you get hungry.

The home team scored the winning touchdown as the crowd cheered them on.

Use a Comma After an Introductory Phrase Only When Needed

At last, the rain began to ease, and the sun came through breaks in the clouds.

The son of a tanner, Grant was everything Lee was not.

After the Labor Day recess, Congress will reconvene.

Feeling ill and confused, he left the dinner table without speaking.

These sentences require no comma:

On the desk you will find your final check and a letter of recommendation.

"For a long time they continued to sit side by side without speaking." (Edith Wharton)

Use Commas to Set off Descriptive and Nonessential Clauses or Phrases Within Sentences

"They were two strong men, these oddly different generals, and they represented the strengths of two conflicting currents that, through them, had come into final collision." (Bruce Catton)

The house on the corner, which was built in the 1880s, will be restored to its original design.

Shakespeare's plays, written nearly four hundred years ago, remain popular in theaters and movies as well as in English courses.

USE COMMAS WITH SOME SINGLE WORDS AND EXPRESSIONS

"Well, Jim's habits and his jokes didn't appeal to Julie . . ." (Ring Lardner, "Haircut")

"Now, I'll read the names—heads of families first." (Shirley Jackson, "The Lottery")

USE COMMAS WITH PARENTHETIC AND TRANSITIONAL EXPRESSIONS

Use commas to set off such expressions as *however, moreover, therefore, nevertheless, after all, by the way, of course, on the other hand, I think.*

"Yet it was not all contrast, after all . . . Furthermore, their fighting qualities were really very much alike." (Bruce Catton)

After all, what you learn is what really matters.

You must, of course, always proofread a paper before handing it in.

COMMAS IN DATES

For expressions of day, month, and year:

July 4, 1776, marks the beginning of the American Revolution.

Registration will take place on September 9, 1994, for the fall semester and on January 12, 1995, for the spring semester.

Do not use commas for expressions of month and year only.

Joan completed graduate school in June 1987, began her legal work in September 1987, and joined our firm in January 1993.

COMMAS WITH ADJECTIVES IN A SERIES

Use a comma when it means *and:*

The little room in Appomattox was "the scene of one of the poignant, dramatic contrasts in American history." (Bruce Catton)

The Regents examinations require you to write thoughtful, well-organized essays.

Do not use a comma if the adjective is part of the meaning of the noun:

She greeted her guests in the large sitting room.

USE COMMAS TO SET OFF QUOTES

"I always used to think," Mrs. Slade continued, "that our mothers had a much more difficult job than our grandmothers." (Edith Wharton, "Roman Fever")

"It isn't fair, it isn't right," Mrs. Hutchinson screamed, and then they were upon her. (Shirley Jackson, "The Lottery")

ADDITIONAL ILLUSTRATIONS OF COMMA USE

If you must sing, sing quietly.
These incidents took place a long, long time ago.

That's not what you meant, is it?
You have everything you need, don't you?

First come, first served.
Now you see it, now you don't.

Shakespeare's tragedy *Macbeth* is one of his best-known plays.
Verdi's only comic opera, *Falstaff,* is the last work he composed.

My sister Anne lives in Seattle; my sister Julia lives in New York.
My only sister, Anne, lives in Seattle.

COMMON ERRORS IN COMMA USE

Do not separate compound elements or isolate essential elements with commas.

Correct: "They greeted one another and exchanged bits of gossip as they went to join their husbands." (Shirley Jackson, "The Lottery")

Faulty: They greeted one another, and exchanged bits of gossip as they went to join their husbands.

Alternative: *They greeted* one another, and *they exchanged* bits of gossip as they went to join their husbands.

Correct: "Whales possess a highly complex language and have developed sophisticated communications systems that transmit over long distances." (Robert Finch)

Faulty: Whales possess a highly complex language, and have developed sophisticated communications systems, that transmit over long distances.

Alternative: *Whales possess* a highly complex language, *and they have developed* sophisticated communications systems that transmit over long distances.

In the faulty examples, the first comma may *look* necessary, but it improperly separates the subject from the second verb; the final clause in each case is essential description and should not be separated from the rest of the sentence. The alternative versions are accurately punctuated and show how the original, correct sentences could be revised into compound sentences.

SUGGESTION: *In all the examples and explanations above, the commas serve one purpose: to make the expression clear on first reading. Insert commas in your own writing as you compose, as you hear the need for them. When you revise, do not be tempted to add commas simply because they look right—chances are, they do not belong.*

The Semicolon

A comma indicates a brief pause between separate elements in a sentence, whereas a semicolon indicates a longer pause between independent statements that form a single sentence. The semicolon may replace *and* or *but* in compound sentences. Here are some of the examples used earlier now revised with semicolons.

I walked slowly; the detail on the beach was infinite.

The luncheon hour was long past; the two had their end of the vast terrace to themselves.

I was not going to talk about Whitewater today; then I thought that if I didn't, you'd think I know something about it; the only way for me to prove that I don't is to talk about it at length; so I will.

In each of these revisions, you can see that the effect of the semicolon is to indicate a cause and effect relationship or to show consequence without stating it directly. This results in forceful and emphatic sentences. The semi-colon also has a formal quality; it creates a feeling of balance and equiva-lence among statements.

> ". . . with a semicolon . . . you get a pleasant little feeling of expectan-cy; there is more to come; read on; it will get clearer." (Lewis Thomas)

The Colon

Use the colon to introduce something: a list, the body of a letter, a quota-tion, or an explanation.

> "Political courage stems from a number of sources: anger, pain, love, hate." (Madeleine Kunin)

> "Mrs. Slade began again: 'I suppose I did it as a sort of joke'—" (Edith Wharton)

> "The purpose of life is to be useful. It is, above all, to *matter:* to have it make some difference that you lived at all." (Leo Rosten)

The Dash

The dash permits you to pause without notice and insert an idea too inter-esting to delay and too important to put in parentheses—but don't overdo it!

> "At some gut level, the art of politics—combative, competitive, self-asserting—is sometimes difficult to integrate with our feminine selves." (Madeleine Kunin)

> "Different as they were—in background, in personality, in underlying aspiration—these two great soldiers had much in common." (Bruce Catton)

> "The wonder of ourselves, of each other, and of life—this is the true subject matter of all novels." (Sandy Asher)

The Ellipsis

The ellipsis is used in quoted passages to show that something has been omitted.

> "The purpose of life is to be useful . . . above all, to *matter*." (Rosten)

When an ellipsis comes at the end of a sentence, the final period must be retained; that is, you will use four periods, not three. The following example shows the use of three ellipses: one in the middle of a sentence and two, each with a fourth period added, at the ends of sentences:

> Mark Van Doren asserts that "Iago's cynicism consists of believing that . . . the passions of men are toys for hum to play with . . . . He likes nothing better than to make plans which other men's emotions will execute . . . ."

The Bracket

Brackets indicate where the writer has added a word or phrase to a quoted passage. Such additions are sometimes necessary to make connections in extended quotes where you have used ellipsis.

> "The persons of the tale were long since types [to Hawthorne], as were their souls' predicaments. The broken law, the hidden guilt, the hunger for confession, the studious, cold heart that watches and does not feel . . . ." (Mark Van Doren)

> Men's passions should lead them to "more and better feeling . . .," but Iago's knowledge of men's hearts transforms those passions into destructive forces, into "toys . . . tools to use." Iago contrives malign "plans which other men's [benign] emotions will execute."

The Apostrophe

The apostrophe has many important uses: to form contractions, to show possession, and to form the plural of numbers, symbols, and letters. Apostrophes are also easily misused. Below are examples of the most common uses.

CONTRACTIONS

The apostrophe takes the place of a missing letter or letters in a contraction:

> It's very warm day. = It is very warm today.

> You don't have to return the book right now. = You do not . . .

Remember that contractions are characteristic of spoken language and are not generally used in formal writing.

The apostrophe is also used to abbreviate dates:

June '82

The Class of '98

POSSESSIVE FORMS OF NOUNS AND PROPER NAMES

You form the possessive of a singular noun or name by adding an apostrophe and an *s*:

The novel's major themes (= The major themes of the novel)

My neighbor's house

Charles's notebook

Dickens's novels

In general, you form the possessive of a plural noun by adding the apostrophe alone:

My neighbors' yards

the jurors' verdict

the witnesses' statements

The Smiths' house

the Davises' horse

NOTE: Be sure to avoid the common error of confusing the possessive form with the plural.

Mark Twain wrote several novels; he did not write "novel's."

The local nursery sells plants; it does not sell "plant's."

SOME PLURALS

Use the apostrophe to form the plurals of letters and some abbreviations:

There were sixteen A's on the last exam.

"Dot your *i*'s and cross your *t*'s."

Mark has earned two Ph.D.'s, each in a different discipline.

TITLES OF WORKS OF LITERATURE

Titles of books and other full-length, separately published works should be set in italics. If you are composing on a typewriter or writing by hand, *underline* such titles. Movies and plays are also set in italics.

The Great Gatsby	*Death of a Salesman*
Huckleberry Finn	*The Glass Menagerie*
To Kill a Mockingbird	*Macbeth*

The names of newspapers and magazines should also be in italics.

The New York Times   *Harper's*   *Newsweek*

Titles of poems, essays, and short stories are set off in quotes.

"The Tell-Tale Heart"	"The Sleeping Giant"
"Roman Fever"	"The Road Not Taken"
"The Lottery"	"Old Photograph of the Future"

A title should not be underlined *and* set in quotes; this is redundant and confusing.

Your own title for an essay or paper should not be underlined; use quotes only for names or phrases actually quoted within the title.

A FINAL NOTE ON PUNCTUATION

The topics reviewed here are meant to offer fundamental guidelines and to illustrate how accurate punctuation helps make writing clear. Review some of the prose passages in other parts of the book for vivid examples of how different authors use punctuation to make their meaning and tone clear.

Chapter 9

VOCABULARY

Formal vocabulary study may begin as early as kindergarten; associating meaning with different sounds begins virtually at birth. As all students have discovered, however, there always seem to be new words to learn. Every novel, essay, or newspaper article we read is likely to include some new expressions or unfamiliar words. Deliberately studying new words and preparing for tests on them is certainly one way to expand our vocabularies, and every serious student has developed a method for such study. But if you do not continue to use those new words—that is, read, speak, and write with them—they may be forgotten soon after the test.

The thousands of words you *know* were acquired through repeated use over time and through association with their contexts, that is, through reading and listening. As you review lists of words and actively work to expand your reading and writing vocabularies, try to learn every new word in a context: associate it with a phrase, an experience, an object or person, an action or incident. Every word you study should create some kind of image for you; if you have no image, you do not truly know the word yet.

The words included on Regents and SAT vocabulary tests are those a high school student in likely to encounter in assigned texts and other works of literature. The new English Regents exam assesses your vocabulary skills in the multiple-choice questions of Parts I–III and by the degree to which you use language effectively in your essays; the exam does not have a separate section on vocabulary. The SAT includes vocabulary questions such as the following. As you choose the answers, say each word to yourself, hear it, think of an image or a context for it.

PRACTICE VOCABULARY TEST

1. **variance**
   (1) authority
   (2) nuisance
   (3) regulation
   (4) difference

2. **entail**
   (1) produce
   (2) involve
   (3) emphasize
   (4) forbid

3. **trudge**
   (1) retreat
   (2) slouch
   (3) plod
   (4) scurry

4. **acme**
   (1) highest point
   (2) final proposal
   (3) detailed explanation
   (4) preliminary investigation

5. **vanquish**
   (1) clean
   (2) criticize
   (3) comfort
   (4) conquer

6. **salve**
   (1) gauge
   (2) ointment
   (3) scar
   (4) bandage

7. **repress**
   (1) insult
   (2) disturb
   (3) subdue
   (4) refuse

8. **trifling**
   (1) useless
   (2) insignificant
   (3) grotesque
   (4) dull

9. **profoundly**
   (1) deeply
   (2) anxiously
   (3) pleasantly
   (4) loudly

10. **insatiable**
   (1) envious
   (2) coarse
   (3) disgusting
   (4) greedy

ANSWERS

1. 4	**3.** 3	**5.** 4	**7.** 3	**9.** 1
2. 2	**4.** 1	**6.** 2	**8.** 2	**10.** 4

LOOKING AT THE QUESTIONS/ANSWERS AND ANALYSIS

The answer to 1 is (4) *difference*. This should offer little difficulty since we associate variance with *variety, variable, variation, vary,* and so on. Think of the phrase "at variance with." Figures in one report can be *at variance with* those in another; language in one document can be *at variance with* language in another.

The answer to 2 is (2) *involve*. Think of the following questions: What does the solution to the problem *entail*? What does this job *entail*?

The word in 3, *trudge,* should bring up images of slogging through snow, mud, or sand; or, of walking when you are very tired. The answer is (3) *plod*. (Do not be distracted by *slouch;* one who trudges might also slouch, but that is not the meaning of the word.)

The answer to 4, *acme,* is (1) *highest point*. Nations, or individuals, may be described as reaching the *acme* of their power or influence.

The word in 5, *vanquish,* should be familiar to most youthful readers. Armies (4) *conquer* opposing forces, and heroes *vanquish* the forces of evil when they overcome or slay them.

For 6, *salve,* think of something that heals. The answer is (2) *ointment*. You may also remember the figurative use of the word, to heal or soothe injured feelings.

The word in 7, *repress*, should be associated but not confused with *oppress* and *suppress*. A people may be *oppressed* by dictatorial rulers; when information or evidence is deliberately withheld, it is *suppressed*. We use *repress* to mean (3) *subdue* feelings or harmful impulses. In each case, the action means to contain, keep down, or stifle.

Something that is 8, *trifling*, is (2) *insignificant* but not useless. We may describe a modest gift as "only a trifle" or reject a trifling comment because it is trivial and unimportant.

The word in 9, *profoundly*, should bring (1) *deeply* to mind fairly easily. We use *profound* or *profoundly* in virtually any context where we would use *deep* and *deeply* in a figurative sense.

Finally, 10, *insatiable*, should instantly suggest "appetites," literal and figurative ones. The answer is (4) *greedy*. Even though someone who is insatiable might also be *disgusting*, that is not the meaning of the word. On any vocabulary test, be careful not to equate the effects of what a word signifies with its definition.

Although you would not go through the detailed process outlined above for every question on a test, it is a process you can use when you are studying words and when you are trying to add them to your working vocabulary. Below are ten more questions in which each word is given in a context. As you can see, the sentence alone does not imply a specific answer; all the choices make sense. Unless the word is completely new to you, however, the sentence should trigger the kind of associations outlined in the discussion of answers above. Questions of this type on the new Regents exam will use words and contexts taken directly from the passage you are listening to or reading.

PRACTICE VOCABULARY TEST (CONT.)

11. The young man had a **debonair** attitude toward life.
    (1) lighthearted
    (2) pessimistic
    (3) childlike
    (4) cautious

12. After so many years of war, the people held little hope for any **armistice**.
    (1) victory
    (2) election
    (3) independence
    (4) truce

13. The judge decided to **mitigate** the criminal's sentence.
    (1) review
    (2) overrule
    (3) lessen
    (4) postpone

14. The teacher asked the **recalcitrant** students to sit down.
    (1) tardy
    (2) unruly
    (3) unhappy
    (4) eager

15. The teacher presented a **synopsis** of the play to the class.
    (1) critique
    (2) history
    (3) summary
    (4) segment

16. **Dissidence** is not usually tolerated by dictators.
    (1) disagreement
    (2) disorganization
    (3) desertion
    (4) democracy

17. No one could **mollify** the lost child.
    (1) identify
    (2) understand
    (3) approach
    (4) soothe

18. The writing was poetic as well as **utilitarian**.
    (1) creative
    (2) entertaining
    (3) witty
    (4) useful

19. She was **inundated** by the work that had been assigned to her.
    (1) overwhelmed
    (2) discouraged
    (3) astounded
    (4) inspired

20. The ex-convicts were engaged in a number of **nefarious** actions.
    (1) pessimistic
    (2) wholesome
    (3) wicked
    (4) regrettable

ANSWERS

11. 1	**13.** 3	**15.** 3	**17.** 4	**19.** 1
12. 4	**14.** 2	**16.** 1	**18.** 4	**20.** 3

At the end of this chapter you will find three collections of words to review or learn. The first includes all the words that have been tested on Regents exams from 1986 through 1998. The second is a list compiled by high school students from their reading of the Op-Ed pages of *The New York Times*. The third, from published book reviews, was also compiled by students. Each list offers the thoughtful reader and writer a rich source of vocabulary in current use.

STUDYING NEW WORDS

Learning in Context

Even the most diligent student cannot reasonably expect simply to memorize—out of context—the hundreds, even thousands, of words on Regents and SAT lists. Recent studies also confirm that vocabulary study confined to lists of words without a context or pattern of association—as with a particular work of literature, for example—does not result in long-term retention. Moreover, the practice of recording dictionary definitions alone gives only general and sometimes misleading information about the meaning and correct use of words. Learning words means learning their precise meanings, connotations, and appropriate context.

Unless you are working with an unabridged dictionary, which often includes illustrative examples in sentences or phrases, you are likely to find in a desk dictionary only brief definitions, general in nature, and possibly a list of synonyms. This limited information is valuable as a *reference,* especially if you are reading a passage and need to know a word's meaning in order to understand the passage. Learning the full meaning of unfamiliar words, however, requires more active study. In the sections below you will find recommendations for ways to prepare and organize your vocabulary study.

ROOTS AND PREFIXES FROM LATIN AND GREEK

Although English is certainly not derived from Greek and Latin only, familiarity with the Greek or Latin forms in English words is often useful to students taking vocabulary tests. Recognition of root meanings in particular may help you determine the correct answer for a word you may not be sure of. Even more important, however, is the value of knowing the Latin and Greek origins of English when you are first studying new words. When you are aware of the meanings of the individual parts of a word you often can form an image for it. Think of the Latin root *spect,* for example. This root means *look into, observe, behold* and, with variations in spelling *spec* and *spic,* is the base of many English words: *inspect, introspect, expect, respect, speculate, spectacle, spectacular, conspicuous*—and many others. Even the word *spy* is related to this Latin root.

When you are looking up words in the dictionary, do not skip over the etymology—the section that shows you in abbreviated form the origin and history of a word. Grouping words by related origin can be a very useful way to organize when you are studying large groups of new words; by using their common origin, you will learn to associate a new word with others you already know. It is the process of forming associations in meaning, forming images, and knowing contexts that permits you to learn efficiently—and to remember—the words you study. (Familiarity with roots and prefixes is also very helpful in understanding spelling patterns, as you will see in Chapter 10).

Listed below, with examples, are many of the Latin and Greek roots found in English. (As you review the meanings of these roots, provide additional examples from your own knowledge; you should also guess about possible examples—then look them up in a dictionary to confirm your guess.) This process is a demonstration of what is meant by *active* vocabulary study. It means you are thinking about a word and associating it with others you know.

As you examine the list of Greek and Latin roots common in English, you should be struck by how familiar many of these forms are. You should also note that all these roots denote specific actions or ideas. Knowing the meanings of these elements as you study new words, or review familiar ones, will give you specific images or experiences to associate with them. This in turn will make the meaning of many words more vivid and easier to remember than will an abstract definition or list of synonyms alone.

LATIN ROOTS

Forms	Meaning	Examples
alter	other	altercation, alternative
ami (amicus)	friend	amiable, amicable, amity
amor	love	amorous, enamored
anima	breath, mind, spirit	animation, unanimous, inanimate, animosity
bell (bellum)	war	bellicose, belligerent, antebellum
cad (cadere), cid	to fall	decay, decadence, deciduous
cap, cip	contain	captivate, capacity, capable
capit (caput)	head	capital, capitol, recapitulate
cede, ceed, cess (cedere)	to move, yield	proceed, accede, exceed, precede, excess, success, procession
cept (capere)	to take, seize, hold	intercept, reception, accept
cid, cis (caedere)	to cut, kill	precise, incisive, homicide
clam, claim (clamare)	to cry, call out	exclaim, proclaim, clamor
clud, clus (claudere)	to shut, close	include, exclusion, recluse
cred (credere)	to believe, loan, trust	creditable, incredible, credulous
culp (culpa)	fault, guilt	culpable, exculpate
cur, curs (currere)	to run	course, cursor, current, incur, precursor, recur
dict (dicere)	to say, tell	dictator, diction, edict, predict
doc (docere)	to teach	doctor, docile, indoctrinate
duc, duct (ducere)	to lead	deduce, induction, conduct
err (errare)	to go, lead astray	error, erroneous, erratum
err (erker)	to travel, wander	errand, arrant, erratic
fac, fact, fect, fic (facere)	to make, do	affect, defect, effect, facsimile, factor, artificial, deficit
fer (ferre)	to bear, carry	inference, offer, reference
fid (fidelitas)	faith, loyalty	infidel, perfidious, diffident
flect, flex (flectere)	to bend	reflex, reflection, flexibility
flu, fluct, flux (fluere)	to flow	affluent, fluctuation, fluent, influence, influx
fund (fundare) (fundus)	to base, bottom	(to) found, fundamental, profundity
fus (fundere)	pour	effusive, foundry, fusion

162

gen (genus) (genare)	kind, sort, birth, to beget	genre, heterogenous, genetic, generate, progenitor, genocide
grad, gress (gradus)	to walk, go, stage or step	digress, graduate, progress, grade, gradient, retrograde
greg (gregis)	flock, herd, group	egregious, gregarious, integrate
her, hes (haerere)	to cling, stick	adhesive, coherence, inherently
ject, jet (jacere)	to throw	inject, projection, jettison
jud, jur, jus (jus)	to judge; to swear just, right; law	abjure, adjudicate, prejudge, jury, justification, perjury
lat (latus)	borne, carried	correlative, related, superlative
leg (legis, lex)	law	legality, legislative
locus	place	location, locale, locomotive
locu, loqu (loqui) locutor	to speak speaker	eloquent, loquacious, soliloquy, interlocutor, locution, obloquy
lude (ludere)	to play	interlude, ludicrous, prelude
mit, mitt, mis, miss (mittere)	to dispatch, send, to let go	emit, permit, remit, submissive, commission, missile, permission
mob, mot (movere)	to move	demote, motivate, promote, commotion, mobility
mor, mort (mortis)	death	immortal, mortality, mortified
ped (pedis)	foot	expeditious, impede, pedestrian
pel, puls (pellere)	to drive, push	compel, dispel, impulse, repel, compulsive, repellent
pend, pens (pendere)	to hang, weigh, pay	append, compensate, dependent, impending, pension, pensive
ple, plet (plere)	to fill	complete, complement, deplete
plen (plenus)	full	plentiful, replete
pon, pos, posit (ponere)	to place, put	component, depose, propose, juxtapostion, impose, opponent
port (portare)	to carry	comport, deportment, purport, portable, portfolio
pot, poten, poss (posse)	to be able	impossibility, omnipotent, potential
rad (radius)	root, spoke (wheel)	eradicate, radical, radiation
rect, reg (regula) (regire)	right, straight to guide, rule	direction, rectified, regal regimen, regime
rupt (rumpere)	to break, burst	disrupt, corrupt, interruption
sat (satis)	enough	dissatisfy, insatiable, saturated
sci (scire)	to know	conscience, omniscient, prescience, scientific
scrib, script (scribere)	to write	describe, inscription, scripture
sect (sectare)	to cut	dissect, intersection
secu, sequ (sequi)	to follow	consequence, obsequious, sectarian, sequel
sed, sid, sess (sedere)	to sit	dissidence, possess, residual, sedation, sedentary
sent, sens (sentire)	to feel	consensus, insensitive, sentient
son (sonus)	sound	consonant, dissonance, sonic, sonogram, sonority, unison

spec, spect, spic (spectare)	to look at, observe	auspicious, conspicuous, expect, inspect, respect, spectacular
spir, spirit	to breathe	inspiration, respiratory, spirit
sta, state, stit (stare)	to stand	constitute, instability, obstacle, stability, status
strict, string (stringere)	to draw tight	constrict, restriction, stringent
sume, sump (sumere)	to take	assume, consume, presumption
tact, tang, ting, tig (tangere)	to touch	contact, contiguous, intangible, tactile, tangential
ten, tain (tenere)	to hold, keep	abstain, pertain, restrain, tenacious, untenable
tend, tens (tendere)	to reach, stretch	contend, intensity, portent, pretentious, tendency
tort (torque)	to twist	contortion, extort, tortuous
tract (trahere)	to draw, pull	distract, intractible, protracted, retraction
ver (veritas)	truth	aver, veracity, verification
vers, vert (vertere)	to turn	adverse, aversion, diversity, inadvertent, reversion, subvert, version, versification
vid, vis (videre) (video)	to see	evident, improvident, supervise, revision, visage, visionary
vit, viv (vivere) (viva)	to live; life	revival, survive, vivacious, unviable
vinc, vict (vincere)	to conquer	conviction, eviction, invincible
voc, voke (vocare)	to call	advocate, equivocal, invocation, provocative, revoke, vocation
volv, volu (volvere)	to roll, turn	convoluted, evolution, revolving

GREEK ROOTS

Forms	Meaning	Examples
anthrop	man, humankind	anthropocentric, misanthropist, philanthropy
arch	rule, ruler	anarchy, patriarchal
astr, astron	star	astronomical, disastrous
bio	life, living things	biography, microbiology
chron	time	anachronistic, chronic
cosm (kosmos)	order, universe	cosmic, microcosm
demo	among the people	democratic, demography
gen	birth, race	genesis, progeny
gno, gnosis	know	agnostic, diagnosis, gnomic
gram, graph	write, writing	epigrammatic, biography
log, logue	word, reason	analogy, illogical, prologue
lect, lex	language, speak	dialect, lexical

lysis	dissolution, destruction	catalyst, paralysis
metr	measure	diametric, metrical
morph	form, shape	amorphous, metamorphose
mne, mnes	memory, remember	amnesty, mnemonic
onym	a name	eponymous, synonym
opti, optic	eye, sight	optical, synopsis
path (pathos)	feeling, suffering	apathy, empathetic, pathetic
ped	child	pediatrician, pedagogy, pedantic
phon	sound	euphony, phonetic, symphonic

Prefixes are units of one or two syllables that are not words in themselves but that have distinct meanings. The addition of a prefix to the beginning of an existing word (what is called a *stem* or *root)* creates a word with an additional meaning. The spelling variations for many of the prefixes listed below are reminders that in English the spelling of a prefix will be altered to match the root to which it is attached. For example, *ad,* which means *to* or *toward,* is attached to many words in English; the *d* often changes to the first letter of the word to which it is added, making the resulting new forms easier to pronounce. (See the examples below as well as those in Chapter 10, Spelling.)

LATIN PREFIXES

Forms	Meaning	Examples*
a, ab, abs	away, from	abdicate, absence, abstraction
a, ad (*ac, af, al, etc.*)	to, toward	absent, acclimate, adherent, alliteration, assign, attribution
ambi	both, around	ambiance, ambiguous, ambidextrous, ambivalent
ante	before	antebellum, antecedent
bene, ben	good, well	beneficial, beneficent, benign
circum	around	circumnavigate, circumstances, circumlocution
co (col, com, cor)	together	coincidence, collaboration, commiserate, correspondence
contra, contro, *counter*	against, opposite	contradiction, controversy, counterfeit, counteract
de	away, down, from	deduction, deterrence, deviate
dis (di, dif)	apart, away; not; separate	disavow, disdain, disappear, disregard, disperse, discern
en (var. of in)	make, put into	enable, enhance, encourage
equ, equi	equal, even	equable, equanimity, equivalence, equivocate
ex (e, ef)	away from, out	efface, effective, ejection, exodus, expiration
in (il, im, ir)	in, within	immersion, impending, innate
in (il, im, ir)	not, without	illegible, imprudent, incognito

165

inter	among, between	intercede, intermediary, interim
magn	great	magnificence, magnanimous
mal	bad, evil	malevolent, malice, malefactor, malign, malignant
ob (oc, of, op)	to, toward; against; over; totally	objection; obdurate, obnoxious; obfuscate; obsolete, obliterate
omni	all	omnipotent, omniscient
per	completely; through	perceive, perdurable, pervasive
post	after	posterity, posthumous
pre	before, in advance	pre-empt, preclude, premonition
pro	before, forward	proclivity, prodigy, profane
re	again	reiterate, reverberate, retort, revise, remember
retro	backward	retrogression, retroactive
se	apart, aside	secession, sedition, select
sub (suf, sup, sus)	from below, under	subsidize, substandard, suffuse, suppress, sustenance
super	above, over	supercilious, superfluous, supervise, supersede
tra, trans	across, beyond	transgression, transcend

GREEK PREFIXES

Forms	Meaning	Examples
a, an	not, without	agnostic, anarchy, apathetic
ana	back, backward according to; through	anagram, anachronistic, anapest analogy, analysis
ant, anti	against, opposite	antipathy, antithesis, antipodes
auto	self	autonomous, autocracy
cata	down	cataclysm, catalyst, catastrophe
dia	through, between	dialect, dialogue, diameter
dys	bad, ill, difficult	dysfunctional, dyspeptic
epi	upon	epicenter, epigram, epilogue
eu	good, well	euphemism, euphoria, eugenics
hetero	different	heterodox, heterogeneous
homo	alike, same	homogeneous, homonym
macro	large, long duration	macrocosm, macroscopic
meta, met	after, beyond; changed	metaphor, metaphysical, metamorphosis
micro	small	microscope, microbe
mon, mono	one, single	monotheism, monolith
pan	all, complete	panacea, pandemonium
pro	before; favorable	prophecy; propitiate
proto	first, primary	protagonist, prototype
sym, syn	together, with	symmetry, synergy, synopsis

* When you review the lists for study at the end of the chapter you will readily see how many words in English are formed with these prefixes. Use those lists to add to the examples offered here.

Here is the first group of vocabulary words from the Regents exams list on page 176. Note how many are formed from the Greek or Latin prefixes reviewed on the previous pages.

abdicate	**ab**errant	**ab**horrent	abridgment
absolve	**ac**claim	**ac**cost	**ac**credit
acme	**ac**quiesce	**ac**quittal	**ad**age
adhere	**ad**junct	**ad**monish	**ad**versity
afflict	agrarian	**al**lot	**al**lure
ally	**alter**cation	amass	**ambi**ance
ambidextrous	**ambi**guous	**ambi**valent	amnesty
amorphous	**ana**chronistic	**an**ecdotes	animation
appease	**ap**prehend	arbitrator	archaic
ardent	armistice	**ar**ray	**ar**rogantly
ascendancy	ashen	**a**spire	assay
astute	**a**sylum	atrocious	audacity
autonomous	avarice	**a**verse	**a**version
avidly	azure		

In many of these examples, the meaning of the original prefix has been absorbed into the meaning of the entire word, in **adage** and **allot**, for example. The highlighted prefixes illustrate, however, how extensively Greek and Latin forms are found in English.

PREPARING NOTE CARDS

Here are samples of detailed note cards for some of the listed words. They show origin, definition, context, and connotation.

---

aberrant, *adj.* [from L. *aberrare*, to go astray, *ab-* from + *errare,* to wander]

deviating from what is true, correct, normal, or typical. Used to describe human behavior, mental lapses; also describes behavior of physical phenomena, esp. in astronomy or physics

"We could not explain the child's *aberrant* behavior; she is normally polite and well-mannered."

"The low scores on last week's chemistry test were an *aberration*; normally the students in this class do very well."

Also, **aberrantly** (adv.) **aberration, aberrance, aberrancy** (n.)

---

adversity, *n.* [from L. *adversus*, turned against, *ad-* from + *versare* to turn]

misfortune, wretched state, poverty, calamity; a condition of extreme hardship

In history and literature, we often read of characters who have "overcome adversity" to lead fulfilling lives or to make notable achievements.

Also, **adverse** (adj.), hostile, harmful, contrary, opposed; conditions and reactions may be described as *adverse.* An **adversary** is an opponent.

> **acquiesce,** *v.i.* [Fr. *acquiescer,* to yield to, from L. *ad-* to + *quiescere,* to be at rest]
>
> To accept, agree to, consent *without protest;* assent *without enthusiasm*
>
> Young people sometimes must *acquiesce* in the demands of their parents. On a committee, some may have to *acquiesce* in the decisions of the majority.
>
> Also, **acquiescence** (n.), **acquiescent** (adj.)

Such comprehensive note cards are not required for all words you wish to study; they are most useful when you intend to make certain words part of your own speaking and writing vocabulary. Most students like to prepare flash cards with synonyms or brief definitions for quick review.

A NOTE ON SYNONYMS AND USING A THESAURUS

As thoughtful students and careful writers know, synonyms are rarely equivalents. Synonyms are words closely related in meaning to a given word, but they should not be considered equally interchangeable with it.

Here is a list of synonyms for **acquiesce** that you might gather from a thesaurus:

accede	accept	agree to	allow
assent	capitulate	come to terms with	comply with
concede	concur	conform	consent
give in	grant	permit	submit
surrender	yield		

This list is very helpful in enriching your understanding of the word, especially because it includes several terms that emphasize that there is a sense of giving in, of reluctance, in **acquiesce**. The closest synonyms in this list are: *accede, come to terms with, conform, give in, yield. Capitulate, submit,* and *surrender* accurately reflect the connotation of the word, but they denote a more forceful sense of defeat than does *acquiesce.* The others, *accept, agree to, concur, consent, permit,* are less precise because they reflect only the general meaning and do not denote the sense of reluctance and the lack of enthusiam inherent in **acquiesce**.

169

Learning to distinguish among variations in meaning and context is an important part of developing your vocabulary. It is also essential to the craft of good writing. In Chapter 5, Writing about Literature, and Chapter 8, Composition, you will find several *synonymies,* which are words grouped by general meaning or connotation. The purpose of the *synonymies* is to help you develop precision and variety in your own writing. You should review those as part of your vocabulary study as well.

ORGANIZING VOCABULARY STUDY

Another way to work with lists such as the ones at the end of this chapter is to *sort* them, much as you would sort playing cards. Depending on the card game you are playing, you might sort a hand by suit, by numerical sequence, or by kind. You can sort a group of words in various ways as well: by part of speech, by connotation, by human or abstract qualities, and so on. Many students create their own flash cards for the words they study, which makes sorting in various ways easy. (See page 168 for sample note cards.)

Here are some suggestions for how you might sort the first group of words from the Regents list (page 176). First, sort by part of speech. In the list below, the *verbs* are printed in bold type:

VERBS:

abdicate	aberrant	abhorrent	abridgment
absolve	**acclaim**	**accost**	**accredit**
acme	**acquiesce**	acquittal	adage
adhere	adjunct	**admonish**	adversity
afflict	agrarian	**allot**	allure
ally	altercation	**amass**	ambiance
ambidextrous	ambiguous	ambivalent	amnesty
amorphous	anachronistic	anecdote	animation
appease	**apprehend**	arbitrator	archaic
ardent	armistice	**array**	arrogantly
ascendancy	ashen	**aspire**	**assay**
astute	asylum	atrocious	audacity
autonomous	avarice	averse	aversion
avidly	azure		

Then classify the group of verbs further as either *transitive* or *intransitive;* that is, according to the nature of the action they denote and the nature of the objects, if any, they take. When you look up these words in a dictionary, they will be identified as *v.i.* or *v.t. Transitive verbs* (*v.t.*) take a direct object; the action is directed from the subject to an object. For example, "She *admonished* (scolded, warned) the unruly child" and "King Midas *amassed* (accumulated) a fortune in gold." *Direct objects,* of course, may be persons and living creatures, or they may be things, even abstractions: "She quickly *apprehended* the danger she was in."

Intransitive verbs (*v.i.*) denote actions that are contained within the subject or that signify what we call states of being: "He *adhered* strictly to his ethical principles." *Adhere* connotes a state of mind, an attitude.

The distinction between transitive and intransitive action is not always easily made, but one way to demonstrate the difference is to make an active statement passive. For example, we can reverse the statement "She admonished the child" and turn it into "The child was admonished by her." The statement above about King Midas can be expressed in the passive as "A fortune in gold was amassed by King Midas." Although transitive actions may be reversed in this way, intransitive actions do not reverse. For example, the sentence "The principles were adhered by him" has no meaning. Some verbs may function both as transitive and intransitive. A simple example is the verb *to sink*: "The small sailboat sank during the heavy storm" (*v.i.*), but "The submarine fired a torpedo that sank the enemy battleship." (*v.t.*).

Most verbs in this first group are transitive, so it would be useful to sort them by the kinds of objects they take; that is, whether they denote actions directed at persons or at things and abstractions. You would, of course, note this information as you look up each unfamiliar word in a dictionary. Here is the list of verbs further sorted:

ACTIONS DIRECTED AT PERSONS:

to **absolve** (free from, relieve) someone of guilt or responsibility

to **acclaim** (praise, honor) a person's performance, action, or work

to **accost** (approach, confront) someone

to **admonish** (caution, scold) someone for misbehavior or inaction

to **afflict** (burden, attack) someone with suffering or illness

to **appease** (conciliate) a person, a nation, or a government

to **apprehend** (catch, capture) a suspect or a criminal

ACTIONS DIRECTED AT THINGS OR ABSTRACTIONS:

to **abdicate** (relinquish, abandon) a throne, a responsibility

to **accredit** (certify, recognize) a school or university, the value of an idea

to **allot** (distribute, assign) funds, resources

to **amass** (gather, accumulate) a fortune, an army

to **append** (add, match) a section, passage, body of information

to **apprehend** (understand, comprehend, capture) an idea, a concept

to **articulate** (verbalize, clarify, explain) ideas, feelings, understanding

to **array** (arrange) a display, a number of objects

to **assay** (measure, evaluate) a task, a situation

to **assert** (declare, claim, affirm, profess) ideas, an opinion, a judgment

INTRANSITIVE ACTIONS:

to **acquiesce** (give in to, agree reluctantly) in demands of others

to **adhere** (hold, cling to, comply) to demands or to principles

to **ally** (join, support) with another person, group, or nation

to **aspire** (strive, seek) to a goal, an achievement

For purposes of study, these verbs could be shuffled, and then resorted, by *connotation*. Which are generally positive in feeling and association, and which are negative? There are many words for which this is not a useful distinction, but appreciation of connotation is often essential to fully understanding the meaning of a word.

POSITIVE:

absolve	acclaim	accredit	adhere
ally	aspire		

NEGATIVE:

abdicate	accost	acquiesce	admonish
afflict	appease		

As you make your notes or compose your flash cards, be sure to include connotation if it is relevant. A dictionary usually does not define a word by its connotation; you must infer it from the meanings and examples offered.

NOUNS:

The *nouns* are in bold type:

abdicate	aberrant	abhorrent	**abridgment**
absolve	**acclaim**	accost	accredit
acme	acquiesce	**acquittal**	**adage**
adamant	adhere	adjunct	admonish
adversary	**adversity**	afflict	affluent
agrarian	allot	**allure**	**ally**
altercation	amass	**ambiance**	ambidextrous
ambiguous	ambivalent	**amnesty**	amorphous
anachronistic	**anecdote**	**animation**	appease
append	apprehend	apprehensive	**arbitrator**
archaic	ardent	**armistice**	**array**
arrogant	articulate	**ascendancy**	ashen
aspire	**assay**	assert	astute
asylum	atrocious	**audacity**	autonomous
avarice	averse	**aversion**	avidly
azure			

As you look at a collection of nouns, try to group them in various ways based on the kinds of things or persons they name. Note that in this group only two, **adversary** and **arbitrator,** name persons. This list, however, includes several political or legal terms that would form a useful group for study:

acquittal	**adversary** (adversarial)	**ally**
amnesty	**arbitrator** (arbitration)	**armistice**
ascendancy	**asylum**	

173

A small group of terms is related to literature:

abridgment   **adage**   **anecdote**

Other terms name attitudes or feelings. (Note the contrast in connotation here.)

POSTIVE

acclaim   **animation**

NEGATIVE

audacity   **aversion**   **avarice**

Finally, there are nouns that name forces, situations, conditions, and other concepts.

acme   **ambiance**   **allure**   **array**

ADJECTIVES:

The *adjectives* are in bold type:

abdicate	**aberrant**	**abhorrent**	abridgment
absolve	acclaim	accost	accredit
acme	acquiesce	acquittal	adage
adamant	adhere	**adjunct**	admonish
adversary	adversity	afflict	**affluent**
agrarian	allot	allure	ally
altercation	amass	ambiance	**ambidextrous**
ambiguous	**ambivalent**	amnesty	**amorphous**
anachronistic	anecdote	animation	appease
append	apprehend	**apprehensive**	arbitrator
archaic	**ardent**	armistice	array
arrogant	articulate	ascendancy	**ashen**
aspire	assay	assert	**astute**
asylum	**atrocious**	audacity	autonomous
avarice	**averse**	aversion	avidly
azure			

Because adjectives modify—that is, qualify, limit, or describe—nouns, a useful way to group them is by the nature of what they describe. For example, some of the adjectives in the list above describe human behavior or *actions:*

aberrant   **abhorrent**   **atrocious**

(all strongly negative in connotation)

Several adjectives describe human *attitudes, feelings, aspects of character:*

NEGATIVE

adamant   **ambivalent**   **arrogant**

POSITIVE

ardent   **astute**   **avid**

Still others characterize *the way people appear or express themselves:*

ambiguous   **ambivalent**   **apprehensive**   **averse**

Language may be:

ambiguous   **anachronistic**   **archaic**

Two adjectives relate to color:

ashen   **azure**

One term, **ambidextrous,** describes a physical characteristic.

This particular group contains no adverb forms, but for many of the adjectives in the list, the adverb is formed by adding -*ly*. For example:

aberrantly   **adamantly**   **ambiguously**   **apprehensively**

astutely   **atrociously**   **avidly**

Reminder: When you prepare your own note cards for study, be sure to include all forms of the word. For example, your notes for **ambivalent** (adj.) would also include **ambivalence** (n.).

These groups overlap and should be combined in different ways as you work through larger numbers of words. The process of sorting, or reshuffling, as new categories and associations occur to you is a very effective way to learn new words. Each time you sort, you are actively thinking about a word in a particular context and are associating it with other words; this process is essential to making a word a permanent part of your reading and writing vocabulary.

VOCABULARY FOR STUDY

Below are lists of words that have been used on Regents exams, on Op-Ed pages, and in book reviews.

Vocabulary from Regents Exams

abdicate	aberrant	abhorrent	abridgment
absolve	acclaim	accost	accredit
acme	acquiesce	acquittal	adage
adhere	adjunct	admonish	adversity
afflict	agrarian	allot	allure
ally	altercation	amass	ambiance
ambidextrous	ambiguous	ambivalent	amnesty
amorphous	anachronistic	anecdotes	animation
appease	apprehend	arbitrator	archaic
ardent	armistice	array	arrogantly
ascendancy	ashen	aspire	assay
astute	asylum	atrocious	audacity
autonomous	avarice	averse	aversion
avid	azure		
badger	barrage	bask	beguile
belied	bemused	benevolent	berate
blatant	bleary	boisterous	brazen
breach	brevity		
cache	carnage	celebrated	chafe
chagrin	charade	charisma	chasm
clandestine	clique	coalition	collate

commencement	commiserate	conception	congeal
consecrate	constrict	converse	convivial
craven	credence	crestfallen	cringe
dauntless	de facto	debonair	decrepit
deduce	deferred	deflect	defunct
deified	deluge	delve	demeaning
denizen	depict	deride	derogatory
desist	desolate	deter	detest
diffuse	dilemma	diminutive	discord
discreet	dissidence	dissuade	divulge
domain	dredge	dynamic	
eccentric	edify	eject	elicit
elude	elusive	embroil	eminence
encore	endorse	endow	enfeeble
enhance	ensnare	entail	entreaty
envoy	equanimity	equilibrium	equitable
equivocal	eradicate	erratic	escapade
euphoric	eviction	exemplary	exodus
exonerate	expedite	exploitation	exulted
facet	fallible	fanatic	fanfare
farcical	feasible	fiasco	fidelity
finesse	finite	flail	fleeting
forage	foreboding	formidable	fortitude
fortuitous	fracas	frugal	futility
garish	garrulous	gaudy	genial
genuine	geriatric	gesticulate	grapple
grate	gratuity	grievously	grisly
guise	guttural		
hallowed	harangue	harrowing	heinous
heretical	hinder	homage	humid

idiosyncrasies	ignoble	illuminate	immutable
impartial	impending	imperative	imperceptible
imperiled	imperious	impertinent	imprudent
inadvertent	inaugural	incensed	incessant
incognito	incompetent	incorrigible	indignant
indisputably	induce	infernal	infringe
ingenuity	inherent	inimitable	innocuous
insatiable	insolent	insomnia	insubordinate
insurgent	inundated	invoked	irate
irksome	irrational	itinerant	

jeer	jocular	jovial	juncture
jut			

lacerated	lackluster	lament	languorously
latent	lateral	lavish	laxity
lesion	lineage	liquidate	loquacious
lucrative	lugubrious	lull	

madcap	maim	malefactor	malice
malleable	marauding	martial	meager
mediate	melancholy	meticulous	militant
misconstrue	misgivings	mitigate	mollify
morose	mortify	mundane	muzzle

nefarious	negligible	nepotism	niche
nimble	nonentity	nostalgia	notorious
nullification	nuptial	nurture	

obliquely	obliterate	obstinate	oligarchy
omnipotent	omniscient	onslaught	opportune
optimum	oscillate	oust	ouster
override			

pacifism   palatable   pandemonium   parable
paraphrase   penchant   perjury   perpetual
perplexity   philanthropic   piety   pinnacle
placid   plague   plausible   plight
poise   precariously   precipice   precludes
prestige   prevail   procrastinate   prodigious
profoundly   proponent   protrude   prowess
proxy   putrid

qualms   quandary

ramification rampant   ramshackle   rancid
rant   rapport   ravenous   recalcitrant
reciprocal   recoil   recrimination   rectify
refute   reminiscent   reparation   repercussion
repress   resolute   retort   revamped
reverberate   revulsion   roster   rouse
rue   ruinous   russet

sacrosanct   salve   sanction   sanctity
saunter   scandalous   scathing   scrupulous
scrutiny   seedy   sheen   shortcomings
shrewd   singularly   skeptical   skulk
sleek   slipshod   smolder   sporadic
squalor   stalwart   stark   stealthily
strew   strut   subliminal   submissive
subside   subsidize   substantiate   subtlety
sullen   sumptuous   superfluous   suppress
surcease   surreptitious   swagger   synopsis

tainted   tally   tawny   tenacity
throng   token   topple   transcend
transient   trauma   traverse   trifling
trudge   tumult

unassuming	uncanny	unnerve	unobtrusive
unpalatable	unscrupulous	utilitarian	

vanquish	variance	vehement	verbatim
verbose	veritable	viable	vigilance
virtually			

waive	warily	weather (vb.)	whack
wield	wily	wrangle	wrath
writhe			

yield

zenith

Vocabulary from Op-Ed Pages

a priori	abdicate	aberration	abrogation
abysmal	abyss	accede	acclimate
accolade	accrue	acrimonious	actuary
acumen	ad hoc	adamant	addled
aegis	affidavit	affront	aggrieved
agnostics	albeit	alleviate	allude (to)
amalgamation	ambivalence	amiss	amorphous
androgyny	annals	annotate	anoint
antidote	antipathy	apathy	append
arbiter	arbitrage	arbitrary	arcane
archetype	archive	ardent	artifice
ascribe	assessment	assimilate	assuage
asylum	au courant	audit	autonomous

barrage	beguile	beleaguered	benighted
bereft	berth	besmirch	bias

bipartisan	blatant	blighted	blunder
brass (slang def.)	brute (vb.)	budgetary	bureaucrats
burgeoning			

cacophony	cajole	callous	canard
candor	canonical/canon	capitulate	cataclysmic
caveat	censure	chasm	chimera
circumspect	civics	clandestine	clerical
coda	coffer	collusion	compliant
complicit	compound (vb.)	compulsion	concede
conciliate	conciliatory	concubine	condone
confrere	conspiratorial	constituent	contemporaries
contend	contender	contingent	conundrum
convene	conversant	conversely	convocation
covet	crafty	craven	credibility
cul-de-sac	cupidity	curtail	cushy
cynical	cynicism		

daunting	debase	decadence	decibel
decree	decry	deferment	defrocked
defunct	deluded	demagogue	demise
demonize	demur	demystify	denounce
denuded	denunciation	deplorable	depredation
deprivation	derail	derangement	deregulation
deride	derisive	despot	deter
detract	didactic	disavow	discernible
discourse	discretion	discretionary	disenchantment
disingenuous	disjointed	dispel	dispirit
disposition	disquieting	dissemble	disseminate
dissident	dissipate	diversity	don (vb.)
doting	Draconian		

earmark	egregious	electorate	elixir
eminence	empathetic	empathy	encapsulate

enclave	enfranchise	enmesh	ennobling
ennui	envoy	epitomize	equanimity
equivocate	eradicate	erode	ethos
eugenics	eviscerate	exhort	exonerate
exorbitant	expenditure	expostulate	expunge
exude			

fallacious	farcical	fedora	feint
fiasco	finagle	firebrand	fiscal
flounder (vb.)	flummoxed	fodder (fig.)*	folly
forlorn	formidable	formulate	fray (n.)
frenetic	fritter (vb.)	frothing	furor
fusillade (fig.)	futility		

gaffe	gag rule	galvanize	garner
gaudy	gauge	gerrymander	glut
gouging	grapple	grim	grotesque
gubernatorial	guffaw		

habeus corpus	hackneyed	hamlet	hapless
harbor (vb.)	heckle	hectoring	heresy
hoosegow (slang)	hubris	hyperbole	

iconography	ideological	idiosyncratic	idyllic
ignominious	ilk	impede	imperil
implement (vb.)	implicit	importune	impunity
incendiary	incessant	incipient	incite
incontrovertible	incumbent	indefatigable	indigenous
indignity	ineptitude	infiltrate	infirmity
inflationary	infuse	inherent	innuendo
inquisitorial	insignia	insular	integrity

---

*In this case, consider the figurative meaning of the words.

interlocking	intransigence	inure	invaluable
inviolate	irk	irredentism	
lacerate	laconic	lambaste	languish
largess	latent	laureate	lebensraum
leery	leitmotif	levitate	litany
lout	lucid		
malady	malaise	malign	manifestation
mantra	martyr	maudlin	megalomaniac
meritorious	meticulous	milieu	mimesis
molder	monolith	morass	moratorium
moribund	morose	mortar	murky
myopic			
nadir	nascent	nexus	nomadic
nuance			
obfuscate	obsolescence	obstreperous	oddity
odious	ominous	omnipresent	oncology
oppression	outlay	overhaul	overt
overweening			
palliative	panacea	pandering	paradox
paramount	parochial	parsimonious	partisan (adj.)
passel	pathology	patrician	pedantic
peevish	pejorative	penchant	perennial
peripheral	pernicious	peroration	perpetuate
perquisite	perversion	pillage	pinnacle
pious	pique	placable/placate	plaudits
plight	plummet	plunder	pogrom
polarization	polemic	polyglot	portend
pragmatism	prattle	preeminent	preempt
preclude	presage	probity	profound

progeny	prohibitive	proliferate	proliferation
propensity	protocol	provocation	prurience
psyche	pugnacity	pundit	purport
purvey/purveyor	pusillanimous	pyrotechnics	

quagmire	qualm	quaver	quibble
quintessential			

rabid (fig.)	rakish	rancor	rapacious
rapprochement	raucous	*realpolitik*	recidivism
reconcile	rectitude	rejoinder	relegate
reparations	replete	resolute	resonance
restorative	retributive	reverberate	reverence
revile	rhetoric	rifle (vb.)	rogue
rudimentary	ruse		

salve (vb.)	sartorial	sashay	scion
scoff	scourge	seamy	self-effacing
sham	shaman	shore up	shudder
siphon	snare	snide	sobriquet
sophomoric	sordid	sorghum	sovereignty
spate	speculative	staggering	stagnation
staid	stark	staunch	steely eyed
stint	stipend	strident	stringent
stymie	subsidize	substantive	subterfuge
sullen	summarily	sumptuary	sunder
supersede	supplant	surfeit	swindle
sword of Damocles	sycophant	synergy	

temporal	temporize	tenacity	tendentious
throng	thwart	torpor	totter
tout	transgression	transitory	treacherous
troupe	tsunami	turbulent	

undergird	undermine	undiluted	unduly
unencumbered	unfettered	unilateral	universality
unprecedented	unrelenting	unscrupulous	usurp
vagaries	venality	veracity	verdant
vestige	vexing	viable	victimize
vigilante	vilify	visceral	vituperation
volatile	voyeurs		
waffling	wallow	wastrels	welter
wheedling	winnow	writ	writhe
wrongheaded			
xenophobia			
zeal	zeitgeist		

Vocabulary from Book Reviews

accolade	accretion	accrue	acerbic
acolyte	acrimonious	acumen	adage
adduce	adherent	adumbrate	adversity
aesthetic	albeit	alluring	amatory
amiable	amok	anapest	ancillary
animus	annotate	antipodes	aphrodisiac
aplomb	apotheosis	arbiter	arbitrary
archaic	ardor	arduous	arsenal
ascetic	asinine	aspire	attenuate
austere	authorial		
banal	barren	bathetic	bedraggled
bemused	bestiality	bevy	bifurcation
blight	blithe	bohemian	boorish
boulevardier	bowdlerize	Byzantine	

cache	cadence	canny	catharsis
caveat	chafe	charisma	chastening
chastise	chic	clandestine	cleric
cloying	coffer	cohere	coherence
colloquial	compendious	compendium	complicity
congenial	consign	contend	contrivance
copious	counterpoise	covert	credo
cribbed	crotchety	cupidity	curmudgeon
cursory			

dash	daunting	debunk	deft
delineate	delude	demigod	denouement
deploy	despotic	detritus	devolve
dichotomy	didactic	discursive	dispense
dispossess	dither	divagation	divergence
droll	duplicity	dysfunctional	dystopia

eccentric	eclectic	edify	egregious
elegy	elocution	elucidate	enclave
encomium	ensconce	entreaty	envisage
epigraph	epitomize	equanimity	eradicate
Eros	eschew	esoteric	espouse
esthetic	ethereal	ethos	evangelical
evocative	exacerbate	exhort	exigency
existential	expansive	expatriate	expurgate
exultant			

fabulist	facsimile	faction	farce
fervid	florid	foray	forbearance
formulaic	fruition	furtive	

galvanize	gamut	gorgon	grapple
guile	gustatory		

hackneyed	hagiography	harrowing	hedonism
hewn (details)			
iconoclast	iconography	idiosyncratic	idyll/idyllic
ignite (fig.)	imminent	imperative	impetus
implacable	impresario	incoherent	incongruous
incur	indelible	indeterminate	indigenous
ineffable	ineffectual	inept	inextricably
insidious	insinuation	insouciance	intelligentsia
intercede	intractable	inured	invidious
irreverent	itinerant		
jarring	jettison	jostle	Joycean
kamikaze			
lacuna	lament	languish	lapidary
largess	libertine	lilting	litigious
loquacious	Lothario	lucid	lucrative
lyricism			
macabre	malaise	malevolent	malign
manifold (adj.)	matrix	mawkish	melodrama
mendacious	mercurial	mien	milieu
minutiae	misogyny	mogul	moldering
mordant	moribund	mosaic	muddle
murky	musing	muster	myopia
naiveté	narcissistic	nascent	natter
nihilism	nimble	nonpareil	non sequitur
noxious	nuance		
obfuscation	opprobrium	ostensible	ostracize

palatable	pantheon	paradigm	pathos
paucity	pedagogical	pelt (vb.)	penchant
penumbra	perdurable	peregrination	perennial
petulance	piety	placebo	plodding
portent	portentous	practitioner	pragmatic
prattle	precocious	premonition	prescient
prevaricate	prodigious	prosaic	protean
punitive	purport		

querulous	query	quintessential	quixotic
quotidian			

rancor	rapacious	rapture	rancor
raucous	reap	recalcitrant	recapitulate
relegate	repatriation	replete	repository
reverence	revile	rhetorical	ricochet
riff	risible	riveting	rudimentary
ruminate			

sagacity	salacious	sally forth	sap (vb.)
savor	scatological	scourge	scuttlebutt
searing	sedentary	self-effacement	sepulchral
shaman	shenanigans	snippet	solicitous
spurn	squander	stanch	standoffish
staunch	stilted	stultifying	sublimate
sublime	subterfuge	succumb	sunder
supercilious	surreptitious	surrogate	symbiosis
symmetry	synoptic		

taut	teeter	temporal	thrall
throng	titillating	torpid	tortuous
traffic (vb.)	transcendent	transient	transitory
transmogrify	travail	treatise	trenchant
trilogy	truism	tweak	

unabashed	uncanny	unfathomable	unflinching
vacillate	valediction	vapid	venal
venality	verisimilitude	vernacular	vicissitude
vignette	vindictiveness	virtuosity	vis à vis
vitriol	voluminous	vortex	votary
waft	welter	wend	whimsy
withal			

Chapter 10

SPELLING

We know how to spell many words because we recognize them from our reading and because we have, from childhood, developed awareness of the conventions of English spelling. Even though English spelling may seem confusing at times, most of the troublesome sounds or patterns reflect the history of English pronunciation and the fact that the English language developed after the forces of William the Conqueror, a Frenchman from Normandy, had invaded and settled in what is now Great Britain. The resulting language is a fusion of Anglo-Saxon, French, and Latin.

SPELLING ON THE NEW REGENTS EXAM

Spelling is no longer a separate part of the Regents examination. Remember, however, that in the guidelines and scoring rubrics for all four parts of the new Regents, the extent to which the writer observes the conventions of standard written English is part of the assessment; this, of course, includes spelling. If you know you have difficulties in spelling, it is important that you use this chapter to review the common patterns of English spelling and to study the list of words commonly misspelled. A word misspelled is a word misused, and egregious spelling errors may affect the scoring of your essays.

AN EXERCISE FOR REVIEW AND PRACTICE

Here is the spelling section from a past Regents exam. In it you will find groups of five words in which one is misspelled. Write each misspelled word correctly in the space provided. This is a useful exercise because it parallels what you do when you proofread your own writing.

QUESTIONS

1 varyed
  sleigh
  precede
  generally
  overrated

  _____

2 omitted
  itchey
  perceive
  intolerant
  carriage

  _____

3 vertical
  defiant
  niece
  dedecated
  egotistical

  _____

4 pleasantly
  arrogant
  athletic
  extended
  commercialy

  _____

5 municipal
  jumble
  dareing
  tariff
  sequence

  _____

6 hesitant
  creamy
  rehabilatate
  bilingual
  fundamental

  _____

7 performance
  uniformity
  legitimate
  predjudice
  reliant

  _____

8 relevence
  interrelated
  pianos
  viewer
  cellar

  _____

9 volume
  acustomed
  casually
  conceded
  fatigued

  _____

10 transparent
   persuasive
   reversable
   prophet
   illiterate

   _____

ANSWER KEY: SPELLING

1. varied
2. itchy
3. dedicated
4. commercially

5. daring
6. rehabilitate
7. prejudice
8. relevance

9. accustomed
10. reversible

SPELLING RULES AND PATTERNS

As you review spelling rules and patterns, you need to be familiar with the following terms:

vowels The letters *a, e, i o, u,* and occasionally *y* signal the vowel, or sustained, sounds in English. The variations in these vowel sounds are spelled as combinations of more than one letter or as combinations with consonants.

consonants In English, the consonant letters and sounds are composed by the following: *b, c, d, f, g, h, j, k, l, m, n, p, q, r, s, t, v, w, x.* In contrast to vowels, consonant sounds do not sustain.

syllable A vowel sound or a combination of a vowel and consonant sounds that makes up a single impulse, or "beat," in a word. Words of one syllable: *think, read, act.* Words of two syllables: *reflect, insist, review.* We regularly use words of six or more syllables: *unintentionally, coincidentally.*

endings Single letters or syllables that indicate grammatical forms, such as noun plurals or verb conjugations. English, in contrast to other languages high school students may study, has relatively few "endings." Among them are: *-s* or *-es* to form plural nouns or to indicate third-person *singular* verb forms, and the verb endings *-ing* and *-ed.*

suffixes Endings used to form new words and different parts of speech: *love, lovely, loveliness; occur, occurrence.* The addition of endings and suffixes to words often alters their spelling. (See next page.)

prefixes Units of one or two syllables that, like suffixes, are not "words" in themselves but have distinct meanings. They are placed at the beginning of existing words, or of what are called *stems* or *roots.* (See the section "Roots and Prefixes from Latin and Greek," Chapter 9, for many examples in English of Latin and Greek roots.) Words formed in this way are spelled to show their meanings: *illogical, overreact, misspell.*

Although most spelling "rules" have exceptions, there are many common patterns for spelling in English. The first group (page 198) involves adding endings or suffixes.

Words That End in Silent *e*

➤ Drop the *e* before adding a suffix or ending that begins with a vowel:

dare	+ -ing	➤ = daring	➤	+ -ed = dared
hope	+ -ing	➤ = hoping	➤	+ -ed = hoped
amuse	+ -ing	➤ = amusing	➤	+ -ed = amused
revise	+ -ion	➤ = revision	➤	+ -ed = revised
advise	+ -able	➤ = advisable,	➤	+ -ed = advised
reverse	+ -ible	➤ = reversible	➤	+ -ed = reversed

➤ When adding *s* or a suffix that begins with a consonant, retain the *e*:

amuse	➤ amuses	➤ amusement
arrange	➤ arranges	➤ arrangement
hope	➤ hopes	➤ hopeless
huge	➤ hugeness	➤ hugely
place	➤ places	➤ placement
spite	➤ spiteful	
sure	➤ surely	

➤ When the word ends in *ce* or in *ge*, retain the *e* when adding *able* or *ous:*

change	➤ changeable
peace	➤ peaceable
service	➤ serviceable
advantage	➤ advantageous
courage	➤ courageous
outrage	➤ outrageous

➤ But drop the silent *e* before adding *ing:*

change	➤ changing
rage	➤ raging
service	➤ servicing
trace	➤ tracing

➤ Note the following **exceptions:**

argue	➤ argument
true	➤ truly
judge	➤ judgment
nine	➤ ninety
whole	➤ wholly

Words That End in y

➤ For words preceded by a consonant, change the *y* to an *i* before adding a suffix:

accompany	➤	accompaniment			
busy	➤	business	➤	busily	
easy	➤	easily			
funny	➤	funnier	➤	funniest	
happy	➤	happiness	➤	happily	
lonely	➤	loneliness			
silly	➤	silliness	➤	sillier	➤ silliest

➤ The same pattern applies when we add *s* to form plural nouns or third-person-singular verb forms:

army	➤	armies
baby	➤	babies
city	➤	cities
marry	➤	marries
try	➤	tries
worry	➤	worries

➤ But retain the *y* before adding *ing, ism, ish*:

baby	➤	babyish	➤	babying
copy	➤	copying		
crony	➤	cronyism		
marry	➤	marrying		
try	➤	trying		
worry	➤	worrying		

➤ For words that end in *y* preceded by a vowel, retain *y:*

annoy	➤	annoys	➤	annoyance	➤	annoyed	➤	annoying	
boy	➤	boys	➤	boyish					
day	➤	days							
destroy	➤	destroys	➤	destroyed	➤	destroying			
monkey	➤	monkeys							
play	➤	plays	➤	played	➤	playing	➤	player ➤
playful									
valley	➤	valleys							

➤ However:

say	➤	says	➤	**said**
pay	➤	pays	➤	**paid**

Double Letters

In writing, we must often stop to think whether to double letters in adding suffixes to words. Here are guidelines to follow.

➤ For one-syllable words that end in a single consonant preceded by a single vowel, *double* the final consonant before a suffix beginning with a vowel:

bat	➤	batter	➤	batting		
big	➤	bigger	➤	biggest		
fit	➤	fitted	➤	fitting	➤	fittest
sit	➤	sitter	➤	sitting		
spot	➤	spotty	➤	spotted		

As you look at the examples, you will see that the effect of the double consonant is to retain the pronunciation of the base word.

➤ Words formed by adding prefixes to one-syllable words follow the same pattern:

outfit	➤	outfitted	➤	outfitter
unwrap	➤	unwrapped		

➤ For one-syllable words that have double vowels or that end in more than one consonant, do *not* double the final consonant:

beat	➤	beating		
neat	➤	neatest		
mail	➤	mailing	➤	mailed
read	➤	reading	➤	reader
fail	➤	failure		
list	➤	listed		
faint	➤	fainted		

➤ However:

quit	➤	quitting

Because *u* must follow the *q*, *-ui* is considered a single vowel.

➤ Do not double the final consonant for words ending in *w, x,* or *y:*

draw	➤	drawing		
mix	➤	mixing		
play	➤	playing	➤	player

It is when we add endings to words of more than one syllable that spelling errors commonly occur.

➤ For words of more than one syllable ending in one vowel and one consonant, double the final consonant before an ending that begins with a vowel *if the last syllable of the base word is accented*:

confer	➤	conferred
infer	➤	inferred
refer	➤	referred
begin	➤	beginning
deter	➤	deterrence
omit	➤	omitted
commit	➤	committed
occur	➤	occurrence
equip	➤	equipped

➤ If the accent is *not* on the syllable to which the ending is added, *do not* double the final consonant:

benefit	➤	benefited		
credit	➤	credited		
open	➤	opening		
happen	➤	happening		
develop	➤	developing	➤	developed
deliver	➤	delivered	➤	delivering

➤ Note how the shift in accent determines spelling:

confer	➤	conference
infer	➤	inference
prefer	➤	preference
refer	➤	reference

Note the following exceptions:

➤ The following words double the final consonant:

program	➤	programmed	➤	programmer
question	➤	questionnaire		
excel	➤	excellence	➤	excellent

➤ Either form is considered acceptable for the following, but the first form, with a single -*l*, is preferred:

canceled	➤	cancelled
traveled	➤	travelled
traveling	➤	travelling

Adding Prefixes and Suffixes

With the exception of the patterns reviewed on the previous pages, which reflect how we pronounce the words, most words formed by adding prefixes and suffixes retain the spelling of each separate part. As a result, the full meaning of the word is reflected in its spelling:

mis + spell + ed	➤	= misspelled (both *s*'s are required)
mis + understand + ing	➤	= misunderstanding
dis + agree + able	➤	= disagreeable
dis + taste + ful	➤	= distasteful
dis + appear + ance	➤	= disappearance
dis + satisfaction	➤	= dissatisfaction
un + necessary	➤	= unnecessary
un + ending	➤	= unending
cool + ly	➤	= coolly
moral + ly	➤	= morally
co + operate	➤	= cooperate
de + emphasize	➤	= de-emphasize
re + entry	➤	= reentry
mean + ness	➤	= meanness
amuse + ment	➤	= amusement

➤ Note that words ending in *c* add a *k* as follows:

panic, panics	➤	panicky, panicked, panicking
mimic, mimics	➤	mimicked, mimicking
picnic, picnics	➤	picnicking, picnickers

Words That Include *ie* or *ei*

➤ Is it *i* before *e* or *e* before *i*? This is the spelling pattern everyone remembers.

i before *e*:

chief   thief   relief   yield

➤ Except after *c*:

   receive   ceiling   conceit

➤ Or, when *ei* sounds long *a*:

   sleigh   neighbor   weigh   veil

There are, however, several **exceptions** to this pattern. They must be memorized:

caffeine	counterfeit	either	financier	foreign
forfeit	leisure	neither	plebeian	protein
seize	sheik	sovereign	surfeit	weird

Noun Plurals

➤ Noun *plurals* are generally formed by adding *s*:

cat   ➤   cats
house   ➤   houses
delay   ➤   delays
piano   ➤   pianos

➤ Nouns ending in *s, sh, ch, x,* and *z,* add *es* to form the plural:

watch   ➤   watches
brush   ➤   brushes
waltz   ➤   waltzes

➤ Nouns ending in the consonant *y*: add *es*:

spy   ➤   spies
lady   ➤   ladies
quantity ➤   quantities

➤ However, do *not* alter the spelling of proper names:

There are two "Sallys" in the junior class.

Shakespeare wrote plays about the "Henrys" of England.

➤ Some words ending in *o* add *es* to form the plural:

echo   ➤   echoes
tomato   ➤   tomatoes

potato	→	potatoes
hero	→	heroes
veto	→	vetoes

➤ Some nouns ending in *f* or *fe* form the plural with *ves*:

calf	→	calves
elf	→	elves
knife	→	knives
life	→	lives
self	→	selves
thief	→	thieves
wife	→	wives

➤ Other nouns change their form internally:

man	→	men
woman	→	women
child	→	children
mouse	→	mice.

➤ In compound expressions, the principal noun is made plural:

sisters-in-law

passers-by

spoonsful

Homophones

Many spelling problems occur because words have syllables whose sounds are alike but could be spelled in more than one way: for example, *cede, ceed, sede*. These are called homophones.

➤ The most common form is *cede:*

precede	concede	antecede	intercede

➤ A few forms are spelled *ceed:*

exceed	proceed	succeed

➤ Only one form is spelled *sede:*

supersede

➤ For *able, ible,* the more common form is *able:*

curable   imaginable   lovable   movable   peaceable

➤ Though fewer in number, there are many common words ending in *ible*:

admissible   compatible   credible   eligible   horrible
intelligible   legible   perceptible possible   visible

➤ There are also words ending in *ance, ant,* or *ence, ent:*

assistant   attendant   dominant   extravagant fragrant
hesitance   ignorance   relevance   resistance

➤ Note, however:

adolescent competent   correspondent   current   frequent
negligence permanence vehemence

➤ Many nouns end in *-er*:

consumer   defender   interpreter   organizer
philosopher

➤ Note, however:

actor   creator   counselor   governor   professor
tailor

NOTE: *The careful writer must memorize the most common spellings. We cannot always use a dictionary or a spellcheck program!*

On the following pages you will find a list of words often confused and an extensive list of words commonly misspelled.

WORDS COMMONLY CONFUSED

Many words in English sound or look very similar to one another. Such words are often "misspelled" as a result of the writer's confusion about them. Here are some of the most commonly confused words; *all are correctly spelled.* Be sure you know their respective meanings.

accept/except

access/excess

adapt/adopt

advice/advise

affect/effect

allusion/illusion

already/all ready

altogether/all together

choose/chose/chosen

cite/sight/site

cloths/clothes

coarse/course

complement/compliment

desert/dessert

device/devise

discreet/discrete

dyeing/dying

elicit/illicit

elude/allude

envelop/envelope

formally/formerly

fourth/forth

hear/here

holy/wholly

hoping/hopping

idle/idol

imminent/eminent/emanate

its/it's

local/locale

loose/lose

medal/meddle/metal/mettle

moral/morale

night/knight

principal/principle

quite/quiet

rain/reign/rein

right/rite

shone/shown

stationary/stationery

than/then

their/there/they're

thorough/through

though/thought

threw/through

throne/thrown

to/too/two

vain/vane/vein

weather/whether

which/witch

who's/whose

your/you're

WORDS COMMONLY MISSPELLED

You will recognize the most familiar and the most notorious spelling demons in this list.

absence	absolutely	academic	accept
acceptance	accessory	accidentally	accommodate

accompanying
accomplish
accuracy
achievement
acknowledge
acquaintance
acquire
across
actually
address
adequately
adherence
adjournment
adjustment
admittance
adolescent
advantage
advantageous
advertisement
advising
against
aggravate
aggravation
aggressive
alleviate
alliance
ally
almanac
already
altitude
amateur
ambassador
amendment
among
analysis
analyze
ancient
angrily
announcement
annually
antagonist
antibiotic
anticipation
antique
anxious
apologetically
apologies
apologize
apology
apostrophe
apparently
appreciate
appropriate
approximate
aptitude
architecture
Arctic
argue
argument
arising
arrangement
article
artistically
ascend
ascent
assassin
assent
assistance
assumption
assurance
atheist
athlete
athletic
attempt
attendance
attractive
audience
authoritative
authority
auxiliary
availability
avalanche
average
awfully
awkward

bachelor
baggage
banana
bankruptcy
bargain
barrel
basement
basically
beautify
becoming
before
beginning
belief
believing
beneficial
benefit
benefited
bibliography
bicycle
biscuit
boring
boundary
breakfast
breath
breathe
bribery
brief
brilliant
Britain
brittle
bruise
budget
buoy
buoyant
bureau
burglar
burglarize
business
businesslike
busy

cafeteria
caffeine
calculator
calendar
calorie
campaign
candidate
cannibal

canoe	capable	capacity	captain
career	carrying	cashier	catastrophe
category	caucus	carefully	cease
ceiling	cellar	cemetery	censor
censure	century	certainly	challenge
changeable	changing	channel	characterize
chauffeur	chief	chimney	chivalry
chloride	cholera	choose	choosing
choral	chose	chuckle	cite
client	closet	clustered	coalition
coherence	collar	college	colonel
column	combustible	comfortable	coming
commencement	commercial	commission	commit
committee	communal	community	companies
comparative	comparison	compatible	compel
compelled	competitive	competitor	comprehensible
conceivable	conceive	concentrate	conception
condemn	condescend	conference	conferred
confidence	confidential	connotation	connote
conqueror	conscience	conscious	consequence
consequently	considerable	considerably	consistency
consistent	conspicuous	contemporary	contempt
contemptible	contemptuous	continual	continuous
contribution	controlled	controlling	controversial
convenience	convenient	convertible	convocation
cool	coolly	cooperate	corollary
corps	correlate	corrode	corrupt
counterfeit	courteous	courtesy	cousin
credible	creditor	credulous	crisis
critical	criticism	criticize	cruel
cruelly	cupola	curiosity	curious
current	curriculum	curtain	customary
customer	cyclical	cylinder	
dangerous	debris	debt	debtor
deceit	deceitful	deceived	decency

decent	deception	decide	decision
default	defendant	defense	defer
deference	deferred	define	definitely
definition	deity	delegate	deliberately
deodorant	dependable	dependent	depth
deputy	descend	descendant	descent
desert	desirable	despair	despite
dessert	destroy	detriment	devastate
developed	development	deviate	device
devise	dexterity	diameter	different
difficult	dilemma	diligent	dining
disappearance	disappointment	disapprove	disaster
disastrous	discern	disciple	disciplinary
discipline	discomfort	discriminate	discriminatory
disease	disillusion	dispatch	disposal
disregard	dissatisfied	dissent	dissimilar
dissipate	divinity	divisible	division
doesn't	dominant	dominate	dormitory
dough	dramatize	drunkenness	due
dully	duly	during	dye
dyeing	dying		

earnest	easily	economically	economy
ecstasy	edge	edgy	edition
editor	effect	efficiency	efficient
eight	eighth	eighty	electoral
elicit	eligible	eliminate	eloquent
elude	emanate	embarrass	embassy
emigrant	emigrate	emphasis	emphasize
emphatic	empirical	employee	encouragement
encouraging	endeavor	enough	entangle
enterprise	entertain	entirely	envelop
envelope	environment	equality	equally
equipment	equipped	equivalent	erroneous
escapade	especially	essential	everything
evidently	exaggerate	exaggeration	exceed

excellence	exceptional	excessive	excitable
excitement	exclusive	exclusively	excursion
exhibit	exhibition	existence	expedite
expedition	experience	experiment	explanation
explanatory	exploit	explore	extension
extraordinary	extravagant	extremely	

facility	fallacious	fallacy	familiar
fantasy	fascinate	fashion	fatality
faulty	favorable	favorite	February
felicity	feminine	feminist	feud
fictitious	fidelity	fiend	fiery
filial	finally	financial	financier
flair	fluent	forbidden	forehead
foreign	forewarn	forgetting	formally
formerly	forth	forty	fourth
fraternity	freight	frequency	frequently
fried	friendless	friendliness	friendly
friendship	fulfill	fulfillment	fundamental
furious	furthermore		

gaiety	gallant	gardener	gaseous
gasoline	generally	generation	generic
genetics	genius	genuine	global
glorious	glossary	goddess	government
governor	gradually	grammar	grandeur
graphics	grief	grievance	grieve
grievous	grocery	guarantee	guidance
guilt	gymnasium		

hammer	handkerchief	handsome	happiness
harassment	harpoon	headache	heard
heathen	heavily	height	heir
hereditary	heroes	heroic	heroine
hindrance	honorable	hopeful	hopeless
hoping	hopping	humidity	humor

humorous	hundredth	hungrily	hurrying
hybrid	hygiene	hypnosis	hypnotism
hypnotize	hypocrisy	hypocrite	hypothesis
hysteria			

icicle	ignorant	illegal	illicit
illusion	illusory	imaginary	imagine
immaculate	immediately	immense	immigrant
immoderate	impressionable	incidentally	incompetent
inconvenience	incredible	indebted	indecisive
indefinite	independence	indispensable	indivisible
indulge	interference	inertia	inevitable
infancy	inferiority	infinite	ingenious
ingenuity	ingenuous	inhabitant	initiative
innocence	inquiry	insistent	inspiration
intelligence	intentionally	interaction	intercede
interrelated	interrupt	intimate	introduce
invisible	ironic	irony	irrelevant
irresistible	irritable	island	isle

jealousy	jewelry	journal	journey
judge	judgment	junction	justifiable
justify			

| kerosene | kindergarten | knight | knowledge |
| kowtow | | | |

laboratory	laborer	launch	lawyer
league	legacy	legible	legislator
legitimate	leisure	leisurely	lenient
library	license	lighten	lightning
likelihood	likely	limb	literary
literature	liveliness	loathe	loneliness
lonely	loose	lose	losing
lottery	lovable	loveless	luncheon
luscious	luxurious	lying	

macaroni	machinery	magazine	magnificent
maintenance	malaria	manageable	management
managing	maneuver	marriage	massacre
mathematics	maximum	meanness	medical
medicinal	medicine	medieval	medley
melancholy	memorable	merchandise	merchant
merger	meteor	mettle	miniature
minimum	minister	miracle	mirror
mischief	mischievous	misdemeanor	misfit
missile	missionary	misspell	monarch
monogram	monopoly	moral	morale
mortgage	mortified	mosquitoes	mountain
movable	muffle	muscle	mysterious
naturally	necessary	necessity	negligent
neighborly	nickel	niece	ninety
ninth	noticeable	notorious	nuclear
nuisance			
obedience	oblige	obnoxious	obscure
observant	obstacle	obtuse	occasionally
occur	occurred	occurrence	official
omission	omitted	opinion	opportunity
opposite	optimism	orchard	ordinarily
organize	originally	outrageous	overrated
owing			
package	pageant	paid	pamphlet
parachute	paradox	paradoxical	paragraph
parallel	paralysis	parcel	parenthesis
parliament	partial	particle	particularly
pastime	patient	patriotic	patriotism
patron	peaceable	peasant	peculiar
pennant	perceive	percentage	perception
perilous	permanence	permanent	permissible
perplex	persistence	persistent	personally

personnel	persuade	persuasion	persuasive
pertinent	philosophy	physical	physician
pianos	picnic	picnicking	piece
pierce	pigeon	pillar	planned
plausible	playwright	pleasant	pledge
plentiful	politeness	politician	popularity
portable	possess	possession	possibility
possibly	potatoes	practicality	prairie
prayer	precede	precedent	precious
predominant	preference	preferred	prejudice
preoccupied	preparation	presence	presidency
prestige	prevail	prevalence	priest
primitive	principal	principles	priority
privilege	probability	probable	procedural
procedure	proceed	professional	professor
prohibitive	prologue	promenade	prominent
promising	pronunciation	propel	propeller
prophecy	proprietor	psychiatrist	psychoanalysis
psychologist	psychosomatic	publicity	punctuation
purchase	purchasing	purgatory	purity
pursue	pursuit		

qualified	qualitative	quandary	quantity
query	questionable	quiet	quite

radiant	ratify	realize	really
recede	receipt	receive	recessive
recognizable	recollect	recommend	recruit
recur	reference	referred	reign
rein	reliable	relieve	reluctance
remembrance	reminisce	repetitious	requirement
requisition	residence	resistance	resolving
resourceful	responsible	restaurant	reveille
rewrite	rhapsody	rhetoric	rheumatism
rhyme	rhythm	ridiculous	rigidity
routine			

sacrifice	safety	salary	satellite
satisfactory	savage	scandal	scarcely
scary	scenery	scent	schedule
schism	scissors	scold	sculptor
secede	secrecy	secretary	seize
seniority	senseless	sensible	sensitive
separate	sergeant	several	shadowy
shady	shepherd	sheriff	shield
shining	shoulder	siege	sieve
significant	simile	simultaneous	sincerely
singular	siphon	skillful	society
solemn	solicit	soliloquy	solos
sophomore	source	sovereign	spaghetti
specimen	spectacles	spectacular	spirited
sponsor	squirrel	statue	stifle
stomach	straight	strategy	strength
strenuous	stressful	studying	submission
subsidy	substantial	substitute	subtle
succeed	successful	successive	sufficient
suffix	summary	superb	surgeon
surprise	susceptible	suspense	suspicion
suspicious	sustained	syllable	syllabus
symbol	symmetrical	sympathize	symphonic
symptom	synonym		

tableau	tailor	technique	temperament
temperature	temporary	tendency	terrific
terrifying	territory	testimony	thematic
theoretical	therefore	thorough	tireless
tobacco	tolerance	tomato	tomatoes
tomorrow	tournament	traction	traffic
trafficked	tragedy	tragic	transfer
transferred	transistor	transitive	transparent
traveler	treachery	treason	treasury
truant	truly	turmoil	twelfth
twilight	typical	tyranny	tyrant

umbrella   unanimous   unconscious   undoubtedly
unison   unnecessary   unprecedented   unveil
urban   urgent   usually   utensil
utterance

vacuum   valleys   valuable   variety
various   varying   vegetable   vehicle
vengeance   vengeful   vicinity   victim
village   villain   villainous   vinegar
volcano   volunteer

warrant   warrior   wary   weapon
weather   weird   whereabouts   whimsical
whistle   wholesome   wholly   woolen
wrangle   wrestle   write   writing
written

yacht   yield

RECOMMENDED READING

The titles listed below, readily available in paperback, represent many of the works widely read and studied in comprehensive high school English courses; the emphasis is on works written in English, primarily by American writers. These titles are recommended to the student seeking to supplement regular course assignments or to prepare independently for the Regents exam. All would be suitable choices for Regents literature questions and would be valuable additions to a student's personal library.

NOVELS

1984	George Orwell
A Farewell to Arms	Ernest Hemingway
A Separate Peace	John Knowles
A Tale of Two Cities	Charles Dickens
A Yellow Raft in Blue Water	Michael Dorris
All the King's Men	Robert Penn Warren
Arrowsmith	Sinclair Lewis
Babbitt	Sinclair Lewis
Billy Budd	Herman Melville
Brave New World	Aldous Huxley
Catch-22	Joseph Heller
Catcher in the Rye	J. D. Salinger
Daisy Miller	Henry James
Deliverance	James Dickey
Ethan Frome	Edith Wharton
Felicia's Journey	William Trevor
Great Expectations	Charles Dickens
Huckleberry Finn	Mark Twain
In Country	Bobbie Ann Mason
Invisible Man	Ralph Ellison
Light in August	William Faulkner
Lord of the Flies	William Golding
Marjorie Morningstar	Herman Wouk
Native Son	Richard Wright
Oliver Twist	Charles Dickens
Ordinary People	Judith Guest
Rabbit, Run	John Updike

Ragtime	E. L. Doctorow
Rebecca	Daphne DuMaurier
Red Badge of Courage	Stephen Crane
Rumors of Peace	Ella Leffland
Sister Carrie	Theodore Dreiser
Slaughterhouse Five	Kurt Vonnegut
So Long, See You Tomorrow	William Maxwell
Song of Solomon	Toni Morrison
Summer	Edith Wharton
The Age of Innocence	Edith Wharton
The Assistant	Bernard Malamud
The Awakening	Kate Chopin
The Bean Trees	Barbara Kingsolver
The Book of Ruth	Jane Hamilton
The Caine Mutiny	Herman Wouk
The Centaur	John Updike
The Chosen	Chaim Potok
The Color Purple	Alice Walker
The Good Earth	Pearl Buck
The Grapes of Wrath	John Steinbeck
The Great Gatsby	F. Scott Fitzgerald
The Joy Luck Club	Amy Tan
The Natural	Bernard Malamud
The Old Man and the Sea	Ernest Hemingway
The Scarlet Letter	Nathaniel Hawthorne
To Kill a Mockingbird	Harper Lee
Tracks	Louise Erdrich
Washington Square	Henry James
World's Fair	E. L. Doctorow

AUTOBIOGRAPHY, ESSAYS, AND OTHER NONFICTION

A Civil Action	Jonathan Harr
A Hole in the Sky	Robert Finch
Angela's Ashes	Frank McCourt
Black Boy	Richard Wright
Cities on the Hill	Frances Fitzgerald
Growing Up	Russell Baker
Hiroshima	John Hersey
Hunger of Memory	Richard Rodriguez
I Know Why the Caged Bird Sings	Maya Angelou
In My Place	Charlayne Hunter-Gault

Iron and Silk	Mark Salzman
Late Innings	Roger Angell
Night	Elie Wiesel
Notes of a Native Son	James Baldwin
Out of Africa	Isak Dinesen
Pilgrim at Tinker Creek	Annie Dillard
Stop Time	Frank Conroy
Such, Such Were the Joys	George Orwell
The Art of Fiction	David Lodge
The Color of Water	James McBride
The Courage of Turtles	Edward Hoagland
The Crack-Up	F. Scott Fitzgerald
The Devils of Loudon	Aldous Huxley
The Duke of Deception	Geoffrey Wolff
The Way to Rainy Mountain	N. Scott Momaday
The White Album	Joan Didion
This Boy's Life	Tobias Wolff
This House of Sky	Ivan Doig
Walden	Henry David Thoreau

Also recommended are collections of essays by the following classic and contemporary authors; they are available in paperback editions:

Ray Bradbury	Malcolm Cowley	Stanley Crouch
Joan Didion	Ralph Waldo Emerson	M. F. K. Fisher
Benjamin Franklin	Ian Frazier	Adam Gopnik
Stephen Jay Gould	Garrison Keillor	Bobbie Ann Mason
John McPhee	H. L. Mencken	Richard Rodriguez
Roger Rosenblatt	Lewis Thomas	Gore Vidal
Eudora Welty	E. B. White	

Recommended anthologies include:

The Art of the Personal Essay, by Philip Lopate, Anchor Books
The Best American Essays 1998, Cynthia Ozick, ed., Houghton Mifflin
The Best American Essays 1997, Ian Frazier, ed., Houghton Mifflin
The Best American Essays 1996, Geoffrey C. Ward, ed., Houghton Mifflin
The Best American Essays 1995, Jamaica Kincaid, ed., Houghton Mifflin
The Best American Essays 1994, Tracy Kidder, ed., Houghton Mifflin
(These collections are published annually and are compiled from essays written
for magazines and journals. They represent a variety of timely subjects and
excellent writing. Earlier editions were published by Ticknor & Fields.)

POETRY

Students are urged to seek out collections of works by poets whom they encounter in class readings and whom they especially admire. Among the many poets who are introduced to high school students and whose work is widely available in paperback collections are the following:

W.H. Auden	Elizabeth Bishop	Louise Bogan
Gwendolyn Brooks	e. e. cummings	Emily Dickinson
T. S. Eliot	Carolyn Forché	Robert Frost
Louise Glück	Donald Hall	Langston Hughes
Denise Levertov	W. S. Merwin	Marianne Moore
Howard Nemerov	Sharon Olds	Sylvia Plath
Adrienne Rich	Theodore Roethke	Carl Sandburg
May Sarton	William Stafford	Richard Wilbur
Nancy Willard	William Carlos Williams	

Currently available paperback anthologies of poetry include:

The Best American Poetry 1998, John Hollander, ed., Simon & Schuster
The Best American Poetry 1997, James Tate, ed., Simon & Schuster
(This series is published annually; most recent editions are available.)
Contemporary American Poetry, Donald Hall, ed., Penguin
The Mentor Book of Major American Poets, Oscar Williams and Edwin Honig, eds., Mentor
The Norton Anthology of Modern Poetry, Richard Ellman and Robert O'Clair, eds. (Norton publishes a wide range of literature anthologies; they are excellent but not inexpensive.)
The Vintage Book of Contemporary American Poetry, J. D. McClatchy, ed., Vintage
The Best of the Best American Poetry 1988–1997, Harold Bloom, ed.

SHORT STORIES

Here is a list of recommended authors whose stories are available in paperback:

Sherwood Anderson	John Barth	Ambrose Bierce
Willa Cather	William Faulkner	F. Scott Fitzgerald
Nathaniel Hawthorne	Ernest Hemingway	Bernard Malamud

Bharati Mukherjee	Joyce Carol Oates	Flannery O'Connor
Edgar Allan Poe	Isaac Bashevis Singer	John Updike
Kurt Vonnegut	Edith Wharton	Eudora Welty
Edgar Wideman		

Collections available in paperback include:

American Short Story Masterpieces, Raymond Carver and Tom Jenks, eds., Laurel/Dell

The Best American Short Stories 1998, Garrison Keillor, ed., Houghton Mifflin

The Best American Short Stories 1997, Annie Proulx, ed., Houghton Mifflin (This series is published annually; the 1992 and 1993 editions were published by Ticknor & Fields.)

The Norton Anthology of Short Fiction, R. V. Cassill, ed.

The Oxford Book of American Short Stories, Joyce Carol Oates, ed.

The Oxford Book of Short Stories, V. S. Pritchett, ed. (incudes British and American writers)

The Vintage Book of Contemporary American Short Stories, Tobias Wolff, ed.

PLAYS

Shakespeare	*Macbeth; Julius Caesar; Othello; As You Like It; Hamlet; King Lear; Much Ado About Nothing; The Tempest; Henry V*
Edward Albee	*Who's Afraid of Virginia Woolf; Zoo Story*
Robert Bolt	*A Man for All Seasons*
Noel Coward	*Blithe Spirit; Private Lives*
Lorraine Hansberry	*A Raisin in the Sun*
William Inge	*Come Back, Little Sheba; Picnic; Bus Stop*
George S. Kaufman/Moss Hart	*You Can't Take It With You*
Jerome Lawrence/ Robert Lee	*Inherit the Wind*
Arthur Miller	*All My Sons; Death of a Salesman; The Crucible; The Price*
Clifford Odets	*Waiting for Lefty; The Country Girl*
Eugene O'Neill	*Long Day's Journey into Night*
Terrence Rattigan	*The Winslow Boy; The Browning Version*
Rod Serling	*Requiem for a Heavyweight*

Peter Shaffer	*Equus; Black Comedy; The Royal Hunt of the Sun*
Neil Simon	*The Odd Couple*
Thornton Wilder	*Our Town; The Matchmaker; The Skin of Our Teeth*
Tennessee Williams	*The Glass Menagerie; A Streetcar Named Desire; Cat on a Hot Tin Roof; Sweet Bird of Youth*
August Wilson	*Fences*

APPENDIX A:
AN INTRODUCTION TO THE NEW YORK STATE ENGLISH LANGUAGE ARTS LEARNING STANDARDS

As part of its revision of New York State standards and graduation requirements, the Board of Regents has adopted the Learning Standards in English Language Arts, and a new Regents Comprehensive English exam has been developed to assess the expectations set forth in those standards. That exam will be administered beginning in June 1999.

The content of the ELA Standards is not new; what is new is the way in which what students should learn is described. The ELA Standards are no longer expressed simply as a list of topics to be "covered"; rather, they are expressed in terms of what students must be able to do. These standards are given in their entirety in Appendix C.

APPENDIX B:
A GLOSSARY OF TERMS

assessment   You may hear teachers and other educators using the term **assessment** instead of test or examination. An **assessment** is more than a simple test (in arithmetic, say) because it seeks to measure a number of skills at one time. Although we continue to refer to the English Regents as an exam or test, its goal is to be a valid **assessment** of a broad range of listening, reading, thinking, and writing skills outlined in the new Learning Standards

audience   In talking about writing, we use the term **audience** to mean the intended readers. Parts I and II of the new Regents exam require that you write an essay or report for a particular group of readers and for a particular purpose.

conventions   This term is found in the **rubrics** (see below) and refers to conventional standards for spelling, punctuation, paragraphing, capitalization, grammar, and usage. You are expected to follow the **conventions** of standard written English in all four parts of the examination.

critical lens   This term is used in Part IV of the revised exam; the critical lens is a quote about a particular way of "looking at" and evaluating works of literature. You will use your interpretation and response to the **critical lens** to compose a literary essay.

guidelines   The **Guidelines** follow the description of each **Task** (see below) and list the specific steps you must take to write a successful essay.

overview   The **Overview** at the beginning of Part I of the Regents exam outlines what is required in that part. Requirements may also be expressed as **Directions** in other parts.

performance indicators   This is the technical term educators use to identify what students should be able to do in order to demonstrate that they have the listening, reading, thinking, and writing skills outlined in the new **Standards.**

rubric   A **rubric** is a descriptive guide to scoring or evaluating an essay, examination, or other task. Many teachers now use **rubrics** in their own courses to show students how their work is assessed or evaluated. You will find the **rubrics** for each part of the Regents exam in Appendix F. Be sure to review these carefully.

situation   Parts I and II of the revised Regents include a **Situation,** a specific context, purpose, and **audience** for the essay, article, or report that you will write.

standards   For students in New York State, The Learning Standards for English Language Arts establishes four broad categories of language skills, states general goals for each, and then outlines **performance indicators** for each. These are described in detail in Appendix D. The revised English Regents exam reflects the emphasis on performance—specific expectations for the intellectual habits you must develop and the skills you must exercise on a habitual basis. (The map in Appendix E outlines the relationship of the **standards** to the **performance indicators**.)

task   The **Task** is what you must actually *do* on each part of the exam. The exam is composed of a series of **tasks** because the revised Regents requires that you *demonstrate* how well you comprehend, analyze, and write.

APPENDIX C: THE ENGLISH LANGUAGE ARTS LEARNING STANDARDS

The standards are identified as four broad areas of language experience, each requiring reading, listening, speaking, and writing.

STANDARD 1: LANGUAGE FOR INFORMATION AND UNDERSTANDING

Listening and reading to acquire information and understanding involves collecting data, facts, and ideas; discovering relationships, concepts, and generalizations; and using knowledge from oral, written, and electronic sources. **Speaking and writing** to acquire and transmit information requires asking probing and clarifying questions, interpreting information in one's own words, applying information from one context to another, and presenting the information and interpretation clearly, concisely, and comprehensibly.

STANDARD 2: LANGUAGE FOR LITERARY RESPONSE AND EXPRESSION

Listening and reading for literary *response* involves comprehending, interpreting, and critiquing imaginative texts in every medium, drawing on personal experiences and knowledge to understand the text, and recognizing the social, historical, and cultural features of the text. **Speaking and writing** for literary *response* involves presenting interpretations, analyses, and reactions to the content and language of a text. Speaking and writing for literary *expression* involves producing imaginative texts that use language and text structures that are inventive and often multilayered.

STANDARD 3: LANGUAGE FOR CRITICAL ANALYSIS AND EVALUATION

Listening and reading to analyze and evaluate experiences, ideas, information, and issues requires using evaluative criteria from a variety of perspectives and recognizing the difference in evaluations based on different sets of criteria. **Speaking and writing** for critical analysis and evaluation requires presenting opinions and judgments on experiences, ideas, information, and issues clearly, logically, and persuasively with reference to specific criteria on which the opinion or judgment is based.

STANDARD 4: LANGUAGE FOR SOCIAL INTERACTION

Oral communication in formal and informal settings requires the ability to talk with people of different ages, genders, and cultures, to adapt presentations to different audiences, and to reflect on how talk varies in different situations. **Written communication** for social interaction requires using written messages to establish, maintain, and enhance personal relationships with others.

APPENDIX D: PERFORMANCE INDICATORS

For teachers, as well as students and parents, the English Language Arts Learning Standards are most meaningfully expressed in what are called **performance indicators,** descriptions of what students are required to do, do habitually, and do on demand. Below are some of the required performance indicators at commencement (Regents exam) level for each standard.

ELA STANDARD 1: LANGUAGE FOR INFORMATION AND UNDERSTANDING

Students are expected to:

Interpret and analyze complex informational texts and presentations, including technical manuals, professional journals, newspaper and broadcast editorials, electronic networks, political speeches and debates, and primary source material, in their subject courses.

Synthesize information from diverse sources and identify complexities and discrepancies in the information.

Use a combination of techniques to **extract salient information** from texts.

Make distinctions about the relative value and significance of specific data, facts, and ideas. **Make perceptive and well-developed connections** to prior knowledge. **Evaluate** writing strategies and presentational features that affect interpretation of the information.

Write research reports, feature articles, and thesis/support papers on a variety of topics. **Present a controlling idea** that conveys an individual perspective and insight into a topic. **Support** interpretations and decisions. **Use** a wide range of organizational patterns.

Revise and improve early drafts by restructuring, correcting errors, and revising for clarity and effect. **Use standard English skillfully,** applying established rules and conventions for presenting information and making use of a wide range of grammatical constructions and vocabulary to achieve an individual style that communicates effectively.

ELA STANDARD 2: LANGUAGE FOR LITERARY RESPONSE AND EXPRESSION

Students are expected to:

Read and view independently and fluently across many genres of literature from many cultures and historical periods. **Evaluate** literary merit based on an understanding of the genre, literary elements, and the literary period.

Identify the distinguishing features of different literary genres, periods, and traditions and use those features to interpret the work. **Read aloud** expressively to convey a clear interpretation of the work.

Recognize and understand the significance of a wide range of literary elements and techniques (including figurative language, imagery, allegory, irony, blank verse, symbolism, stream-of-consciousness), and use those elements to interpret the work.

Understand how multiple levels of meaning are conveyed in a text. Produce literary interpretations that **explicate** the multiple layers of meaning.

Write original pieces in a variety of literary forms, using the conventions of the genre and using structure and vocabulary to achieve an effect.

Use standard English skillfully and with an individual style.

ELA STANDARD 3: LANGUAGE FOR CRITICAL ANALYSIS AND EVALUATION

Students are expected to:

Analyze, interpret, and evaluate ideas, information, organization and language of a wide range of general and technical texts . . . across subject areas, including technical manuals, professional journals, political speeches, and literary criticism.

Evaluate the quality of the texts . . . from a variety of critical perspectives within the field of study. **Make precise determinations** about the perspective of a particular writer.

Present well-developed analyses of issues, ideas, and texts . . . . **Make effective use** of details, evidence, and arguments . . . to influence and persuade an audience.

Use standard English, a broad and precise vocabulary, and the formal conventions of formal oratory and debate.

ELA STANDARD 4: LANGUAGE FOR SOCIAL INTERACTION*

Students are expected to:

Engage in conversations and discussions on academic, technical, and community subjects, anticipating listeners' needs and skillfully addressing them.

Express their thoughts and views clearly with attention to the perspectives and voiced concerns of others in the conversation. **Use** appropriately the language conventions for a wide variety of social situations.

Use a variety of print and electronic forms for social communication with peers and adults. **Make effective use** of language and style to connect the message with the audience and context.

You will find a map to the standards and performance indicators in Appendix E and the scoring rubrics for each part of the exam in Appendix F.

---

*This standard is not formally assessed in the new Comprehensive English Regents Exam.

APPENDIX E:
A MAP TO THE ENGLISH LANGUAGE ARTS STANDARDS AND PERFORMANCE INDICATORS

	Task	Standard	Performance Indicators
PART I	(a) Extended written response to a speech (b) Multiple-choice questions on key ideas (5–6)	Listening and writing for information and understanding	Interpret and analyze complex informational texts and presentations... Use a combination of techniques to extract salient information from texts... Make distinctions about the relative value and significance of specific data, facts, and ideas Write...research reports, feature articles, and thesis/support papers on a variety of topics... Present a controlling idea that conveys an individual perspective and insight into the topic Use a wide range of organizational patterns... Support interpretations and decisions... Use standard English skillfully...
PART II	(a) Extended written response to informational materials (text and visual) (b) Multiple-choice questions on basic comprehension (salient information, vocabulary, and interpretation) (8–10)	Reading and writing for information and understanding	Interpret and analyze complex informational texts and presentations... Use a combination of techniques to extract salient information from texts... Make distinctions about the relative value and significance of specific data, facts, and ideas Write...research reports, feature articles, and thesis/support papers on a variety of topics... Present a controlling idea that conveys an individual perspective and insight into the topic Use a wide range of organizational patterns... Support interpretations and decisions... Use standard English skillfully...
PART III	(a) Extended written response to two linked passages of different genres (b) Multiple-choice questions on key ideas, details, and vocabulary (8–10)	Reading and writing for literary response	Read...independently and fluently across many genres of literature Identify the distinguishing features of different literary genres...and use those features to interpret the work Recognize and understand the significance of a wide range of literary elements and techniques... and use those elements to interpret the work Produce literary interpretations that explicate the multiple layers of meaning Use standard English skillfully...
PART IV	Extended written response to literature read for school	Reading and writing for critical analysis and evaluation	Analyze, interpret, and evaluate...a wide range of...texts... Evaluate the quality of texts...from a variety of critical perspectives Make precise determinations about the perspective of a particular writer... Present...well-developed analyses of issues, ideas, and texts... Make effective use of details, evidence, and arguments... Use standard English skillfully...

APPENDIX F: SCORING RUBRICS

PART I: LISTENING AND WRITING FOR INFORMATION AND UNDERSTANDING

Quality	Responses at this level: 6	Responses at this level: 5	Responses at this level: 4	Responses at this level: 3	Responses at this level: 2	Responses at this level: 1
Meaning: the extent to which the response exhibits sound understanding, interpretation, and analysis of the task and text(s)	—reveal an in-depth analysis of the text —make insightful connections between information and ideas in the text and the assigned task	—convey a thorough understanding of the text —make clear and explicit connections between information and ideas in the text and the assigned task	—convey a basic understanding of the text —make implicit connections between information and ideas in the text and the assigned task	—convey a basic understanding of the text —make few or superficial connections between information and ideas in the text and the assigned task	—convey a confused or inaccurate understanding of the text —allude to the text but make unclear or unwarranted connections to the assigned task	—provide no evidence of textual understanding —make no connections between information in the text and the assigned task
Development: the extent to which ideas are elaborated using specific and relevant evidence from the text(s)	—develop ideas clearly and fully, making effective use of a wide range of relevant and specific details from the text	—develop ideas clearly and consistently, using relevant and specific details from the text	—develop some ideas more fully than others, using specific and relevant details from the text	—develop ideas briefly, using some details from the text	—are incomplete or largely undeveloped, hinting at ideas, but references to the text are vague, irrelevant, repetitive, or unjustified	—are minimal, with no evidence of development
Organization: the extent to which the response exhibits direction, shape, and coherence	—maintain a clear and appropriate focus —exhibit a logical and coherent structure through skillful use of appropriate devices and transitions	—maintain a clear and appropriate focus —exhibit a logical sequence of ideas through use of appropriate devices and transitions	—maintain a clear and appropriate focus —exhibit a logical sequence of ideas but may lack internal consistency	—establish, but fail to maintain, an appropriate focus —exhibit a rudimentary structure but may include some inconsistencies or irrelevancies	—lack an appropriate focus but suggest some organization, or suggest a focus but lack organization	—show no focus or organization
Language Use: the extent to which the response reveals an awareness of audience and purpose through effective use of words, sentence structure, and sentence variety	—are stylistically sophisticated, using language that is precise and engaging, with a notable sense of voice and awareness of audience and purpose —vary structure and length of sentences to enhance meaning	—use language that is fluent and original, with evident awareness of audience and purpose —vary structure and length of sentences to control rhythm and pacing	—use appropriate language, with some awareness of audience and purpose —occasionally make effective use of sentence structure or length	—rely on language from the text or basic vocabulary, with little awareness of audience or purpose —exhibit some attempt to vary sentence structure or length for effect, but with uneven success	—use language that is imprecise or unsuitable for the audience or purpose —reveal little awareness of how to use sentences to achieve an effect	—are minimal —use language that is incoherent or inappropriate
Conventions: the extent to which the response exhibits conventional spelling, punctuation, paragraphing, capitalization, grammar, and usage	—demonstrate control of the conventions with essentially no errors, even with sophisticated language	—demonstrate control of the conventions, exhibiting occasional errors only when using sophisticated language	—demonstrate partial control, exhibiting occasional errors that do not hinder comprehension	—demonstrate emerging control, exhibiting occasional errors that hinder comprehension	—demonstrate a lack of control, exhibiting frequent errors that make comprehension difficult	—are minimal, making assessment of conventions unreliable —may be illegible or not recognizable as English

228

PART II: READING AND WRITING FOR INFORMATION AND UNDERSTANDING

QUALITY	6 Responses at this level:	5 Responses at this level:	4 Responses at this level	3 Responses at this level:	2 Responses at this level:	1 Responses at this level:
Meaning: the extent to which the response exhibits sound understanding, interpretation, and analysis of the task and document(s)	—reveal an in-depth analysis of the documents —make insightful connections between information and ideas in the documents and the assigned task	—convey a thorough understanding of the documents —make clear and explicit connections between information and ideas in the documents and the assigned task	—convey a basic under-standing of the docu-ments —make implicit con-nections between information and ideas in the documents and the assigned task	—convey a basic understanding of the documents* —make few or superficial connections between information and ideas in the documents and the assigned task	—convey a confused or inaccurate understanding of the documents —allude to the documents but make unclear or unwarranted connections to the assigned task	—provide no evidence of understanding —make no connections between information in the documents and the assigned task
Development: the extent to which ideas are elaborated using specific and relevant evidence from the document(s)	—develop ideas clearly and fully, making effective use of a wide range of relevant and specific de-tails from the documents	—develop ideas clearly and consistently, using relevant and specific details from the documents	—develop some ideas more fully than others, using specific and relevant details from the documents	—develop ideas briefly, using some details from the documents	—are incomplete or largely undeveloped, hinting at ideas, but references to the documents are vague, irrelevant, repetitive, or unjustified	—are minimal, with no evidence of development
Organization: the extent to which the response exhibits direction, shape, and coherence	—maintain a clear and appropriate focus —exhibit a logical and coherent structure through skillful use of appropriate devices and transitions	—maintain a clear and appropriate focus —exhibit a logical sequence of ideas through use of appro-priate devices and transitions	—maintain a clear and appropriate focus —exhibit a logical sequence of ideas but may lack internal consistency	—establish, but fail to maintain, an appropriate focus —exhibit a rudimentary structure but may include some inconsistencies or irrelevancies	—lack an appropriate focus but suggest some organization, or suggest a focus but lack organization	—show no focus or organization
Language Use: the extent to which the response reveals an awareness of audience and purpose through effective use of words, sentence structure, and sentence variety	—are stylistically sophis-ticated, using language that is precise and engaging, with a notable sense of voice and awareness of audience and purpose —vary structure and length of sentences to enhance meaning	—use language that is fluent and original, with evident awareness of audience and purpose —vary structure and length of sentences to control rhythm and pacing	—use appropriate language, with some awareness of audience and purpose —occasionally make effective use of sentence structure or length	—rely on language from the documents or basic vocabulary, with little awareness of audience or purpose —exhibit some attempt to vary sentence structure or length for effect, but with uneven success	—use language that is imprecise or unsuitable for the audience or purpose —reveal little awareness of how to use sentences to achieve an effect	—are minimal —use language that is incoherent or inappropriate
Conventions: the extent to which the response exhibits conventional spelling, punctuation, para-graphing, capitalization, grammar, and usage	—demonstrate control of the conventions with essentially no errors, even with sophisticated language	—demonstrate control of the conventions, exhibiting occasional errors only when using sophisticated language	—demonstrate partial control, exhibiting occasional errors that do not hinder comprehension	—demonstrate emerging control, exhibiting occasional errors that hinder comprehension	—demonstrate a lack of control, exhibiting frequent errors that make com-prehension difficult	—are minimal, making assessment of conventions unreliable —may be illegible or not recognizable as English

*If the student addresses only one document, the response can be scored no higher than a 3.

229

PART III: READING AND WRITING FOR LITERARY RESPONSE

QUALITY	6 Responses at this level:	5 Responses at this level:	4 Responses at this level:	3 Responses at this level:	2 Responses at this level:	1 Responses at this level:
Meaning: the extent to which the response exhibits sound understanding, interpretation, and analysis of the task and text(s)	—establish a controlling idea that reveals an in-depth analysis of both texts —make insightful connections between the controlling idea, the ideas in each text, and the elements or techniques used to convey those ideas	—establish a controlling idea that reveals a thorough understanding of both texts —make clear and explicit connections between the controlling idea, the ideas in each text, and the elements or techniques used to convey those ideas	—establish a controlling idea that shows a basic understanding of both texts —make implicit connections between the controlling idea, the ideas in each text, and the elements or techniques used to convey those ideas	—establish a controlling idea that shows a basic understanding of the texts* —make few or superficial connections between the controlling idea, the ideas in the texts, and the elements or techniques used to convey those ideas	—convey a confused or incomplete understanding of the texts —fail to establish a controlling idea —allude to the texts but give no examples of literary elements or techniques	—provide minimal evidence of textual understanding —make no connections between ideas in the texts and literary elements or techniques
Development: the extent to which ideas are elaborated using specific and relevant evidence from the text(s)	—develop ideas clearly and fully, making effective use of a wide range of relevant and specific evidence from both texts	—develop ideas clearly and consistently, using relevant and specific evidence from both texts	—develop some ideas more fully than others, using specific and relevant evidence from both texts	—develop ideas briefly, using some evidence from the texts	—are incomplete or largely undeveloped, hinting at ideas, but references to the text are vague, irrelevant, repetitive, or unjustified	—are minimal, with no evidence of development
Organization: the extent to which the response exhibits direction, shape, and coherence	—maintain the focus established by the controlling idea —exhibit a logical and coherent structure through skillful use of appropriate devices and transitions	—maintain the focus established by the controlling idea —exhibit a logical sequence of ideas through the use of appropriate devices and transitions	—maintain a clear and appropriate focus —exhibit a logical sequence of ideas but may lack internal consistency	—establish, but fail to maintain, an appropriate focus —exhibit a rudimentary structure but may include some inconsistencies or irrelevancies	—lack an appropriate focus but suggest some organization, or suggest a focus but lack organization	—show no focus or organization
Language Use: the extent to which the response reveals an awareness of audience and purpose through effective use of words, sentence structure, and sentence variety	—are stylistically sophisticated, using language that is precise and engaging, with a notable sense of voice and awareness of audience and purpose —vary structure and length of sentences to enhance meaning	—use language that is fluent and original, with evident awareness of audience and purpose —vary structure and length of sentences to control rhythm and pacing	—use appropriate language, with some awareness of audience and purpose —occasionally make effective use of sentence structure or length	—rely on language from the text or basic vocabulary, with little awareness of audience or purpose —exhibit some attempt to vary sentence structure or length for effect, but with uneven success	—use language that is imprecise or unsuitable for the audience or purpose —reveal little awareness of how to use sentences to achieve an effect	—are minimal —use language that is incoherent or inappropriate
Conventions: the extent to which the response exhibits conventional spelling, punctuation, paragraphing, capitalization, grammar, and usage	—demonstrate control of the conventions with essentially no errors, even with sophisticated language	—demonstrate control of the conventions, exhibiting occasional errors only when using sophisticated language	—demonstrate partial control, exhibiting occasional errors that do not hinder comprehension	—demonstrate emerging control, exhibiting occasional errors that hinder comprehension	—demonstrate a lack of control, exhibiting frequent errors that make comprehension difficult	—are minimal, making assessment of conventions unreliable —may be illegible or not recognizable as English

*If the student addresses only one text, the response can be scored no higher than a 3.

230

PART IV: READING AND WRITING FOR CRITICAL ANALYSIS

QUALITY	6 Responses at this level:	5 Responses at this level:	4 Responses at this level:	3 Responses at this level:	2 Responses at this level:	1 Responses at this level:
Meaning: the extent to which the response exhibits sound understanding, interpretation, and analysis of the task and text(s)	—provide an interpretation of the "critical lens" that is faithful to the complexity of the statement and clearly establishes the criteria for analysis —use the criteria to make an insightful analysis of the chosen texts	—provide a thoughtful interpretation of the "critical lens" that clearly establishes the criteria for analysis —use the criteria to make a clear and reasoned analysis of the chosen texts	—provide a reasonable interpretation of the "critical lens" that establishes the criteria for analysis —make implicit connections between the criteria and the chosen texts	—provide a simple interpretation of the "critical lens" that suggests some criteria for analysis —make superficial connections between the criteria and the chosen texts*	—provide a confused or incomplete interpretation of the "critical lens" —may allude to the "critical lens" but do not use it to analyze the chosen texts	—do not refer to the "critical lens" —reflect minimal analysis of the chosen texts or omit mention of texts
Development: the extent to which ideas are elaborated using specific and relevant evidence from the text(s)	—develop ideas clearly and fully, making effective use of a wide range of relevant and specific evidence and appropriate literary elements from both texts	—develop ideas clearly and consistently, with reference to relevant and specific evidence and appropriate literary elements from both texts	—develop some ideas more fully than others, with reference to specific and relevant evidence and appropriate literary elements from both texts	—develop ideas briefly, using some evidence from the texts	—are incomplete or largely undeveloped, hinting at ideas, but references to the text are vague, irrelevant, repetitive, or unjustified	—are minimal, with no evidence of development
Organization: the extent to which the response exhibits direction, shape, and coherence	—maintain the focus established by the critical lens —exhibit a logical and coherent structure through skillful use of appropriate devices and transitions	—maintain the focus established by the critical lens —exhibit a logical sequence of ideas through the use of appropriate devices and transitions	—maintain a clear and appropriate focus —exhibit a logical sequence of ideas but may lack internal consistency	—establish, but fail to maintain, an appropriate focus —exhibit a rudimentary structure but may include some inconsistencies or irrelevancies	—lack an appropriate focus but suggest some organization, or suggest a focus but lack organization	—show no focus or organization
Language Use: the extent to which the response reveals an awareness of audience and purpose through effective use of words, sentence structure, and sentence variety	—are stylistically sophisticated, using language that is precise and engaging, with a notable sense of voice and awareness of audience and purpose —vary structure and length of sentences to enhance meaning	—use language that is fluent and original, with evident awareness of audience and purpose —vary structure and length of sentences to control rhythm and pacing	—use appropriate language, with some awareness of audience and purpose —occasionally make effective use of sentence structure or length	—rely on basic vocabulary, with little awareness of audience or purpose —exhibit some attempt to vary sentence structure or length for effect, but with uneven success	—use language that is imprecise or unsuitable for the audience or purpose —reveal little awareness of how to use sentences to achieve an effect	—are minimal —use language that is incoherent or inappropriate
Conventions: the extent to which the response exhibits conventional spelling, punctuation, paragraphing, capitalization, grammar, and usage	—demonstrate control of the conventions with essentially no errors, even with sophisticated language	—demonstrate control of the conventions, exhibiting occasional errors only when using sophisticated language	—demonstrate partial control, exhibiting occasional errors that do not hinder comprehension	—demonstrate emerging control, exhibiting occasional errors that hinder comprehension	—demonstrate a lack of control, exhibiting frequent errors that make comprehension difficult	—are minimal, making assessment of conventions unreliable —may be illegible or not recognizable as English

*If the student addresses only one text, the response can be scored no higher than a 3.

MODEL REGENTS EXAMINATIONS

MODEL EXAMINATION 1

Part I—Sample

Student Copy

Overview: For this part of the test, you will listen to a speech about an author's memories of an island in South Carolina, answer some multiple-choice questions, and write a response based on the situation described below. You will hear the speech twice. You may take notes anytime you wish during the readings.

The Situation: Your English class is learning about authors whose lives are strongly influenced by a specific place. Your teacher has asked you to write an essay about author Pat Conroy and the ways in which his life was influenced by a specific place. In preparation for writing your essay, you will listen to a speech Pat Conroy made about his memories of an island in South Carolina. Then use relevant information from this speech to write your essay.

Your Task: Write an essay for your English class showing how Pat Conroy's life was influenced by a specific place.

Guidelines:

- Tell your audience what they need to know to help them understand how Pat Conroy's life was influenced by a specific place

- Use specific, accurate, and relevant information from the speech to support your discussion

- Use a tone and level of language appropriate for an essay for English class

- Organize your ideas in a logical and coherent manner

- Be sure to indicate any words taken directly from the speech by using quotation marks or referring to the speaker

- Follow the conventions of standard written English

Passage

I have written, in part, to honor a landscape I carry with me wherever I go. Though I have traveled all over the world, it is the smell of the tides and marshes of Beaufort County, South Carolina, that identifies and shapes me. Its seeds and grasses grow along the margins of my books. Its soft mosses hang, like laundry, from my high-strung prose.

I sometimes feel that Fripp Island and I grew up together, formed a pact of great intimacy during my final years of high school, and have maintained an alliance throughout my adult life despite many travels, false starts, and driftings of the spirit. A Marine colonel and his son first took me to Fripp on a fishing expedition the summer between my 15th and 16th year, and it was my first step on a sea island totally isolated from the mainland. It was an island as God made it, and nothing else, pristine as time itself. The sea islands of South Carolina shoulder up against the Atlantic, and the trees and the vegetation on these islands are wind-shaped and salt-burnt and stunted by the great storms and swells resulting from this initial encounter with the continent. They are the first line of defense against hurricanes and those deep-throated storms out of the Northeast.

When I graduated from Beaufort High School, workers had just completed the bridge to Fripp Island, and I had a free run of the island that same summer. The president of the Student Council, Bruce Harper, sold real estate that first year land was for sale, and I remember him complaining that they would never sell a single lot with the prices so outrageously high. In my own memory, I think that oceanfront property was selling for $2,500 a lot during those hot, long-ago days. Bruce and I would golf when he got off work, then go for long swims in the ocean on a beach where not a single house had gone up. The sun would turn our bodies gold as it settled to the west of the marshes, and I thought I would be young forever.

My mother, Peg Conroy, walked the shoreline of Fripp every day for the last five years of her life and collected basketfuls of seashells that she would place in the clear globes of lamps. Those lamps are now treasures her children keep because we love to associate our mother with the sea, the crashing of waves, the gathering up of beauty, and of light itself.

It was my mother who chose Fripp Island as our family beach, and it was where she was living when she died in 1984. She taught us that nature was simply another way of approaching God. When I asked her why buzzards never gathered over the corpses of loggerheads or pilot whales, she explained that the putrescence of red meat, and not seafood, is what attracted vultures to southern roadsides in the first place. "A matter of preference," she said. "Your father likes steak. I like shrimp."

My mother was afraid of hurricanes and bought her Fripp house near the golf course, so she could watch the small convoy of golfers sail past her house in their squat, pragmatic carts. That flow of humanity made her less lonely and provided her with an endless supply of free golf balls lost in the shrubbery of her yard. Years later, I bought my own house facing a saltwater lagoon where I watch ospreys hunt fish in my backyard, then take their catch up into the trees to eat them heads first. I have seen great blue herons kill and eat snakes and huge eels. The alligators have developed a fondness for domesticated dog, and the raccoons find garbage cans better hunting grounds than the toad-haunted wetlands. I woke up one bright fall morning and counted 300 egrets surrounding my lagoon in some mating ritual that looked like a dream of snow.

Because I came to Beaufort County when I was a boy, my novels all smell of seawater. I watch things closely here, and I try to get the details right. I write about the great salt marshes and pretend I am that marsh. I do the same with the ocean, the horseshoe crab, the flock of brown pelicans, the beach-strewn kelp, the half-eaten stingray. I try to inhabit the soul of things, before I write about them, the way my mother taught me.

There are other beaches, other oceans, but my mother staked out Fripp forever for her children. When she was dying, with her seven children gathered around her, Peggy, our mountain-born mother, said, "When I'm gone and you cross the bridge over to Fripp, look out toward the ocean. If you see whitecaps, that'll be me, that'll be your mother, waving, letting you know I'm still here with you."

Directions: Use your notes to answer the following questions about the passage read to you. The questions may help you think about ideas and information you might use in your writing. You may return to these questions anytime you wish.

1   The speaker's opening lines serve to

    1 list a series of problems
    2 acknowledge a source of inspiration
    3 describe a plan of organization
    4 argue a point of view

2   Pat Conroy's first trip to Fripp Island, at age 15, was for the purpose of

    1 hiding   3 fishing
    2 writing   4 studying

3　The phrase "pristine as time itself" implies that Conroy was impressed by the island's

    1　history　　　　　　　　3　size
    2　potential　　　　　　　4　purity

4　According to Conroy, plants on the island are affected by

    1　hurricanes　　　　　　3　snowstorms
    2　drought　　　　　　　　4　earthquakes

5　According to Conroy, what was happening not long after his graduation?

    1　The beach was becoming polluted.
    2　The island was becoming developed.
    3　His mother was dying.
    4　His friends were leaving.

6　Conroy associates his mother with the

    1　marsh　　　　　　　　3　turtles
    2　bridge　　　　　　　　4　waves

7　Conroy implies that his house near the lagoon is a good place to

    1　watch ships　　　　　　3　observe wildlife
    2　entertain company　　　4　play golf

8　According to Conroy, he tries to "inhabit the soul of things" as a way to

    1　recreate the details of the island
    2　improve the design of the bridge
    3　protect the habitat of the sea creatures
    4　encourage the use of other beaches

Review **The Situation** and read **Your Task** and the **Guidelines.**
Then write your response.

Note:　The operational examination will include only 5–6 questions on Part I. Additional questions are included here to suggest a fuller range of possible question types.

Part II Task, Text, and Questions—Sample

Directions: Read the article and study the chart on the following pages, answer the multiple-choice questions, and write a response based on the situation described below. You may use the margins to take notes as you read. You may use scrap paper to plan your response.

> **The Situation:** You are a member of the youth editorial board of a new international English-language magazine for high school students. The board is considering whether to use American English or British English in the magazine's articles and advertising. As the United States representative on the board, you are submitting a written argument at the next board meeting telling why you believe the magazine should be written in American English.

Your Task: Write an argument to be submitted to the editorial board of a new international magazine for high school students. Using relevant information from the text **and** the chart, explain why you believe the magazine should use American English in its articles and advertising.

Guidelines:

- Tell the youth editorial board what they need to know about American and British English to understand your argument

- Explain why you believe the magazine should use American English, rather than British English, in its articles and advertising

- Use specific, accurate, and relevant information from the article **and** the chart to support your argument

- Use a tone and level of language appropriate for an argument to be submitted to a magazine editorial board

- Organize your ideas in a logical and coherent manner

- Be sure to indicate any words taken directly from the article by using quotation marks or referring to the author

- Follow the conventions of standard written English

Like many Russians, Ilya Bezouglyi learned English the way his teachers preferred, British style. But after being laughed at in Canada for using the word "chaps," and after a year of graduate study in the United States, Mr. Bezouglyi says that he and his English are "pretty much
(5) Americanized."

The "Americanization" of English is happening around the world today, from Africa to Britain itself. American English is seeping into the nooks and crannies of English everywhere thanks to education, business, Hollywood, and the Internet.
(10) Although British English—which many countries consider to be the "real thing"—is widely taught around the world, what those learners use in their private lives is more influenced by the United States. As a result, "American English is spreading faster than British English," says Braj Kachru, a linguist in India and a founder and co-editor of the journal
(15) *World Englishes.*

In television broadcasts alone, the United States controlled 75 percent of the world's programming as recently as 1993, beaming *Sesame Street* to Lagos, Nigeria, for example.

Americans also outnumber Britons: People are more likely to
(20) encounter one of the 260 million Yanks than one of the 55 million Brits. "It's more practical to speak and understand American English these days," says Bezouglyi, who adds there are more Americans than Britons in Russia today.

The spread of American English began in the decades after World
(25) War II. Experts say the simultaneous rise of the United States as a military and technological superpower and the receding of the British empire gave many in the world both the desire and option to choose American English. English in general has spread during that time as well. More than 1 billion people are thought to speak it as a native, second, or
(30) foreign language. Among the roughly 350 million native English speakers, the American version is spoken by about 70 percent.

"There's no question that Britain made English an international language in the 19th century with its empire," says Bill Bryson, an American author of several books on the history of English. "But it's
(35) Americans that have been the driving force behind the globalization of English in the 20th century" because of their commercial and cultural clout, he says.

Examples of the influence of American English include:
• Young people in Europe, Asia, and Russia use it in casual
(40) conversation—including the notorious United States export, "you guys"—even when many of them have been taught British English. "As far as I can see, it's exactly equivalent to wearing Nike baseball caps, or Air Jordan shoes," says Mr. Bryson, who listened to teenagers speak with American accents in the Netherlands recently. "It's a kind of linguistic
(45) badge."
• In Brazil, people often ask for courses in "American," rather than English, according to Bernabe Feria, head of curriculum and development for Berlitz International in Princeton, New Jersey.
• In Nigeria, years of trade with the United States—and contact that
(50) blossomed in the 1960's with the Peace Corps—have greatly increased the

use of American English. It is now spoken along with British English, a leftover of British colonial rule.

• In Cairo, as recently as 1984, some university students received lower grades if they used American spellings instead of British. Since
(55) then, there has been an increase in the number of teachers in Egypt trained by Americans. "You can well imagine that nobody gets a red line through their paper for spelling 'center' with an 'er' anymore," says Richard Boyum, the head of English-language teaching activities at the United States Information Agency (USIA).
(60) • In Thailand, the standard in both schools and the English-language press is British English. But university teachers may speak English with an American accent because they have studied in the United States.

• The British Broadcasting Corporation (BBC), long the promoter of proper British English, now includes Americans in its broadcasts. Its
(65) English-language teaching programs feature Americans in broadcasts that go to countries where American English is favored, such as South Korea.

American invasion

Britain has not been immune to the spread of American English, either. More words that were exclusively American are now found in the
(70) speech and writing in both countries, says Norman Moss, compiler of an American-British/British-American dictionary called "What's the Difference?" "Once 'guy' and 'campus' were almost unknown in Britain," he says. Today they are widely used.

Britons are also increasingly saying "movie" instead of "film."
(75) Computer-related words are more frequently spelled the American way: program, without the British addition of "me" on the end, for example. And the American phrase "the bottom line" is encroaching on its British equivalent "at the end of the day."

"We tend to take them [Americanisms] over if they are useful and
(80) reject them if they are not," offers Geraldine Kershaw, a senior English-teaching consultant to the British Council, a government-sponsored agency that operates British-English teaching centers worldwide.

Linguists note that the mixing of British and American English in Europe has given rise to a "mid-Atlantic" English, a more neutral
(85) language that is less identifiable with either country.

In some European countries, both kinds of English are now accepted and taught. Some learners prefer American English because they believe it has fewer regional accents and dialects than British English does, experts say, and therefore is easier to understand and use.
(90) Still, the USIA—which advises countries on English teaching but does not teach it directly—and its British counterpart, the British Council, argue that the languages are not in competition. "I don't think there is a fierce contest going on between the two kinds of English," says Ms. Kershaw of the British Council. She notes that there are very few differences
(95) between the two.

English as a commodity

But the question of who is teaching the world to speak English is no small matter. The hunger for the language has made English teaching a

big business. "English has become an economic commodity," says Dr.
(100) Kachru, who runs the Center for Advanced Study at the University of
Illinois in Champaign.

Some estimates place the revenues of the worldwide industry at about
$10 billion annually. That includes teaching, textbooks, and materials,
and money spent by foreign students who choose to attend schools in
(105) English-speaking countries as a result of learning the language.

The dollar amount will likely get much bigger if predictions by the
British Council that more than 1 billion people will be learning English
by 2000 prove true. Markets that are expected to contribute to the rise
include Russia and China. China alone is estimated already to have
(110) between 200 million and 400 million people who speak some form of
English.

Currently, much of the English taught in Europe, India, and parts of
Asia and Africa is British or British-influenced. American English is
favored in Latin America, Japan, and South Korea. But linguists note that
(115) often those learning the language just want English—they don't care what
kind. English is often studied by people whose primary purpose is not to
speak to Americans or Britons, says Dr. Feria of Berlitz. They need to
speak with other non-native speakers, using English as a common
language, experts say.
(120) Nevertheless, English teaching generates more than $1.1 billion
annually for Britain. Last year, the British Council launched its English
2000 program. One of its aims is to attract more foreign students to
Britain through promotion of British English and culture worldwide.

Australia is also in the game, adding an estimated $415 million
(125) annually to its economy from teaching English. It, too, has become more
aggressive recently, establishing English-teaching centers in Asia as a
way to attract foreign students to Australian universities.

Although the United States government discontinued its involvement
in direct English teaching in the 1970's, the United States still attracts
(130) 450,000 students and scholars to American schools each year. They, in
turn, become a powerful dissemination vehicle (in addition to bringing
more than $7 billion annually to the American economy). In addition, it
is thought that those who learn one kind of English or another, especially
when they learn it while immersed in the culture of a country, are more
(135) likely to buy the goods of that country in the future.

Muscovite Bezouglyi is a case in point. He reads *Newsweek* magazine
and frequents a newly opened American bookstore in Russia. He says he
chooses to read American publications because he better understands
"what they're writing about and their English."
(140) As English continues to spread, some experts say, a form of it could
become the common language of the world. But multilingualism is also on
the rise, suggesting that English may not be the only language to prevail.

David Crystal, a linguist from Wales and author of the *Cambridge
Encyclopedia of the English Language,* says that the way English is
(145) changing now, if it does become the global language, "it's going to be
American-English-dominated, I have no doubt."

—K. Campbell

DIFFERENCES BETWEEN AMERICAN ENGLISH AND BRITISH ENGLISH

Spelling		Word Usage		Pronunciation	
American	British	American	British	American	British
honor	honour	truck	lorry	• retaining sound of flat "a"	• change sound to broad "a"; for example "man" would be pronounced with the sound of "a" in "father"
favor	favour	windshield	windscreen		
color	colour	railroad	railway	• keeping the "r" sound in all words	• dropping the "r" sound in most words—"lord" sounds like "laud"
theater	theatre	muffler	silencer		
center	centre	spark plugs	sparking plugs	• shortening of the "o" sound in words such as "not," "lot," "top," "hot," so they sound like the "a" in "father"	• retaining an open "o" sound, pronounced with the lips rounded in those same words
traveler	traveller	elevator	lift		
wagon	waggon	hardware	ironmongery		
defense	defence	gasoline	petrol	• unaccented syllables are pronounced more clearly	• unaccented syllables shortened or suppressed so that "secretary" is pronounced "secret 'ry" or "necessary" is pronounced "necess 'ry"
offense	offence	mail	post		
ax	axe	lawyer	barrister	• which syllable is accented sometimes differs—American pronunciations: "lab' oratory," "advertise' ment"	• British pronunciations: "labor' atory," "adver' tisement"
plow	plough	garbage collector	dustman		
tire	tyre	long-distance call	trunk call		
story	storey	expressway	motorway	• Americans speak more slowly with less variety of tone	• The British speak more quickly with more variety of tone
jail	gaol	divided highway	dual carriageway		

Chart compiled from information in *A History of the English Language* by Albert C. Baugh and Thomas Cable, Third Edition. Englewood Cliffs, NJ, Prentice-Hall Inc., 1978.

Directions: Answer the following questions. The questions may help you think about ideas and information you might use in your writing. You may return to these questions anytime you wish.

1 In line 9, the word "Hollywood" is used to signify

   1 warm climate   3 American geography
   2 urban life   4 popular media

2 What factor in the spread of American English is illustrated by the reference to Americans in Russia (lines 21 through 23)?

   1 technology   3 population
   2 culture   4 history

3 In lines 26 and 27, the phrase "the receding of the British empire" probably refers to the

   1 loss of British colonies   3 decline of British culture
   2 reduction of British   4 deterioration of British
      population   government

4 What characteristic of American English is illustrated by the reference to Nike baseball caps (line 42)?

   1 versatility   3 beauty
   2 trendiness   4 practicality

5 The reference to the "red line" (line 56) is used to illustrate the

   1 prestige of Cairo   3 importance of British
      universities   literature
   2 strictness of Egyptian   4 acceptance of American
      teachers   spelling

6 According to the article, the use of American English in Britain is becoming

   1 controversial   3 commonplace
   2 competitive   4 costly

7 The author uses bullets (•) as a way to

   1 note supporting details   3 contrast opposing arguments
   2 omit repetitive phrases   4 question common assumptions

8 In line 108, the word "markets" refers to countries that want to buy

1 industrial technology 3 consumer products
2 language instruction 4 business expertise

9 Which situation demonstrates the use of English as a common language?

1 A Russian watches an English movie with Russian subtitles.
2 A Korean and a German have a conversation in English.
3 An American teaches English classes in Japan.
4 A Mexican reads a Spanish translation of an English poem.

10 According to the author, English-speaking countries seek foreign students because those students

1 encourage responsibility in government
2 raise the standards of education
3 stimulate changes in the culture
4 add money to the economy

11 According to the chart, one characteristic of British English is a tendency to

1 speak slowly with little variety in tone
2 shorten the "o" sound
3 drop the "r" sound
4 clearly pronounce unaccented syllables

12 According to the chart, one example of British-English spelling is

1 plough 3 offense
2 theater 4 color

After you have finished these questions, review **Your Task** and the **Guidelines** and write your response. Use scrap paper to plan your response.

Note: The operational examination will include only 8–10 questions on Part II. Additional questions are included here to suggest a fuller range of possible question types.

Part III Task, Texts, and Questions—Sample

Directions: Read the passages on the following pages (a poem and an excerpt from a story) and answer the multiple-choice questions. Then write the essay described in "Your Task." You may use the margins to take notes as you read and scap paper to plan your response.

Your Task:

> After you have read the passages and answered the multiple-choice questions, write a unified essay about the effects of war on the soldiers who do the fighting as revealed in the passages. In your essay, use ideas from **both** passages to establish a controlling idea about the effects of war on the soldiers who do the fighting, use evidence from **both** passages to develop your controlling idea, and show how each author used specific literary elements or techniques to convey ideas.

Guidelines:

- Use ideas from **both** passages to establish a controlling idea about the effects of war on the soldiers who do the fighting, as revealed in the passages

- Use specific and relevant evidence from **both** passages to develop your controlling idea

- Show how each author uses specific literary elements (for example, theme, characterization, structure, point of view) or techniques (for example, symbolism, irony, figurative language) to portray the effects of war on the soldiers who do the fighting

- Organize your ideas in a logical and coherent manner

- Use language that communicates ideas effectively

- Follow the conventions of standard written English

*Note: Only one sample of a Part III task is included in this Sampler.

Passage I

Our brains ache, in the merciless iced east winds that knive us . . .
Wearied we keep awake because the night is silent . . .
Low, drooping flares confuse our memory of the salient . . .
Worried by silence, sentries whisper, curious, nervous,
(5)   But nothing happens.

Watching, we hear the mad gusts tugging on the wire,
Like twitching agonies of men among its brambles.
Northward, incessantly, the flickering gunnery rumbles,
Far off, like a dull rumour of some other war.
(10)   What are we doing here?

The poignant misery of dawn begins to grow . . .
We only know war lasts, rain soaks, and clouds sag stormy.
Dawn massing in the east her melancholy army
Attacks once more in ranks on shivering ranks of gray,
(15)   But nothing happens.

Sudden successive flights of bullets streak the silence.
Less deadly than the air that shudders black with snow,
With sidelong flowing flakes that flock, pause and renew,
We watch them wandering up and down the wind's nonchalance,
(20)   But nothing happens.

Pale flakes with fingering stealth come feeling for our faces—
We cringe in holes, back on forgotten dreams, and stare, snow-dazed.
Deep into grassier ditches. So we drowse, sun-dozed,
Littered with blossoms trickling where the blackbird fusses.
(25)   Is it that we are dying?

Slowly our ghosts drag home: glimpsing the sunk fires, glozed[1]
With crusted dark-red jewels; crickets jingle there;
For hours the innocent mice rejoice: the house is theirs;
Shutters and doors, all closed: on us the doors are closed,—
(30)   We turn back to our dying.

Since we believe not otherwise can kind fires burn;
Nor ever suns smile true on child, or field, or fruit.
For God's invincible spring our love is made afraid;
Therefore, not loath, we lie out here; therefore were born,
(35)   For love of God seems dying.

Tonight, His frost will fasten on this mud and us,
Shrivelling many hands, puckering foreheads crisp.
The burying-party, picks and shovels in their shaking grasp,
Pause over half-known faces. All their eyes are ice,
(40)   But nothing happens.

—Wilfred Owen

---

[1]glazed over

245

Passage II

They carried USO stationery and pencils and pens. They carried Sterno, safety pins, trip flares, signal flares, spools of wire, razor blades, chewing tobacco, statuettes of the smiling Buddha, candles, grease pencils, *The Stars and Stripes,* fingernail clippers, bush hats, bolos, and much more.

(5) Twice a week, when the resupply choppers came in, they carried hot chow in green mermite cans and large canvas bags filled with iced beer and soda pop. They carried plastic water containers, each with a two-gallon capacity. Mitchell Sanders carried a set of starched tiger fatigues for special occasions. Henry Dobbins carried Black Flag insecticide. Dave

(10) Jensen carried empty sandbags that could be filled at night for added protection. Lee Strunk carried tanning lotion. Some things they carried in common. Taking turns, they carried the big PRC-77 scrambler radio which weighed 30 pounds with its battery. They shared the weight of memory. They took up what others could no longer bear. Often, they

(15) carried each other, the wounded or weak. They carried infections. They carried chess sets, basketballs, Vietnamese-English dictionaries, insignia of rank, Bronze Stars and Purple Hearts, plastic cards imprinted with the Code of Conduct. They carried diseases, among them malaria and dysentery. They carried lice and ringworm and leeches and paddy algae

(20) and various rots and molds. They carried the land itself—Vietnam, the place, the soil . . . dust that covered their boots and fatigues and faces. They carried the sky . . . the stink of fungus, and decay, all of it, they carried gravity.

—Tim O'Brien

Directions: Answer the following questions. The questions may help you think about the ideas you might want to use in your essay. You may return to these questions anytime you wish.

Passage I (the poem)—Questions 1–7 refer to Passage I.

1 The mood conveyed in the first stanza is one of

   1 mystery   3 peacefulness
   2 foreboding   4 confusion

2 Lines 13 and 14 (Dawn . . . gray) refer to

   1 storm clouds   3 hungry rats
   2 advancing soldiers   4 enemy tanks

3 In stanza 4 of the poem the dominant figure of speech is

   1 onomatopoeia   3 oxymoron
   2 personification   4 alliteration

4 In lines 6 through 20, the soldiers are bombarded by

   1 overwhelming hunger   3 painful memories
   2 merciless weather   4 paralyzing fear

5 Lines 17 through 19 suggest that the action of the snowflakes is

   1 puzzling   3 erratic
   2 noisy   4 threatening

6 The statement "Slowly our ghosts drag home" (line 26) refers to dead comrades as well as

   1 injured animals   3 suffering survivors
   2 living relatives   4 absent soldiers

7 The repetition of the phrase "But nothing happens" underscores the soldiers' feelings of

   1 fear   3 anger
   2 hopelessness   4 indifference

Passage II (the excerpt from a story)—Questions 8–12 refer to Passage II.

8   Throughout Passage II, "they" refers to

   1   soldiers   3   civilians
   2   trains   4   ambulances

9   The variety of items the men carried reflects their desire to

   1   make friends   3   sell products
   2   bribe villagers   4   maintain morale

10   The repetition of the expression "they carried" helps establish a feeling of

   1   relentlessness   3   suspense
   2   monotony   4   disappointment

11   The word "gravity" (line 23) is used to mean

   1   earthly delights   3   weighty matters
   2   fond memories   4   unexplained forces

12   The organization of this passage is characterized by a movement from

   1   literal to figurative   3   emotion to reason
   2   past to present   4   far to near

After you have finished these questions, review **Your Task** and the **Guidelines** and write your response to Part III. You may use scrap paper to plan your response.

Note: The operational examination will include only 8–10 questions on Part III. Additional questions are included here to suggest a fuller range of possible question types.

Part IV Task—Sample

Your Task: Write a critical essay in which you discuss two works of literature you have read from the particular perspective of the statement that is provided for you in the "critical lens." In your essay, provide a valid interpretation of the statement, agree or disagree with the statement as you have interpreted it, and support your opinion using specific references to appropriate literary elements from the two works. You may use scrap paper to plan your response.

Critical Lens:

> "The test of a courageous person is the ability to bear defeat without losing heart."

Guidelines:

- Provide a valid interpretation of the critical lens that clearly establishes the criteria for analysis

- Indicate whether you agree **or** disagree with the statement as you have interpreted it

- Choose **two** works you have read that you believe best support your opinion

- Use the criteria suggested by the critical lens to analyze the works you have chosen

- For **each** work, do not summarize the plot but use specific references to appropriate literary elements (for example, theme, characterization, structure, language, point of view) to develop your analysis

- Organize your ideas in a unified and coherent manner

- Specify the titles and authors of the literature you choose

- Follow the conventions of standard written English

Scoring Key for Multiple-Choice Questions

Part I—Sample

1	2
2	3
3	4
4	1
5	2
6	1
7	3
8	1

Part II—Sample

1	4
2	3
3	1
4	2
5	4
6	3
7	1
8	2
9	2
10	4
11	3
12	1

Part III—Sample

1	2
2	1
3	4
4	2
5	3
6	3
7	2
8	1
9	4
10	1
11	3
12	1

MODEL EXAMINATION 2

Part I—Sample

Student Copy

Overview: For this part of the test, you will listen to a speech about being well-educated for today's world, answer some multiple-choice questions, and write a response based on the situation described below. You will hear the speech twice. You may take notes anytime you wish during the readings.

The Situation: As president of the Student Council, you have been asked to write an article for the junior high school newspaper to help eighth graders select the courses and activities to pursue in high school in order to be well-educated for today's world. In preparation for writing your article, listen to a speech given by J. Peter Kelly, president of a steel company, to an audience of science students. Then use relevant information from this speech to write your article.

Your Task: Write an article for the junior high (middle school) newspaper in which you advise eighth graders on how to select courses and activities in high school in order to become well-educated for today's world.

Guidelines:

- Tell your audience what they need to know to help them select appropriate courses and activities to pursue in high school

- Use specific, accurate, and relevant information from the speech to support your discussion

- Use a tone and level of language appropriate for an essay for a junior high school newspaper

- Organize your ideas in a logical and coherent manner

- Be sure to indicate any words taken directly from the speech by using quotation marks or referring to the speaker

- Follow the conventions of standard written English

Passage

A quote I heard many times when I was your age and which I now know traces back to Sir Francis Bacon, one of our earliest scientists, or philosophers as they were then called, is the statement, "Knowledge Is Power." Today I believe that the fuller, more correct statement is: "the application of knowledge is power." As you pursue your math, science or engineering studies, I'd like you to keep in mind a few things on the application side of these pursuits. Yes, we need mathematicians, scientists and engineers, and we need people with exceptional levels of capability who will earn Ph.D.'s in these disciplines. You should also know that we need many more people who will be what I call scientifically and technically literate. These people will not necessarily acquire Ph.D.'s in the sciences, but they will be highly successful in fields as diverse as sales, finance, law, manufacturing and business management. In fact, the list is virtually endless. I hope you get the idea. The study of science, math and technology subjects will broaden your opportunities in life, not narrow them. However, a failure to be scientifically literate will greatly limit your future opportunities.

My point is, do not stop pursuing an interest in the sciences, math or technology areas simply because you may decide you do not want to be a scientist, a mathematician or an engineer. A solid foundation in these disciplines will be an excellent foundation for an extraordinarily broad range of career choices.

But now let me broaden this discussion a little bit more and address two areas of personal concern. Again, to the students, I assume that at this point in time you have high personal aspirations. You should, and your presence here this evening says that you do. But unfortunately, we as human beings tend to focus on what we enjoy and find easy and comfortable, and too often we are tempted to ignore the rest.

Well, if you truly aspire to be something more than a star, solo performer, that is to effectively participate in a group activity; to lead an entire organization or even lead a small part of one; or to play a significant role in your community, then you must also develop your communication skills. You must be able to write effectively, and you must be able to speak effectively. And now at your present age is when you should be developing these competencies. Surfing the Internet may be fine and it has its own jargon, but you must be able to move away from the keyboard and speak effectively. If you are to be a leader, you must be able to explain, persuade, and, in short, communicate your vision to others. You must develop the ability to make others share your vision, and help you realize your dream. If you are not comfortable speaking to a group, or if you know that you are not effective when you speak or write, then I urge you in the strongest terms possible, to address these issues as vigorously as you would pursue any other learning discipline. Effective communication skills can be developed.

Let me be very clear about this subject. You do not have to do this, but let me also be clear, if you do not do it, if you are not a good communicator, you will not achieve your full potential, and, there will be many, many opportunities that you will not be able to realize.

My second concern is this: as a scientific and technical society, we have done a much better job of answering the question of "how can we do something?" than we have of answering the much deeper question of "should we do something?" We know how to make weapons of awesome, destructive power; we know how to efficiently perform abortions and euthanasia; and we know how to use technology to support life almost indefinitely. We know how to do an endless array of amazing things, but knowledge, scientific or otherwise, does not necessarily imply wisdom.

The greater question is, do we know whether we should do any of these things at all? And do we even know how we should go about developing answers to those higher questions, and who is it that should be answering these questions.

So to the students I urge, yes, study science, math and technology, but make time to read some history, study some philosophy, enjoy some Shakespeare, grow in your understanding of whatever you believe about your maker and your reason for being here in this world at this time. Do not educate yourself so narrowly that you are excluded from those greater considerations of "should we?"

Let me give you an example. Today there is technology available, for exorbitant sums of money, to reduce by incredibly small amounts various pollutants in the air. But that same amount of money might enable large numbers of our population to simply eat regularly, enjoy decent housing or receive proper medical care. Well, how should that money be spent? Who should decide? Too often today the majority of the scientific community which has a real grasp of the technical or economic merits of a subject sit by silently while those with a particularly strong social agenda and little appreciation of the technical merits are most communicative and have the greatest influence upon the decision makers. Tonight I am urging you to equip yourself to intelligently participate in the whole dialogue to help us make the best decision, the right decision. We will need your balanced, reasoned and educated involvement. But you will have to decide whether you will educate yourself so as to be a worthy participant and valuable contributor to the dialogue.

Directions: Use your notes to answer the following questions about the passage read to you. The questions may help you think about ideas and information you might use in your writing. You may return to these questions anytime you wish.

1   According to the speaker, the power or knowledge lies in its

    1   accumulation   3   use
    2   accuracy   4   limits

2   The speaker assumes that the members of his audience have studied

    1   math and technology   3   business and manufacturing
    2   history and philosophy   4   writing and speaking

3   According to the speaker, communication skills are necessary for an individual to

    1   achieve stardom   3   earn money
    2   accomplish goals   4   use technology

4   The speaker implies that the answer to "how can we do something?" depends on a knowledge of

    1   philosophy   3   literature
    2   history   4   science

5   The speaker uses the examples of weapons and life support to illustrate a need for

    1   locating cheaper energy   3   asking deeper questions
    2   developing better technology 4   inventing safer procedures

6   The speaker uses rhetorical questions in order to

    1   raise doubts about the future of science
    2   stimulate thinking about ethical issues
    3   challenge assumptions about the value of education
    4   avoid providing obvious answers

7   The speaker criticizes members of the scientific community for their lack of

    1   concern for financial   3   patience toward non-
        matters   scientists
    2   appreciation for art and   4   involvement in social
        music   issues

8 The speaker implies that the question of how to spend public money can best be answered by people with a

1 broad base of knowledge   3 bold financial plan
2 strong social agenda   4 high level of intelligence

Review **The Situation** and read **Your Task** and the **Guidelines.**
Then write your response.

Note: The operational examination will include only 5–6 questions on Part I. Additional questions are included here to suggest a fuller range of possible question types.

Part II Task, Text, and Questions—Sample

Directions: Read the text and study the graphs on the following pages, answer the multiple-choice questions, and write a response based on the situation described below. You may use the margins to take notes as you read. You may use scrap paper to plan your response.

The Situation: A community health clinic has invited students in your school to write health-related articles for its newsletter. You decided to write an article discussing factors that influence teenage smoking and the implications of those factors for reducing teenage smoking.

Your Task: Write an article for the community health newsletter. Using relevant information from the text and graphs, discuss the factors that influence teenage smoking and the implications of those factors for reducing teenage smoking.

Guidelines:

- Tell your audience what they need to know about factors that influence teenage smoking

- Discuss the implications of those factors for reducing teenage smoking

- Use specific, accurate, and relevant information from the text **and** the graphs to develop your discussion

- Use a tone and level of language appropriate for an article for a community health newsletter

- Organize your ideas in a logical and coherent manner

- Be sure to indicate any words taken directly from the article by using quotation marks or referring to the author

- Follow the conventions of standard written English

Researchers calculate that teenage smoking rates, after declining in the 1970's and leveling off in the 1980's, have climbed sharply over the last five years. Although everything from why the trend began to what might stop it is disputed, it adds up to a huge health problem for the country and a public relations disaster for the tobacco industry.

Teenage smoking rates are still lower than in the 1970's, but they are rapidly increasing. According to the most recent edition of the University of Michigan's Monitoring the Future Survey, last year the percentage of 12th graders who smoked daily was up 20 percent from 1991. This annual study is widely followed by tobacco researchers. The rate among 10th graders jumped 45 percent, and the rate for 8th graders was up 44 percent between 1991 and 1996.

At current smoking rates, five million people now younger than 18 will eventually die of tobacco-related illnesses, according to the most recent projections from the Centers for Disease Control and Prevention in Atlanta.

Rising youth smoking rates have been cited by the Food and Drug Administration and President Clinton as evidence that the industry is marketing its products to youths and should be restricted by the F.D.A. The rates are also fueling demands in many states and nationally for higher taxes on tobacco, based on research showing that price increases typically discourage teenage smokers.

Just what has caused the teenage smoking rate to rise so sharply is hotly debated. The tobacco industry says the increase is due to a broad range of social forces. Industry officials note that other kinds of risk-taking among teenagers, especially the use of marijuana and other drugs, have risen more sharply than tobacco use. The industry also cites teenagers' naturally rebellious reaction to the increasing efforts to stop them from smoking.

Critics of the tobacco industry agree that rebelliousness and other forces are at work. But they say the industry itself is the most important factor. The industry's spending on domestic advertising and promotions soared from $361 million in 1970, to $4.83 billion in 1994, a 250 percent increase after adjusting for inflation, according to the latest data published by the Federal Trade Commission.

Just how that huge pie has been divided is a secret closely guarded not only from critics but even among companies in the industry. Much of the money goes into promotions to encourage retailers to run sales or to display particular brands and signs more prominently. Tobacco companies say they have adopted practices to focus their messages on adults, like requiring that all models be—and look—older than 25.

But critics like John Pierce, head of the Cancer Prevention Center at the University of California at San Diego, say it is most telling that spending rose most rapidly in the 1980's, when the decline in youth smoking was halted. They also point to research showing that children have been strongly attracted to some of the biggest marketing campaigns, notably R.J. Reynolds Tobacco's use of the ever-hip Joe Camel and Philip Morris' use of the rugged Marlboro man and the Marlboro Adventure team, a merchandise promotion.

The surge in teenage smoking in the 1990's coincided with a sharp expansion by both Reynolds and Philip Morris in giveaways of items like

T-shirts in return for coupons accumulated by buying their cigarettes. Research showed that the companies had limited success in preventing distribution of the merchandise to children—30 percent of teenage smokers have it—and that the items are just as appealing to teenagers as to adults.

Tobacco companies say critics grossly exaggerate the effects of their marketing. They point out that teenage smoking is also rising in countries where most forms of advertising have been banned.

The latest indicator of the distance between the two sides is Philip Morris' creation of a record company—Woman Thing Music—to promote its Virginia Slims brand. The company will be selling bargain-priced compact discs by its female artists along with its cigarettes. Its first artist, Martha Byrne, a nonsmoking actress from the soap opera *As the World Turns,* is on a concert tour. She is appearing in venues where only those older than 21 are allowed.

Making matters worse, some critics say, is that Hollywood's long love affair with smoking seems to be heating up. Cigars are being widely used to symbolize success in movies like *The Associate,* with Whoopi Goldberg. And even though today's stars are not inseparable from their cigarettes the way Humphrey Bogart, Bette Davis, and James Dean were, actors who show up puffing on cigarettes include John Travolta and Uma Thurman as anti-heroes in *Pulp Fiction,* and Winona Ryder as a Generation X drifter in *Reality Bites.* Leonardo DeCaprio went so far as to light up as Romeo in last year's updated *Romeo and Juliet.*

Whether smoking in films contributes to the teenage trend or simply picks up on it is one of many questions. Teenagers say that movie and music stars do shape their sense of what is "cool" and that a desire to be cool is often a reason the youngest smokers first try cigarettes. But many researchers doubt that an effect can be reliably measured.

Moreover, high school students who smoke regularly say it is so common that no one thinks of it as cool. Some concede that they enjoy doing something forbidden, but more often they cite a desire to relieve stress or to stay thin, the taste, or simply the need to fill time as reasons they kept smoking to the point of becoming addicted. Many, like David Bernt of Oak Park, agree with the industry's contention that its marketing had nothing to do with the decision to smoke but that it does influence brand choice.

"If I buy anything but Camel, it feels like I wasted money because I collect Camel cash," he said, referring to the coupons that can be redeemed for Camel merchandise.

The increased smoking rates since 1991 are expected to translate into tens of thousands of additional early deaths because one out of three teenage smokers is expected to develop fatal tobacco-related illnesses. About 46,000 more 8th graders are smoking at least half a pack a day than would have been smoking had the rate remained at its 1991 level, and 250,000 more have smoked within the last 30 days than would have at the 1991 rate, judging from the application of census data to results from the Monitoring the Future surveys. And because of the rising smoking rate since 1991, an extra 110,000 10th graders are half-a-pack-a-day smokers, and nearly 366,000 more of them have smoked in the last 30 days.

—B. Feder

Graph 1

Half a Pack
At an Early Age

Percentage in each grade who told surveyors that they smoke at least half a pack of cigarettes a day.

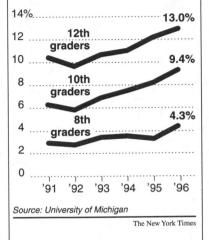

14%.............................. **13.0%**

12th graders

10th graders

8th graders

9.4%

4.3%

'91 '92 '93 '94 '95 '96

Source: University of Michigan

The New York Times

Graph 2

Teen-Age Smoking
Makes a Comeback

The number of 12th graders who try cigarettes has declined over the last two decades, but the number who smoke occasionally and who develop heavier habits has increased sharply in recent years.

Of 12th graders surveyed

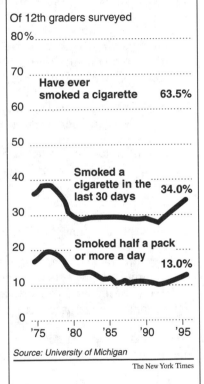

80%..................................

70 ....

Have ever smoked a cigarette **63.5%**

60 ....

50 ....

40 ....
Smoked a cigarette in the last 30 days **34.0%**

30 ....

20 ....
Smoked half a pack or more a day **13.0%**

10 ....

0

'75   '80   '85   '90   '95

Source: University of Michigan

The New York Times

Directions: Answer the following questions. The questions may help you think about ideas and information you might use in your writing. You may return to these questions anytime you wish.

1   Rising youth smoking rates have led the FDA to propose

   1   a national anti-smoking campaign
   2   a federal lawsuit against the tobacco industry
   3   restrictions on marketing tobacco products to teenagers
   4   denial of insurance coverage for smokers

2   The text implies that one result of raising taxes on tobacco is that

   1   the FDA will restrict tobacco sales
   2   retailers will lower cigarette prices
   3   tobacco companies will advertise less
   4   teenagers will buy fewer cigarettes

3   Tobacco industry officials imply that a major factor in teenage smoking is the tendency of teenagers to

   1   misunderstand cigarette warnings
   2   believe cigarette advertisements
   3   engage in risky behavior
   4   imitate their parents

4   The "secret" mentioned in line 34 refers to the

   1   ways in which advertising money is spent
   2   amount of money spent on advertising
   3   results of increased advertising
   4   reasons for increased advertising

5   According to the text, teenage smoking increased at the same time that the tobacco industry increased its promotion of

   1   long, slim cigarettes   3   more effective filters
   2   giveaway items   4   reduced nicotine cigarettes

6   The text mentions Humphrey Bogart and James Dean as examples of movie stars who

   1   died of tobacco-related illnesses
   2   were usually pictured with a cigarette
   3   urged fans not to smoke
   4   refused to smoke on screen

7 The text implies that Hollywood may influence teenagers to smoke by

   1 shaping their sense of what is trendy
   2 indirectly advertising cigarettes in movies
   3 selling cigarettes in movie theaters
   4 giving them false information

8 The anecdote about David Bernt implies that marketing techniques influenced Bernt to

   1 start smoking   3 become addicted
   2 buy a certain brand   4 decide not to smoke

9 What is the main purpose of the text?

   1 to criticize the tobacco industry
   2 to persuade readers not to smoke
   3 to offer solutions to the problem of teenage smoking
   4 to report on the increase in teenage smoking

10 Graph 1 shows a steady increase in the

   1 age at which teenagers start to smoke
   2 number of teenagers who smoke heavily
   3 price of tobacco products
   4 earnings of tobacco companies

11 What does Graph 2 imply about 12th graders in 1995?

   1 About forty percent of them did not smoke at all.
   2 About forty percent of them developed tobacco-related illnesses.
   3 Twelfth graders smoked primarily on weekends.
   4 Twelfth graders started smoking in elementary school.

12 According to Graph 2, the sharpest decrease in teenage smoking occurred during which years?

   1 late 1930's   3 late 1970's
   2 late 1960's   4 late 1990's

After you have finished these questions, review **Your Task** and the **Guidelines** and write your response. Use scrap paper to plan your response.

Note: The operational examination will include only 8–10 questions on Part II. Additional questions are included here to suggest a fuller range of possible question types.

Part III Task, Texts, and Questions—Sample

Directions: Read the passages on the following pages (a poem and an excerpt from a memoir) and answer the multiple-choice questions. Then write an essay described in "Your Task." You may use the margins to make notes as you read and scrap paper to plan your response.

Your Task:

> After you have read the passages and answered the multiple-choice questions, write a unified essay about conflicting attitudes toward the elderly as they are revealed in the passages. In your essay, use ideas from **both** passages to establish a controlling idea about attitudes toward the elderly, use evidence from **both** passages to develop your controlling idea, and show how each author used specific literary elements or techniques to convey ideas.

Guidelines:

- Use ideas from **both** passages to establish a controlling idea about conflicting attitudes toward the elderly, as revealed in the passages

- Use specific and relevant evidence from **both** passages to develop your controlling idea

- Show how each author uses specific literary elements (for example, themes, characterization, structure, point of view) or techniques (for example, symbolism, irony, figurative language) to portray the conflicting attitudes toward the elderly

- Organize your ideas in a logical and coherent manner

- Use language that communicates ideas effectively

- Follow the conventions of standard written English

Note: This Task is adapted from a pilot version of the new Regents exam developed by the New York State Education Department.

Passage I

Grandpa

Grandpa he was a man
he taught me the things that
    mattered
how to eat oxtail soup before
(5)   fishing on Saturday morning to
keep you warm how to
cast a line into a
streamful of angered anglers and
be the only one to
(10)   come home with anything worth
bragging about how to
set teeth in any saw and
dovetail a joint in a
chair leg and roof a
(15)   house and weld a
straight seam on a
kitchen pipe and make a
home out of a
workshop out of a
(20)   two-car garage and
smoke Granger's tobacco and
love work and kids and
fishing for "a Man's
life is his work and
(25)   his work is his life" and
once you take away his work
you pull the plug of his life
and it takes too long
for it to drain silently away.
(30)   One day they came and
told him to go home and
rest old man it's time
that you retire he begged
them "let me stay" but
(35)   they of course knew best for
everyone knows at sixty-five all
men are old and useless and
must be cast off to
rot so he came home and
(40)   tried to fish and
couldn't and tried to joke and

couldn't and tried to live and
couldn't. Every morning he was
up at four and cooked breakfast
    for
(5) grandma and warmed up the house
    and
went to the workshop and
filed saws for neighbors but
they told him to stop that too
so he put all his tools away and
(10) cleaned up the workshop and
came into the house for his daily afternoon nap and
died. They didn't know
what I knew because he
didn't tell them but
(15) he showed them
Grandpa he was a man.

W.M. Ransom

Passage II

A Celebration of Grandfathers

Rudolfo A. Anaya

Buenos dias le de Dios, abuelo. God give you a good day, grandfather. This is how I was taught as a child to greet my grandfather, or any grown person. It was a greeting of respect for the old ones.

The old people I remember from my childhood were strong in their beliefs, and as we lived daily with them, we learned a wise path of life to follow. They had something important to share with the young, and when they spoke, the young listened. These old abuelos and abuelitas had worked the earth all their lives, and so they knew the value of nurturing, they knew the sensitivity of the earth . . . . They knew the rhythms and cycles of time, from the preparation of the earth in the spring to the digging of the *acequias* that brought the water to the dance of harvest in the fall. They shared good times and hard times. They helped each other through the epidemics and the personal tragedies, and they shared what little they had when the hot winds burned the land and no rain came. They learned that to survive one had to share in the process of life . . . .

My grandfather was a plain man, a farmer from the valley called Puerto de Luna on the Pecos River. He was probably a descendant of those people who spilled over the mountain Taos, following the Pecos River in search of farmland. There in that river valley he settled and raised a large family.

Bearded and walrus-mustached, he stood five feet tall, but to me as a child he was a giant. I remember him most for his silence. In the summers my parents sent me to live in that valley, there where only the flow of the river and the whispering of the wind marked time. For me it was a magical place.

I remember once, while out hoeing the fields, I came upon an anthill, and before I knew it I was badly bitten. After he had covered my welts with the cool mud from the irrigation ditch, my grandfather calmly said: "Know where you stand." That is the way he spoke, in short phrases, to the point.

One very dry summer, the river dried to a trickle; there was no water for the fields. The young plants withered and died. In sadness and with the impulse of youth I said, "I wish it would rain!" My grandfather touched me, looked up into the sky and whispered, "Pray for rain." In his language there was a difference. He felt connected to the cycles that brought the rain or kept it from us. His prayer was a meaningful action, because he was a participant with the forces that filled our world; he was not a bystander. A young man died at the village one summer. A very tragic death. He was dragged by his horse. When he was found, I cried, for the boy was my friend. I did not understand why death had come to one so young. My grandfather took me aside and said: "Think of the death of the trees and the fields in the fall. The leaves fall, and everything rests, as if dead. But they bloom again in the spring. Death is only this small transformation in life."

These are the things I remember, these fleeting images, few words.

I remember him driving his horse-drawn wagon into Santa Rosa in the fall when he brought his harvest produce to sell in the town. What a tower of strength seemed to come in that small man huddled on the seat of the giant wagon. One click of his tongue and the horses obeyed, stopped or turned as he wished. He never raised his whip. How unlike today, when so much teaching is done with loud words and threatening hands.

I would run to greet the wagon, and the wagon would stop. "Buenos dias te de Dios, mi hijo" he would answer and smile, and then I could jump up on the wagon and sit at his side.

Then I, too, became a king as I rode next to the old man who smelled of earth and sweat and the other deep aromas from the orchards and fields of Puerto de Luna. We were all sons and daughters to him. But today the sons and daughters are breaking with the past, putting aside los abuelitos. The old values are threatened most where it comes to these relationships with the old people. If we don't take the time to watch and feel the years of their final transformation, a part of our humanity will be lessened.

I grew up speaking Spanish, and oh! how difficult it was to learn English. Sometimes I would give up and cry out that I couldn't learn. Then he would say, "Ten paciencia." Have patience. Paciencia, a word that said that someday we would overcome . . . "You have to learn the language of the Americanos," he said, "Me, I will live my last days in my valley. You will live in a new time."

A new time did come; a new time is here. How will we form it so it is fruitful? We need to know where we stand. We need to speak softly and respect others, and to share what we have. We need to pray not for material gain, but for rain for the fields, for the sun to nurture growth, for nights in which we can sleep in peace, and for a harvest in which everyone can share. Simple lessons from a simple man. These lessons he learned from his past, which was as deep and strong as the currents of the river of life.

He was a man; he died. Not in his valley but nevertheless cared for by his sons and daughters and flocks of grandchildren. At the end, I would enter his room, which carried the smell of medications and Vicks. Gone were the aroma of the fields, the strength of his young manhood. Gone also was his patience in the face of crippling old age. Small things butchered him; he shouted or turned sour when his expectations were not met. It was because he could not care for himself, because he was returning to that state of childhood, and all those wishes and desires were now wrapped in a crumbling, old body.

"Ten paciencia," I once said to him, and he smiled. "I didn't know I would grow this old," he said . . . I would sit and look at him and remember what was said of him when he was a young man. He could mount a wild horse and break it, and he could ride as far as any man. He could dance all night at a dance, then work the acequia the following day. He helped the neighbors; they helped him. He married, raised children. Small legends, the kind that make up every man's life.

He was ninety-four when he died. Family, neighbors, and friends gathered; they all agreed he had led a rich life. I remembered the last years, the years he spent in bed. And as I remember now, I am reminded that it is too easy to romanticize old age. Sometimes we forget the pain of the transformation into old age, we forget the natural breaking down of the body. My grandfather pointed to the leaves falling from the tree. So time brings with its transformation the often painful wearing-down process. Vision blurs, health wanes; even the act of walking carries with it the painful reminder of the autumn of life. But this process is something to be faced, not something to be hidden away by false images. Yes, the old can be young at heart, but in their own way, with their own dignity. They do not have to copy the always-young image of the Hollywood star . . . .

I returned to Puerto de Luna last summer to join the community in a celebration of the founding of the church. I drove by my grandfather's home, my uncles' ranches, the neglected adobe washing down into the earth from whence it came. And I wondered, how might the values of my grandfather's generation live in our own? What can we retain to see us through these hard times? I was to become a farmer, and I became a writer. As I plow and plant my words, do I nurture as my grandfather did in his fields and orchards? The answers are not simple.

---

abuelos and abuelitas: grandfathers and grandmothers
acequias: ditches
mi hijo: my son
los abuelitos: the grandparents

Directions: Answer the following questions. The questions may help you think about the ideas you might want to use in your essay. You may return to these questions anytime you wish.

Passage I (the poem)—Questions 1–4 refer to Passage I.

1   The dominant mood in the first part of the poem (lines 1–29) is one of

   1   regret   3   curiosity
   2   admiration   4   confusion

2   In line 30, "they" probably refers to Grandpa's

   1   family   3   wife
   2   neighbors   4   employers

3   Lines 26–29 are an example of

   1   alliteration   3   allusion
   2   metaphor   4   personification

4   The tone in lines 35–39 is best described as

   1   sad   3   ironic
   2   angry   4   humorous

Passage II (the memoir)—Questions 5–8 refer to Passage II.

5   In this passage, the writer develops the story of his grandfather primarily through

   1   diaries   3   memories
   2   stories others told him   4   letters

6   The author feels that young people today

   1   continue to honor their grandparents' values
   2   may be losing the values of their grandparents
   3   should continue to work the land as their ancestors did
   4   should live more modern lives

7   The development of the second paragraph of the passage is character-ized primarily by use of

   1   metaphor and simile   3   repetition
   2   allusion   4   irony

8 In the next to last paragraph, when the author says, ". . . it is too easy to romanticize old age," his attitude is essentially

1 sympathetic   3 mournful
2 resentful   4 defiant

After you have finished these questions, review **Your Task** and the **Guidelines** and write your response to Part III. You may use scrap paper to plan your response.

Part IV Task—Sample

Your Task: Write a critical essay in which you discuss two works of literature you have read from the particular perspective of the statement that is provided for you in the "critical lens." In your essay, provide a valid interpretation of the statement, agree or disagree with the statement as you have interpreted it, and support your opinion using specific references to appropriate literary elements from the two works. You may use scrap paper to plan your response.

Critical Lens:

> "The best literature is about the old universal truths, such as love, honor, pride, compassion, and sacrifice."
> —William Faulkner (adapted)

Guidelines:

- Provide a valid interpretation of the critical lens that clearly establishes the criteria for analysis

- Indicate whether you agree or disagree with the statement as you have interpreted it

- Choose **two** works you have read that you believe best support your opinion

- Use the criteria suggested by the critical lens to analyze the works you have chosen

- For **each** work, do not summarize the plot but use specific references to appropriate literary elements (for example, theme, characterization, structure, language, point of view) to develop your analysis

- Organize your ideas in a unified and coherent manner

- Specify the titles and authors of the literature you choose

- Follow the conventions of standard written English

Scoring Key for Multiple-Choice Questions

Part I—Sample

1	3
2	1
3	2
4	4
5	3
6	2
7	4
8	1

Part II—Sample

1	3
2	4
3	3
4	1
5	2
6	2
7	1
8	2
9	4
10	2
11	1
12	3

Part III—Sample

1	2
2	4
3	2
4	3
5	3
6	2
7	3
8	1

INDEX

College-bound students can rely on Barron's for the best in SAT II test preparation...

Every Barron's SAT II test preparation manual contains a diagnostic test and model SAT II tests with answers and explanations. Model tests are similar to the actual SAT II tests in length, format, and degree of difficulty. Manuals also present extensive subject review sections, study tips, and general information on the SAT II. Manuals for foreign language tests, priced slightly higher than the others, come with audiocassettes or CD's that present listening comprehension test sections and additional practice material.

All books are paperback.